# THE CITY OF REFUGE

Rudolph Fisher; by permission of
The New York Public Library, Special Collections

# THE CITY OF REFUGE
## The Collected Stories of Rudolph Fisher

Edited with an Introduction by
John McCluskey, Jr.

University of Missouri Press
Columbia, 1987

Library of Congress Cataloging-in-Publication Data
McCluskey, John.
The city of refuge.
Bibliography: p.
1. Fisher, Rudolph, 1897–1934.   2. Authors,
American—20th century—Biography.   3. Physicians—
United States—Biography.   I. Title.
PS3511.I7436Z78   1987   813'.52 [B]   86–19314
ISBN 0-8262-0630-1 (alk. paper)

∞™ This paper meets the minimum requirements of
the American National Standard for Permanence of Paper
for Printed Library Materials, Z39.48, 1984.

For Jane Ryder Fisher

# Preface

This volume is intended to present a collection of the published works of Dr. Rudolph Fisher and to give an overview of his life and of the themes that his short and long fiction addressed. Every effort has been made to see that these reproductions of the stories are as consistent as possible with their original printings. Because Fisher was such a master at presenting dialect, it was thought unwise to tamper with the stories as he knew them for the sake of modernizing or standardizing spelling or punctuation. Some thought was given to including a glossary such as Fisher himself provided with *The Walls of Jericho*. However, except for one or two instances, possibly unfamiliar words or phrases are clarified by context.

As mentioned in the introduction, developed discussions of the work and career of Fisher are scant, beyond the biographical and critical sketches provided in a number of anthologies. Students of his work will want to know the study by Melvin Tolson, "The Harlem Group of Negro Writers" (cited in the text), which contains a brief chapter on Fisher. In addition, Dr. Eleanor (Queen) Tignor's "A Study of Rudolph Fisher's Prose Fiction" (M.A. thesis, Howard University, 1961), and Leonard J. Deutsch's "Rudolph Fisher's Unpublished Manuscripts: Description and Commentary" (*Obsidian* 6 [1980]) are useful and readable studies of Fisher's fiction.

I wish to thank the many people who contributed to this volume. The following librarians and archivists were very helpful: Lisa Brower, Richard Schoonover, and Christa Sammons, Beinecke Rare Book and Manuscript Library, Yale University; Eugene R. Lehr and Marla Muse, Library of Congress; Wilmer Baatz and Kathy Talalay, Indiana University libraries; Esme Bhan and Thomas C. Battle, Moorland-Spingarn Research Center, Howard University; Diana Lachatanere and Natasha Russell, Schomburg Center for Research in Black Culture, New York Public Library; and Olivia Martin, Western Reserve Historical Society. I especially thank Martha Mitchell of Brown University Library, who took a very kind personal interest in the project.

The following provided information and insight into Fisher's medical career and research publications: Alice T. Davis (Executive Director, Howard University Medical Alumni Association); Dr. James Holland (Indiana University); Dr. Wilbert C. Jordan (Los Angeles); Dr. Russell Miller (Dean, College of Medicine, Howard University); Dr. John Robb (Indianapolis); and David Saumweber (National Academy of Sciences).

In addition to those cited in the text, the following people provided various doses of information, helpful criticism, and hospitality: Marvel Cooke, Elton Fax, Michael Harper, James Hatch, Robert Hemenway, Bruce Kellner, Henry Louis-Gates, Terence Martin, Carolyn Mitchell, Grace "Bunny" Patterson, Louise Patterson, and Thomas Wirth.

Two faculty research grants from the Office of Research & Graduate Development, Indiana University-Bloomington, supported the initial archival work and the preparation of the final manuscript.

My wife, Audrey, endured and encouraged throughout this project, which at times must have seemed interminable.

Finally, I must thank Mrs. Jane Ryder Fisher for generously sharing her memories and material of her life and her husband's.

J.M.
Bloomington, In.
1 November 1986

# CONTENTS

# INTRODUCTION

The story goes that in a taxi traveling from Brooklyn to Manhattan one night in the early 1920s sat Edwin Coates, Frank Turner, Paul Robeson, and Rudolph Fisher—respectively, a future educator, an educator-administrator, an actor-singer-activist, and a physician-writer. All the passengers were black and young; so was the driver. The weather was foul—windy, raining heavily—and the cab made several fishtailing stops. As the cab roared off from one of these breath-stealers, Robeson leaned forward and cautioned the driver, his bass voice cutting through the groan of the cab's motor with the solemnity of a foghorn, "Driver, do be careful. If anything happens to us, you will set the race back three generations." Then he sat back, chuckling. The driver got the message and, perhaps counting himself among such proud company, eased up on the accelerator. Despite his anonymity, he deserves our appreciation today for his newfound caution.[1]

Autobiographies and cultural histories have described the additional obstacles and hazards, even if less dramatic, that faced early Afro-American artists and professionals. Even as late as the twenties, one obstacle was a lack of confidence in the significance of formal art produced by Afro-Americans, as well as in the vernacular of Afro-America. There was a need to affirm the forms and expressions of folk culture; at the same time there was the challenge to stretch literary forms to achieve—more than atmosphere or self-pity—a truer synthesis with black culture than before. At a time when fiction in the urban context seemed to require, singly or in combination, wailing jazz, bad gin, or flashing razors—a new-style minstrelsy—black writers were once again challenged to peel away the old clothing of stereotypes and project the complexity and variety of black Americans. Rudolph Fisher was one of several writers in his generation who met this challenge squarely.

1. Francis (Frank) Turner, telephone interview, 7 February 1984. Turner was a friend of Fisher's, a teacher, and later a deputy superintendent in the New York Public School system. He lives in New York City.

Dr. Rudolph Fisher was one of the Harlem Renaissance writers who attempted to affirm the complexity of black urban culture while steering clear of exotica and oversentimentality, two dangers of his moment. Though he is generally listed among the brighter lights of the Harlem Renaissance, his name is often fitted among those of Langston Hughes, Claude McKay, Nella Larsen, et al., as if it were part of, say, the roster for a large law firm. Because the roster has grown so familiar, our eyes glide along the list without slowing. Yet Fisher deserves better. In just less than ten years, fifteen of his short stories were published. Of these, "The City of Refuge," his first, and "Miss Cynthie" are the best known today. Both were included in *The Best American Short Stories* collections for their respective years of publication. Fisher was also the author of two novels, *The Walls of Jericho* and *The Conjure Man Dies*. The first novel has been touted as one of the more successful Harlem novels of the period; the second is a successful detective novel and the earliest black detective novel published in book form.[2] It was adapted for the stage and was produced posthumously as part of the Federal Theater Project.

As a fiction writer Fisher deserves our attention for the wealth of voices he brought to life. In his detective fiction he mapped out the terrain for Chester Himes and Ishmael Reed, two later writers of detective fiction. Further, Fisher's work can instruct us on the complexities of urban life and of a community moving through rapid social changes. More specifically, his pieces demonstrate the importance of the integration of the rural past (tradition) with the urban present and future (modernity).

Fisher himself can serve as a case study of how a formally trained intellect expands to embrace the enduring aspects of a folk culture. To put it another way, it is intriguing to assess his integration of the culture of his formal training with the culture of his experience as a black man in urban America. A fascinating part of this dynamic is the encounter of the sensibilities of a scientist and practicing medical specialist with those of a creative writer. However, the central point, the guiding question, is what he made of it all and how the interior debate, if we can term it as such, was shaped as fiction.

Rudolph John Chauncey Fisher was born on 9 May 1897 in Washington, D.C., to Reverend John W. and Glendora Williamson Fisher. As a Baptist minister, Reverend Fisher had pastored at a number of churches along the

---

2. Fisher wrote two plays. *The Vici Kid* centered on a small-town gambler. *Golden Slippers* combined features from light opera, musical comedy, and melodrama (see n. 17, below). I am not aware of the production of either play or of the location of the scripts.

Though not in book form, John Edward Bruce's "Black Sleuth" could be called the first detective story by a black writer. The story was serialized in *McGirt's Reader* during 1907–1908.

eastern seaboard as far south as Washington, D.C., and as far north as Fall River, Massachusetts. Rudolph had an older brother, Joseph, and an older sister, Pearl, born at different waystations on the eastern sojourn. At the time of Rudolph's birth, the family was living in Providence, Rhode Island. Mrs. Fisher had left Providence to have the child delivered in Memphis, her hometown. Accompanied by Pearl, she got only as far as Washington before she went into labor, and it was in a Washington hospital that Rudolph was born.[3]

In 1903 the family moved to New York, but by 1905 they had resettled in Providence. Rudolph Fisher attended public schools in Providence and graduated from Classical High School. While in high school he won high honors in scholarship and was a member of the debating team. By the end of his senior year, his interest in both literature and science was established. By the end of his career at Brown University in 1920, this interest in two areas of thought seemingly diametrically opposed would be a passion.

While at Brown, Fisher proved himself equally talented in biology and English; in fact, he did exceptionally well in all his courses, which included subjects as diverse as Latin, public speaking, and military engineering. By the time he graduated he had been elected to Phi Beta Kappa, Sigma Xi, and Delta Sigma Rho honorary fraternities. He won the Caesar Misch Prize in German, the Carpenter Prize in public speaking, and the Dunn Premium for the student with the highest standing in courses in rhetoric, English composition, and public speaking. In 1925 he would describe his academic feat in a self-mocking tone: "Brown University, a most generous institution, gave me a great many prizes and scholarships, the degree of A.B. and A.M. in 1919 and 1920, and all of the keys—Phi Beta Kappa, Delta Sigma Rho and Sigma Xi. There was undoubtedly an oversupply that year."[4]

Having established a reputation as a public speaker and debater, in addition to his achievements as a student, Fisher was elected by his classmates to the honored post of class day orator. Also, he was elected by the faculty to be commencement day speaker. Thus, on the afternoon of 18 June 1919, Rudolph Fisher followed two other classmates and addressed the faculty, graduating seniors, and guests on the subject "The Emancipation of Science." Fisher's talk focused on the development of science through the ages of religious dominance and social upheaval. The speech is noteworthy be-

---

3. Here I defer to Mrs. Jane Ryder Fisher (phone conversation of 22 October 1984), though in his master's thesis, Melvin Tolson reported that Fisher's mother was traveling to be with her family in Little Rock. Melvin Tolson, "The Harlem Group of Negro Writers," master's thesis, Columbia University, 1940, p. 64.
4. "Horizon," *The Crisis* 30 (1925):132.

cause, more than professing a bright young man's ideals, it foreshadows Fisher's own attempts in two narratives to integrate two modes of thought into one catholic sensibility. In terms of cultural history, the speech paints in broad strokes the birth pangs of modernity, with science and rationalism bursting the confines of superstition and religious domination. A portion of the typescript puts the matter squarely:

> As thinking Christians, we strive not to bring men to heaven, but to bring heaven to men, and with that the aim of science is identical. It is the oneness of purpose that brings science and religion into harmony—a harmony which permits science to devote its energies not to self-protection, but to the making of life worth living. Devoutly revering its supreme ruler, which is law; persistently upholding the prin ciples of its savior, which is evolution; and constantly comforted by its holy spirit, which is truth, science is at least free to serve mankind. Is there any finer liberty than that?[5]

The next academic year Fisher remained at Brown to take his masters in biology with courses exclusively in biology, chemistry, and physics. Again he did exceptionally well. He applied and was accepted to Howard University Medical School for the term beginning September 1920.

I should add here that by the summer of 1919 Fisher had met Paul Robeson, with whom he would remain friends for many years. With Rudolph playing the piano and arranging while Paul sang, they toured the eastern seaboard in the hopes of raising money for college tuition. Though the trip was hardly a financial success, it did bring together two ebullient and versatile talents. Oddly enough, there is no mention of their friendship—indeed the friendship of the families—in any texts on Robeson.[6]

By the time Fisher arrived at Howard Medical School, it had been operating for some fifty-two years; a year later, university president Durkee could boast that it was "the only class A medical school for colored youth in America."[7] Fisher did well in his work as a medical student, graduating in 1924 with highest honors in a class of twenty-seven. It is significant that he took courses in roentgenology during both his sophomore and junior years, for several years later he would operate an X-ray laboratory in New York. Just as important, however, is the fact that during his senior year in medical school Fisher started writing "The City of Refuge," which was to be his first

5. Rudolph Fisher, "The Emancipation of Science," typescript in possession of Mrs. Jane Ryder Fisher, pp. 7–8.

6. William H. Robinson, Jr., preface to *The Walls of Jericho* by Rudolph Fisher (New York: Arno, 1969), v. Further comments on travels with Robeson and the relationship with the Robeson family are drawn from phone conversations with Mrs. Jane Fisher (8 January, 25 June 1984, 25 May 1985).

7. Rayford Logan, *Howard University: The First Hundred Years, 1867–1967* (New York: New York University Press, 1969), 213.

published story. Late each afternoon, he would work on the piece at the Library of Congress, revising it until he decided to send it off to the *Atlantic Monthly* late in the spring of 1924. His satisfaction with the story encouraged him, so that by the time he started his internship at Freedman's Hospital in Washington, he was already working on "The South Lingers On," "Ringtail," and the much lengthier "High Yaller," which won the Amy Spingarn Prize for fiction in 1926.

By 1924 he had met Jane Ryder, a graduate of Miner's Teachers College and a grade-school teacher in Washington, D.C. By then the personable and handsome Fisher was popular among the daughters of Washington's black professionals. Yet in this case his reputation for brilliance and wit had not preceded him. Even though Jane was not immediately swept off her feet, by the second semester of Fisher's senior year in medical school, Jane was accompanying him on his late-afternoon jaunts to the Library of Congress, and the couple was married a year after their initial meeting. A son, Hugh, was born in 1926. With his disarming wit, Rudolph promptly nicknamed him "the new Negro." [8]

Fisher was awarded a National Research Council Fellowship in September 1925. The one-year grant was for $2,300, and he was to work in bacteriology with Dr. Frederick P. Gay at the College of Physicians and Surgeons, Columbia University. His research interest was the influence of ultraviolet rays on viruses. His fellowship began on 6 October, and by the following fall he had co-authored an article on the actions of ultraviolet light on bacteriophage and filterable viruses. In April 1926 he was granted a one-year extension of the fellowship and an additional $200. In 1927 another article, published in the *Journal of Infectious Diseases*, treated the resistance of different concentrations of a bacteriophage (now known to be viruses that infect bacteria) to ultraviolet rays. Because his fellowship was due to expire in October 1927, Fisher applied for a one-month extension to carry him through until be began work in November at the Vincent Sanitarium in New York. That request was denied.

While a research fellow, Fisher helped shape some of the skits for what Langston Hughes described as an "intimate Negro revue, to star Paul Robeson and to present many of the then unexploited Negro folk-songs." [9] The revue was never produced, because, in the meantime, Robeson scored on the London stage and refused to return to New York. What is important, however, is Fisher's ability to carry through work on ultraviolet rays, musical sketches, and short fiction simultaneously. Some of this versatility was sug-

8. "Ebony Flute," *Opportunity* 4 (August 1926):261.
9. Langston Hughes, *The Big Sea* (New York: Hill and Wang, 1963), 240.

gested in a brief autobiographical sketch that appeared in the August 1927 issue of *McClure's Magazine*: "An A.B. degree from Brown University in '19 urged me into art and an A.M. degree in '20 urged me into science; and so I studied medicine to heal my fractured ambition. An M.D. degree in '24 saved my life by permitting me to write both fiction and articles for literary journals and research reports for the scientific journals."[10]

During the late 1920s, before going into private practice in his own lab on 7th Avenue in Harlem, he worked at Bronx Hospital and at Mt. Sinai Hospital. By 1930 he was serving as secretary of the corporation and as head of the department of roentgenology at International Hospital in Manhattan. He had also moved his private practice to his new home in Jamaica, Long Island.

X-ray technology advanced rapidly during Rudolph Fisher's lifetime. In the year of his birth the first full-length X-ray of the human body was completed by William Morton. In 1934, the year of Fisher's death, the first X-ray diffraction photograph was taken, and X-ray spectroscopy was introduced, increasing our knowledge of crystal and molecular composition. Nonetheless, during the 1920s, roentgenology, the study and use of X-rays in the treatment of disease, was in its infancy. Though there were dangers to the operators of X-ray equipment—such as overexposure of the fingers and the hands to radiation—there is no evidence that Fisher ever suffered from such problems.

The deepening of the Depression affected Fisher's practice on Long Island. He worked by referrals, yet hard times lessened visits to physicians of any kind. His work at International Hospital had ended by 1932. Yet during 1930–1934, Dr. Fisher continued to write, often removing his heavy leaded apron and gloves to write between appointments. He published five adult stories, two children's stories, book reviews for the *New York Herald-Tribune*, and one novel. He also worked on two plays, neither of which was, to my knowledge, produced. This count does not include the unpublished stories. One of these was "War Hero," a short story on a returning war veteran, which was planned for *Esquire*.[11] It would have been one of very few fiction pieces about a black soldier who served in World War I. A trilogy of novels on three sons of an African chieftain was talked about. The novels would have charted the lives of three sons who were educated in Europe and America. We can discover the seeds for such a work in the background of N'gana Frimbo, the complex character in *The Conjure Man Dies*. Unfortunately, however, this ambitious project was never realized.

10. "The Author! Author! Page," *McClure's Magazine* 59 (August 1927):6.
11. Pearl Fisher, "Rudolph Fisher," three-page typescript prepared for Schomburg Collection, New York Public Library, 1951, p. 2.

Rudolph Fisher

In the late 1920s, during late evenings with his wife or friends, Fisher visited the many cabarets, speakeasies, nightclubs, and theaters in Harlem. According to his widow, they would visit the Savoy "especially on bad nights" to listen to music. All the while Fisher would be observing, mentally noting the conversations and gestures of those in the audience. Not that he did this with the cool detachment of, say, a clinician, for he was wise enough to know that such detachment could cause suspicion. And after all, who could sit still for long while the bands of Chick Webb, Fess Williams, or Fats Waller were in full swing?

"Bud," as he was known to his friends and family, knew the dance and theater crowd well, and this was attested to in the details of such pieces as "Common Meter" and "Miss Cynthie." Most of this crowd might have been surprised to learn that he was a physician. With other contemporaries, whether scholars or fellow writers, he was equally popular. Langston Hughes described him as follows:

> The wittiest of these New Negroes of Harlem, whose tongue was flavored with the sharpest and wittiest humor, was Rudolph Fisher, whose stories appeared in the *Atlantic Monthly*. His novel, *Walls of Jericho*, captures but slightly the raciness of his own conversation. He was a young medical doctor and x-ray specialist, who always frightened me a little, because he could think of the most incisively clever things to say—and I could never think of anything to answer.[12]

At another point in *The Big Sea*, Hughes recalls a visit to a doctor and his referral to Fisher.

> The doctor suggested that I go to Rudolph Fisher for the x-ray photographs, but I knew that my writer-friend, Bud, would be full of clever witticisms of a sort that I could never find repartee for when I was in a normal state of mind, let alone now—with my mind in the far-off spaces and my stomach doing flops. So I went to another Harlem specialist I did not know.[13]

Others who knew him during this period described him fondly, though with less sense of intimidation than Hughes. His friend Frank Turner described him as a "fine looking young man. He was clever, witty, with a contagious, ready laugh."[14] Edwin Coates, another passenger in that taxi from Brooklyn to Manhattan, described him similarly: "a fine looking man, tall."[15] Poet May Miller Sullivan taught in Baltimore, as, for a period, did Fisher's sister Pearl. Sullivan was a member of "The Scribblers," a literary club that invited Fisher down to read from his work. In turn he encouraged

12. Hughes, *The Big Sea*, 240
13. Ibid., 328
14. Frank Turner, telephone interview, 7 February 1984.
15. Edwin Coates, telephone interview, 16 January 1984.

the group and heard some of their pieces. She describes him as "tall, hand-some, and a great tale-teller." He was a "regular guy" with a good voice.[16] Vincent McHugh of the *Providence Journal* interviewed him in 1930 and described him as "tall, well-muscled." Still further, McHugh noted, "The planes of his features in repose had a dark grace; and his voice, quickened with humor and indefinable warmth, . . . was singularly potent in its sugges-tion of character, and singularly hospitable to understanding."[17] Sterling Brown, appointed at Howard University in 1930, knew of him and related that he had heard from Charles Johnson, a Fisk sociologist, that Fisher was a student of black humor and kept a card file on black jokes.[18] For Bruce Nugent (Richard Bruce), Fisher was something of an idol, "innovative, hu-morous."[19] Arthur P. Davis, a reviewer of *The Conjure Man Dies* and a col-league of Sterling Brown, knew of Fisher only through his brother, John, who attended medical school in the class immediately after Fisher's. Davis reported that the adjective his brother repeated most often when discussing Fisher was *brilliant*.[20]

Fisher's wit and familiarity with Harlem nightlife are demonstrated most directly in an essay published in 1927. Originally entitled "The Complexion of Negro Nightclubs," this frequently anthologized piece was published as "The Caucasian Storms Harlem" in the *American Mercury*. Fisher notes that Harlem's many cabarets were catering to largely white audiences during the latter half of the decade. Of course, this was in sharp contrast to the all-black clubs he first encountered in New York during the summer of 1919. The new arrangement was based on profits to the club owners, and Fisher speculates, before rejecting the idea, that the popularity of "Shuffle Along" and its many Broadway imitations was what had sent herds of whites stam-peding into the Harlem clubs. He entertains more seriously the possibility that the nightly slumming was a fad, a temporary diversion. It is but a short step to extend this to include the attitudes toward black art more generally. To use critic Sterling Brown's terms, the "exotic primitive" was but a jazzed-up version of the "contented slave" with Harlem as the backdrop.

Fisher ends the piece on a poignant, if not faintly optimistic note:

Willingly would I be an outsider in this if I could know that I read aright—that out of this change in the old familiar ways some finer thing may come. Is this interest akin to that of the Virginians on the veranda of the plantation's big house—sitting

16. May Miller Sullivan, telephone interview, 13 April 1984.
17. Vincent McHugh, "The Left Hand of Rudolph Fisher," *Providence Journal* (5 March 1930).
18. Sterling Brown, telephone interview, 3 October 1983.
19. Bruce Nugent, telephone interview, 26 April 1985.
20. Arthur P. Davis, telephone interviews, 13 April 1984 and 15 May 1985.

genuinely spellbound as they hear the lugubrious strains floating up from the Negro quarters? Is it akin to that of the African explorer, Stanley, leaving a village far behind, but halting in spite of himself to catch the boom of its distant drum? Is it significant of basic human responses, the effect of which, once admitted, will extend far beyond cabarets? Maybe these Nordics at last have tuned in on our wave-length. Maybe they are at least learning to speak our language.[21]

In terms of access and possibility, a truly integrated cabaret might well have served as the twenties' metaphor of democratic participation. This would have meshed with Fisher's hopes, apparently, at this stage of his career. However, a thorough "blackening of the Nordic" was not to be, as Fisher himself demonstrated in his first novel, *The Walls of Jericho*, which I will treat briefly later. The cabaret scene, obligatory as it seems in the work of F. Scott Fitzgerald, Carl Van Vechten, Claude McKay, and others, remained as lively backdrop, and the common meter of the jazz served more as a powerful narcotic than as a significant cultural referent.

Despite Fisher's speculation on a shared idiom, one can ask how signifi-cant the *actual* lives and experiences of Harlemites (the doorman? the waiter? the dancers?) were to the short-term refugees from downtown. Be-yond the fixed image of black life as exotica, how well did the nightly visi-tors come to know the private lives of those around them, to know that even before the Depression Harlem was sliding toward economic decay? Critic after critic suggests that they did not learn this, even if they cared to. Despite the popularity of black musical and literary forms during the twenties, one must look hard and long to find any immediate benefits to the community. Thus, Langston Hughes's wry comment is telling: "The ordinary Negroes hadn't heard of the Negro Renaissance. And if they had, it hadn't raised their wages any."[22]

More startling perhaps is the fact that so few writers used Harlem exten-sively as a backdrop for their fiction. Of course, it is probable that, because none of the writers of the Harlem Renaissance was born *and* reared there, they had not deeply integrated its rituals and rhythms into their working sensibilities. It is the South of Zora Neale Hurston and Jean Toomer and the other varied regions of Hughes that we recall most vividly from the period's fiction. Though admittedly Toomer's knowledge of and experience in the South were scant, he was able to discover and, like Hurston, project power-fully evocative imagery of the region. This was rarely the case for Harlem fiction written during the period. Certainly, if we borrow another idiom, there was little in the fiction to match the range of Duke Ellington's textures

21. Rudolph Fisher, "The Caucasian Storms Harlem," *American Mercury* 11 (August 1927):398.
22. Hughes, *The Big Sea*, 228

as presented in such pieces as "Harlem Flat Blues," "Harlem Speaks," and "Take the A Train." Perhaps the image of a sensuous and joyous Eden (with evil lurking in the shadows) was too deeply felt to be uprooted in so short a time. Perhaps it was enough for the first generation of black urban writers to only suggest the possibilities that later writers like Richard Wright, Ann Petry, and Ralph Ellison—to name just a few—would develop.

It is one of Rudolph Fisher's achievements that he delivered Harlem's breadth and vitality so consistently and extensively. Of all the Renaissance fiction writers, it is to him we must turn time and time again to get the flavor, the music, and the poetry of the 1920s "black capitol of the world."

## THE SHORT STORIES

The short fiction of Dr. Rudolph "Bud" Fisher might be neatly categorized for presentation to a contemporary audience, but like all categories these would be merely for convenience, for the noting of emphases. In this volume, I have grouped the short fiction into two movements—"The Quest" and "The New Land." The first movement offers portraits that treat first or early encounters with Harlem. The new arrivals are rushed through the blur, screech, and bumps of the city and are still feeling their way. Most often, blind trust and intuition are their only guides. They have arrived with great hope, and they struggle to maintain that hope despite disappointments. The conflict of values is sharply drawn in these pieces, and in this battle zone Fisher's use of satire is most effective. The second movement presents those stories in which the principal characters are more familiar with Harlem and its codes. The struggles of these characters often involve salvaging personal integrity from a corrosive cynicism.

Within these movements it is possible, of course, to identify even narrower concerns. However, none of these concerns or emphases is discrete. Throughout this body of work there are overlapping emphases, as there must be in the collected works of any writer, emphases that haunt the specific artistic imagination with the ease of dreams.

One group of stories focuses on city etiquette and generally dramatizes the ambitions and woes of the newcomer to Harlem. I suggest especially "City of Refuge," "Ringtail," "Promised Land," "South Lingers On," and the two children's stories, "Ezekiel" and "Ezekiel Learns." A second group deepens the theme of transition by introducing the specific figure of the ancestor who actively struggles to keep some sense of integrity clear to her young charges. The stories "Promised Land," "Guardian of the Law," and "Miss Cynthie" are representative of this category. A third group treats the problems of Harlemites without the influence of the ancestor and with violence a real threat to personal and communal unity. Common to these pieces is the active force of music, whether as foreshadowing agent, as metaphor, or as balm. In some cases the wisdom of the musical statement substitutes for that of the ancestor. Equally common is the collective cabaret/dance-hall scene. "Common Meter," "Backslider," and "Blades of Steel" include most of the elements defining this series.[23] A fourth group, much smaller than the other three, contains stories that treat caste and class as areas of tension. "High Yaller," "Fire by Night," and "Dust" emphasize these aspects most explicitly. Each of these groups of stories will be discussed in greater detail below.

Finally, there is the long detective story "John Archer's Nose," which is a sequel of sorts to Fisher's second novel, *The Conjure Man Dies*. It is so unlike the rest of the fiction that I will discuss it with the novel. I also urge that the piece, taken with the second novel, offers the fullest persona Fisher was able to develop.

In "City of Refuge," King Solomon Gillis has fled to Harlem from the fictional Waxhaw, North Carolina, home also of Miss Cynthie in a later story.[24] (In "Ezekiel," the home is Waxhaw, Georgia.) As he emerges from the subway, he is assaulted by the blur of Harlem sounds and colors. He is too quickly befriended by Mouse Uggams, a "home-boy," and is soon working in a grocery store. Mouse has arranged for Gillis to sell dope, though Gillis has no idea he is doing anything illegal. He believes firmly in the down-home commitments to friends, newfound or otherwise. Gillis is caught at this trade, arrested in a cabaret, and, after a struggle, led toward jail at the story's end. Throughout this quickly moving story, Fisher supplies many flashes of humor. One of the best examples exploits the clash of dialects so keenly shown in the piece. Gillis has stopped on the street to figure out the direction of a rooming house. Mouse eases up to give directions and eventually befriends him for his own purposes.

"See that second corner? Turn to the left when you get there. Number forty-five's about halfway down the block."
"Thank y', suh."
"You from—Massachusetts?"

23. For a more detailed discussion of the roles of the ancestor figure and secular music in Fisher's short fiction, see my "Aim High and Go Straight: The Grandmother Figure in the Short Fiction of Rudolph Fisher," *Black American Literature Forum* 15 (1981): 55–59; and "Healing Songs: Use of Secular Music in the Short Fiction of Rudolph Fisher," *CLA Journal* 26 (1982):191–203.
24. A typescript for "The City of Refuge" is held in the Brown University Library Archives and tells the story in a slightly different way.

"No, suh, Nawth Ca'lina."

"Is 'at so? You look like a Northerner. Be with us long?"

"Till I die," grinned the flattered King Solomon.

The joke, of course, rests on the crude drawl of the outsider in the face of the street-wise ex-immigrant's slick come-on. Similarly, Fisher juxtaposes the voice of the West Indian stockboy ("Who you call nigger, mon?") with that of Gillis ("How you know dis' is me?"). He even introduces the voice of the Italian immigrant, Gabrielli ("Dope?. .What 's a dis, dope?"). The dissonance of this ensemble of urban immigrant voices defines the relationships among the characters and their limited understanding of the codes of the streets. In this piece only the voices of Mouse and the policeman ("Are you coming without trouble?") communicate with a complete knowledge of that code, even if antagonistic.

Two images of power and possibility especially snag the imagination of Gillis: the flashing green stockings of a passing woman and the sight of a black policeman directing traffic, gruffly giving directions to white folks. With these twin images—sexual glitter and reversed authority—overriding the most powerful ones from the rural South he had known—mob violence and economic repression—Gillis takes on the twentieth-century city.

Many of the ingredients common to Fisher's stories are provided in this first published piece—the displaced person, the quick-paced action, the cabaret scene, and swift violence. What is missing here that was present in another 1925 piece, "The South Lingers On," is the ancestor—the steadying voice of tradition. In "City of Refuge" that voice is partially played out in Gillis's consciousness as he reflects in fragments on the hostile South:

> "Know whut dey done? Dey killed five o' Mose Joplin's hawses 'fo he lef'. Put groun' glass in de feed-trough. Sam Cheevers come up on three of 'em one night pizenin' his well. Bleesom beat Crinshaw out o' sixty acres o' lan an' a year's crops. Dass jess how 't is. Soon 's a nigger make a li'l sump'n he better git to leavin.' An' 'fo long ev'ybody 's goin' be lef'!"

But Solomon is alive with no guide except a con man who deserts him at the end.

Beneath it all is a subtle, yet devastating, critique of the city and the tragedy of self-delusion. Posing no rural and sentimental alternative, this story is an early statement on personal disintegration. Yet the specific flashes of humor overwhelm the tragedy.

The tableau of the outsider trying to maneuver among those more familiar with the city code is similar in Fisher's next published pieces, "Ringtail," "The South Lingers On," and "High Yaller." Originally published in a special edition of *Survey Graphic* in March 1925, "The South Lingers On" is a series of five sketches that introduce the difficulty of communication among the generations, among urban Northerners and transplanted rural Southerners, among the devoutly religious and their exploiters or detractors. The second vignette was deleted when the series was published as "Vestiges" in *New Negro* late the same year.

Both "Ringtail" and "High Yaller" introduced the notion of vengeance, which will be taken up in the discussion of a later piece. What is interesting in these first pieces are the tensions between the Afro-American and the West Indian, which force the action for "Ringtail," and the tensions of color, which are the cause of distress in "High Yaller." Fisher did not return to either theme as a dominant factor in any later published fiction. The latter story echoes the familiar theme of a black passing as nonblack handled in earlier works by William Wells Brown, Charles Chesnutt, James Weldon Johnson, as well as by Fisher's contemporary, Nella Larsen. Considered as too long for H. L. Mencken's *American Mercury*, the story was introduced to *Harper's* with the help of Walter White.[25] The piece eventually appeared in *The Crisis*, where it later won the 1926 first-place Amy Spingarn Prize in the fiction contest sponsored by that magazine. It is interesting to note that the three judges for that contest were Charles Chesnutt, Sinclair Lewis, and H. G. Wells. Both Lewis and Wells placed the story well ahead of three other submissions. Chesnutt praised the plot and Fisher's ambitions for the piece, but, before offering his rankings, said, "To me at least the theme is not convincing."[26]

In one of his most daring unpublished stories, "The Man Who Passed," Fisher treats the passing theme humorously, but from another angle. Peuryn Joel is a white reporter sent to Harlem to pass for black. His editor wants a "descriptive article with plenty of local color." A series of sobering experiences sends Joel back downtown with a more sympathetic view of black life. Incidentally, by the end of the decade the passing story and the theme of color obsession with their attendant oversentimentality were ripe for the swords of the satirists George Schuyler (*Black No More*) and Wallace Thurman (*The Blacker the Berry*).[27]

The majority of Fisher's short fiction, however, sought to portray black intragroup dilemmas involving areas beyond skin color, with class conflict frequently more important than color. We see that in his first four published

25. Rudolph Fisher, letters to Walter White, 5, 11, and 15 February 1925, Personal Correspondence of Walter White/National Association for the Advancement of Colored People Collection. Manuscript Division, Library of Congress.
26. "Words of the Judges," *The Crisis* 31 (1926):276.
27. Fisher did comment on the work of his fellow satirists. See "Harlem Manor," rev. of *Infants of the Spring* by Wallace Turman, and "A Novel That Makes Faces," rev. of *Black No More* by George Schuyler.

pieces, all appearing in 1925, when, again, he was also an intern and later a research fellow, he was to stake out the territory he would explore, often with the eye of a skillful and affectionate surveyor. There is the estrangement often compounded by age and by culture, and the destructive impulses of revenge and social violence with their potential for communal disintegration. In his more mature pieces Fisher would seek ways to bond the community, to heal the rifts and tensions that Harlem experienced while defining itself as a community. To this end I suggest that he was aiming to paint a broad canvas—wedding the best in the traditional ethos with the promise of the modern age as experienced in the city.

The second group of stories involves the presence and force of the ancestor, in all cases an older female figure, a grandmother. Though the grandmother figure does not always explicitly describe the communal loyalties and cohesion of the black community in the rural South, she does occasionally comment on this in the context of urban violence and fragmentation. In most cases she leans on the steadying chords of spirituals, which are occasionally drowned out by the blare of the blues.

Fisher's first portrayal of the grandmother figure was in the vignette "Majutah" in "The South Lingers On." In this sketch as well as in "The Promised Land," the older woman appears helpless to guide her young charges around the snares of city life. In "The Guardian of the Law," the grandmother is far more active and emerges as a savior in several ways. This series culminates in the wonderful "Miss Cynthie." Easily as popular as "City of Refuge," this story was first published in *Story* magazine in June 1933 and has since appeared in numerous anthologies of Afro-American literature. In "Miss Cynthie," Fisher avoids the melodrama of "Guardian of the Law" and the resignation of both "Majutah" and "Promised Land," creating a tender portrait of the tough-spirited Miss Cynthie.

Miss Cynthie comes to New York to visit her grandson, Dave Tappen. She has never been to New York, indeed has never traveled out of the South before, though, unlike King Solomon Gillis, she is blessed with a great deal of mother-wit. At the train station she tells a redcap that he may take her bags but that she will hold on to her umbrella.

> "Always like to have sump'm in my hands when I walk. Can't never tell when you'll run across a snake."
> "There aren't any snakes in the city."
> "There's snakes everywhere, chile."

Such a caution distinguishes her instantly from Gillis. Like Gillis, however, she has brought her baggage of hope and faith to the city. She knows that Dave is a success, and she anticipates a respectable profession. He invites her to a theater where she learns that he is a highly successful dancer and singer. At first, she enters the theater with much trepidation: "She entered the sudden dimness of the interior as involuntarily as in a dream." She is shocked by what she considers the sinful nature of the musical revue and the crowd's response. She is even more surprised when Dave and his girlfriend, Ruth, cavort onstage. When he first appears onstage, after thunderous applause, Dave taps out a rhythm and sings a song taught to him years before by Miss Cynthie. Then he quiets the audience to tell them of the source of his success. It is Miss Cynthie who has taught him to do "like a church steeple—aim high and go straight." He may not have succeeded in a field of which she approved, but he has achieved, nonetheless.

As Dave is singing his secular, childhood song, Miss Cynthie watches its effect on the members of the audience. They are transformed from a loud and sinful crowd to a gathering of children, children who share Dave's memory and remember perhaps a similar song, a similar love and caring. Miss Cynthie concludes that "they didn't mean no harm" in their fervent appreciation of the revue. The crowd, Dave, and Miss Cynthie are brought together in a magic moment of love. Her understanding of an essential innocence and idealism, including her own, that can endure the whirl of city life is important for her acceptance of Dave's work. Dave's singing and recognition of Miss Cynthie—the recognition of a caring tradition—have allowed all present to touch and recall an important dimension of themselves.

In the second draft of an unpublished story entitled "Lindy Hop," probably written during 1932–1933, the grandmother enters a dance contest. It is a desperate gesture to save her granddaughter from winning and reaping awards that will surely lead her to a life of sin. While the grandmother's younger partner dances the contemporary dances, the grandmother dances the traditional dances: the reel, quadrille, schottische, and cakewalk. To the delight of the crowd, agility, speed, and gusto are offset by precision, steadiness, and grace. Youth is balanced by age.[28] It is Fisher's unmistakable point throughout this series of stories that the achievement of this balance—between the insights of tradition and the bold restlessness of the new age—is a significant basis for optimism about the directions of a new community.

The stories in the third group look even more closely at the rift within the community. Humor fades into the background; melodrama, already introduced in the earliest stories, steps forward, center stage. While they explore the theme of personal vengeance, the pieces I have grouped together here seek not only the resolution of personal fragmentation but also a means of

---

28. I draw upon the second version of "Lindy Hop." Two complete versions in typescript and one incomplete handwritten version are housed at the John Hay Library at Brown University.

communal healing. In these pieces we have a typical, though not stock, cabaret dance scene. As related earlier, in "City of Refuge" this setting is the backdrop of Gillis's final confusion. In "High Yaller," the music from the cabaret operates as an ironic frame around, and refrain within, the story. "Backslider" (1927), "Blades of Steel" (1927), and "Common Meter" (1930) develop in their separate ways concerns already well established in the earlier stories. Yet, in these two pieces, Fisher utilizes secular music in ways significantly different than before.

I will focus on "Common Meter" here. In this story the business of the protagonist Bus Williams is music. Williams and Fessenden "Fess" Baxter are rivals for the crowd's adulation and the attention of Miss Jean Ambrose. As in "High Yaller," the opening scene is a dance hall and Fisher moves swiftly to introduce the main conflict. The climax of the story is the battle of the bands, with the leader of the winning band to receive a large victory cup and, presumably, the undivided attention of Miss Ambrose. The reader learns that the drum heads of Tappen, Bus's master percussionist, have been sliced, rendering the drums useless. The devious Fess will stop at nothing to win. When the audience responds poorly to the first two of the scheduled three numbers, Bus is desperate to find a means to catch up with and surpass Fess's score. Identifying with his desperation, Jean provides the key: play a blues tune and turn it into an old-fashioned shout in which the audience can join in clapping and shouting. The stomping feet of the musicians thus take the place of the pulse of the bass drum. The transformation of the audience is instantaneous. They become one with the music and, further, one with a collective past.

> They had been rocked thus, before, this multitude. Two hundred years ago they had swayed to the same slow fateful measure, lifting their lamentation to heaven, pounding the earth with their feet, seeking the mercy of a new God through the medium of an old rhythm, zoom-zoom. They had rocked so a thousand years ago in a city whose walls were jungle, forefending the wrath of a terrible Black God who spoke in storm and pestilence, had swayed and wailed to that same slow period, beaten on a wild boar's skin stretched over the end of a hollow tree trunk.

Bus's orchestra reconstructs the moment that profoundly ties past to present. The blues tune, "St. Louis Blues," strikes a sociohistorical chord that resonates toward the sacred. Far more than serving as a frame and internal refrain then, secular music here explicitly connects an individual's call of romantic despair with the response of control. Here ritual summons collective memory. One recalls similar effects frequently dramatized in narrative poetry. Sterling Brown's "Ma Rainey," for example, portrays the effect of the great blues artist's performances on the crowd:

"O Ma Rainey
Sing yo' song;
Now you's back
Whah you belong,
Git way inside us,
Keep us strong.[29]

True ritual defines and strengthens the group.

In "Blades of Steel," song lyrics help to color, if not direct, the story's central action, and "a curious mingling of the secular and religious" is achieved. Both "Common Meter" and "Blades of Steel," however, used secular lyrics not only to reflect the deepest yearnings of the group but also to alter group and individual consciousnesses in seemingly indifferent or antagonistic contexts.

The fourth group of Fisher's stories concerned caste and class as areas of tension. In one of the few discussions of the short fiction of the Harlem Renaissance, Robert Bone emphasizes the pastoral as a means by which black writers reconciled a number of issues: the conflict of cultures (urban North and rural South), the conflict of classes, and the conflict of races.[30] The result of all this, Bone contends, is the suspension of class divisions. "In recoiling from the values of the white middle-class, black writers sought an alternative value system in the 'lower' world of negro folk culture. Pastoral, with its characteristic inversion of values, was an ideal instrument for this theme."

When he applies this notion to Fisher's work, Bone is correct in identifying the healing spirit as an emphasis. However, he overstates the case when he describes the extent to which Fisher is "torn" between two value systems, that of the street and that of middle-class respectability. This theory might apply to, say, "Fire By Night," but the greater part of Fisher's work, not to speak of the several accounts of his life, does not bear this out. Indeed, as I attempted to suggest earlier, personally and professionally the alliance was an easy one.

Bone's notion of an inversion of values is equally misleading. Reading the pieces in this group, and in fact all the stories, I see not the attempt to show the superiority of black life, as Bone calls it, but a self-assured effort to view the black urban experience as worthy of exploration in its own right. We do not get exotics ready to Charleston at the first lick from a hot trumpet, nor do we get the stereotyped country cousins sitting in the shade and humming all day. We do get vital statements on individuals searching for an ethic in a

29. Sterling Brown, "Ma Rainey," *Collected Poems of Sterling Brown* (New York: Harper and Row, 1980), 62.
30. Robert Bone, *Down Home* (New York: G. P. Putnam's Sons, 1975), 109–59.

time of rapid socioeconomic change. Fisher did not view the modern city as a symbol of civilization or hell. I suggest he viewed the city as frontier, that space between wilderness and civilization. Only through the humanizing and clarifying effect of specific traditional elements as demonstrated in the stories could the urban experience be a liberating and enlightening one. Though the pace may be more leisurely in his two novels, the tensions identified within the short stories are still evident.

## THE NOVELS

B. A. Botkin, in the conclusion of his review of *The Walls of Jericho*, was perhaps the first to address Rudolph Fisher's style as one of the lighter touch.

> Those who look here for the passion that might be expected of on the inside looking out will be as disappointed as those who demand perspective of one on the outside looking in. His is a frankly hedonistic attitude, eschewing protest, poetry, and pity alike. Here are the suave aplomb and easy assurance of one at home in his subject, the self possession of self-understanding, the adroit irony and clever banter of, if not exactly the light, at least the lighter touch.[31]

At any rate, the term has stuck and is often used by more recent critics when addressing Fisher's work. Certainly among Harlem Renaissance satirists his tone and shadings are somewhat less pessimistic than those of Wallace Thurman and less caustic than those of George Schuyler.

The *Walls of Jericho* (1928) presents a Harlem panorama. We are introduced to nearly every layer of social class as Fisher knew them during the late 1920s. The passing theme and class conflict are introduced in ways often comic. Still further, it is a novel that attempts to hold together its many disparate parts through the exploration of the notion of self-delusion. However, the work centers on an evolving relationship between "Shine," a piano-mover, and Linda, an ambitious maid. Shine deludes himself about the possibilities for vengeance from a fellow black. All this is fueled by a metaphor crystallized late in the book. With Linda, Shine listens to a minister shape the story of Joshua and the walls of Jericho. The minister eloquently delivers his point about the continuous struggle against self-delusion. He compares the knowledge of self to Jericho, "chief city of every man's spiritual Canaan." The possession of the soul can be gained only when struggle encouraged by something new threatens some falsely secure sense of self.

Prepared for this wisdom by his involvement with Linda, who challenges him to accept his vulnerability, Shine takes the Jericho metaphor to heart in

31. B. A. Botkin, "The Lighter Touch in Harlem," rev. of *The Walls of Jericho*, *Opportunity* 6 (1928):346.

the last third of the book. He struggles to maintain his tough facade for his friends and at the same time come to grips with his underlying tenderness. This is shown not only in the love relationship but also in his inability to seriously injure two rivals—one apparent (Merrit), the other real (Patmore)—in later action. The characteristic Fisher arrangement of the love triangle and vengeance on the part of the spurned male is acted out here, as in much of the short fiction. In the supreme moment when Shine has Patmore helpless before him, as Eight-Ball has Dirty Cozzens in "Blades of Steel," he hesitates, then releases him. No blues lyric stays his hand, however—only his own sense of compassion freed by his love for Linda.

Most important to Shine's development, however, is his newly gained ability to state the metaphor in his own terms. In recounting the story to Jinx and Bubber as one might recount some bizarre, if comic, ritual, he manipulates the description of the service and sermon to rob it of its deeper meaning. Later, however, he can tell Linda that she is far less hardheaded than she pretends, and he is slowly growing to accept that truth about himself also. Near the novel's end he can state: "The guy that's really hard is the guy that's hard enough to be soft."

Jinx and Bubber, the comic duo who work with Shine, voice the irreverent views of the street crowd on a wide range of subjects. At a few points their banter comes across as a contrived set piece during which dramatic action and narration are frozen. Their dialogue, while consistently quick-paced and playful, too often calls attention to them as opposed to the insight provided by a rapier-tongued Harlem chorus. Perhaps it was this tendency and the lack of any consistent voice with Fisher's own sophistication that prompted W. E. B. DuBois to say in his review of the novel:

> Mr. Fisher does not yet to write of himself and his own people; of Negroes like his mother, his sister and his wife. His real Harlem friends and his own soul nowhere yet appear in his pages, and nothing that can be mistaken for them. The glimpses of better class Negroes which he gives us are poor, ineffective make-believes. One wonders why? Why does Mr. Fisher fear to use his genius to paint his own kind as he has painted Shine and Linda? [32]

One can only imagine DuBois's reaction to a story by Rudolph's sister, Pearl, published in October 1928, the month before DuBois's review of *The Walls of Jericho*. The story, "High Falutin'," does not treat the "better class of Negroes" either.[33] Perhaps the blood of familial imagination was thicker than the water of class loyalty.

32. W. E. B. DuBois, "The Browsing Reader, rev. of *The Walls of Jericho*, *The Crisis* 35 (1928):374. For an article in the same vein see Allison Davis, "Our Negro 'Intellectuals,'" *The Crisis* 35 (1928):268–86.
33. Pearl Fisher, "High Falutin'," *Opportunity* 6 (1928):301–3.

At any rate, a work should be judged by how successfully the writer has worked with the material he has chosen. Fisher is not the first nor will he be the last writer to refuse to write in depth about his current social class. If the characters ring falsely and represent types or caricatures rather than vibrant characters who demand our concern, then that is the point where we make our claims for aesthetic evasion and nowhere else. That is the point where talent, powers of observation, imagination, and empathy have failed the writer.

Incensed by DuBois's review, Wallace Thurman addressed this issue during his brief commentary on the novel.

> The entire universe is the writer's province and so are all the people therein, even lower class Negroes, and if they happen to attract the writer there is no reason why he shouldn't write about them. Nor is it implied here that all Negro writers should write only of "the half world above 125th Street," for such an implication would be just as ridiculous as the one being constantly made by Dr. DuBois.[34]

The black bourgeoisie, no less than the white, comes in for criticism in *The Walls of Jericho*. Their fantasy that "dicty-hood" places them closer to whiteness, their pallid commitment to less fortunate blacks, and their pomposity are all spoofed with quick and telling strokes. However, Fisher focuses his judicious satire on the relationships between blacks and whites. More specifically, he focuses on the presumptions and actions of one Agatha Cramp. Insensitive and patronizing, she is a forerunner to Mrs. Ellsworth in Langston Hughes's "The Blues I'm Playing" and Mrs. Dalton in Richard Wright's *Native Son*. The play on such imposing ignorance, spiced with the slightest hint of sexuality, would receive its most extensive riff in Chester Himes's bawdy *Pinktoes*. Most such portraits belie the DuBoisian notion that racial harmony can be encouraged by sustained contact and dialogue among the leading spokesmen from both races. Good intentions mask much.

More important than Fisher's devastating portrait of Agatha Cramp, however, is its context. Chapters 7–12 constitute the longest scene in the novel, and the setting is the General Improvement Association's annual costume ball. With the proceeds going to black-uplift programs, this event offers the greatest variety of participants of any Harlem social functions. "One great common fellowship in one great common cause," as the narrator states in chapter 7. Yet we soon learn from descriptions of the seating arrangement that democracy is not at work. The powerful sit high, and the "rats" sit low.

Recalling Fisher's comments at the conclusion of "The Caucasian Storms Harlem" on the possible blackening of the Nordics, one can conclude that in

---

34. Wallace Thurman, "High, Low, Past and Present," *Harlem* 1 (1928):31–32.

its best moments the dance floor can serve as a metaphor of democratic participation. Access is freely given, participation is open to all, and possibility in terms of the choice of partners and the personality achieved through dance and dress (many wore costumes) is available insofar as etiquette will allow. However, in the novel the vantage points allowed by the seating arrangement provide not understanding but further self-delusion, with that of Agatha Cramp and her guides reigning supreme. The music does not bind the participants in any significant way, and it is where the dancers go after the music ends that is most revealing. The irony is dramatic and shifts toward sarcasm.

> Ordinary Negroes and rats below, dicties and fays above, the floor beneath the feet of the one constituting the roof over the heads of the other. Somehow, undeniably, a predominance of darker skins below, and just as undeniably, of fairer skins above. Between them, stairways to climb. One might have read in that distribution a complete philosophy of skin color, and from it deduced the past, present, and future of this people. . . . Out on the dance floor everyone, dickty and rat, rubbed joyously elbows, laughing, mingling, forgetting differences. But whenever the music stopped everyone immediately sought his own level.
> One great common fellowship in one great common cause.[35]

More generally, the dance hall/cabaret, like its music—its narrative?—received various uses in Fisher's stories. In "City of Refuge" it is the site of Gillis's final confusion. In "Fire by Night" it is the literal battleground of class conflict. Its anticipation by the three principal characters is the key factor leading to violence in "Blades of Steel." In only two published pieces does this setting define communal harmony. As mentioned earlier, in "Common Meter," Bus's blues unite the crowd around the pulse of racial memory. In "Miss Cynthie," differences in age and values are rendered irrelevant. Miss Cynthie sits on high but, unlike Agatha Cramp, is willing to look closely at the stage and at those below. This music-space is more than backdrop; it is a site of possible transformation and insight. Those who do not profit from the occasion will presumably never profit.

At the end of *Walls of Jericho* Miss Cramp has decided that the plight of the Irish Republic will be her cause for the season. "Shine" and Linda have drawn close, with marriage a distinct possibility. Merrit, the "black" and blond lawyer, functions as their "angel," helping to establish Shine in his own trucking business. Thus, rifts, predicated on self-delusions both individual and communal, are healed for the moment.[36]

35. Rudolph Fisher, *The Walls of Jericho* (New York: Arno Press, 1969), 73–74.
36. I agree with David L. Lewis's excellent summation in his *When Harlem Was in Vogue* (New York; Knopf, 1981), 230.

Fisher's second novel, *The Conjure Man Dies*, which received far briefer reviews and was generally taken less seriously than his first novel, offers two of his most engaging characters. In an enthusiastic review, Arthur P. Davis drew attention to the plot ("startling in it cleverness") as well as to the characters of Frimbo ("a striking creation"), Jinx, and Bubber. Of John Archer he said:

> Dr. Archer is a good authentic detective story type. With his likeable personality, his penchant for dropping into an exaggeratedly pedantic and technical vocabulary, he is of the type of Van Dine's Philo Vance and Carolyn Wells' Fleming Stone—detective fiction heroes that may be used in a series of such works. He has the human quality that will bear the strain of repetition, and we sincerely hope that Dr. Fisher will carry him on.[37]

In another favorable review, a *Time* writer proved himself capable of some mystery writing, as the following two sentences demonstrate: "His (Fisher's) detective story is one of the first by a Negro and with an all-Negro cast. Negroes are suitable for mystery stories because they are hard to see in the dark[!] and because white folk not knowing much about them, believe them primitively prone to violence"[38] (exclamation added). If Dubois and the others were indignant or befuddled by Fisher's unwillingness to treat the lives of the middle and professional classes in a sympathetic or complex manner, one might speculate that they would be even more indignant when Fisher tried his hand at the mystery novel. Because this novel, its stage adaptations, and "John Archer's Nose" may be less familiar to readers, I will treat them all together.

During the 1920s the American detective story was in its infancy. Though most critical literature of the period cited Edgar Allen Poe as the father of the mystery story, the genre enjoyed far more success in Europe, specifically in England and France, than in America. The critical literature of the period also displayed a rampant defensiveness over the question of whether the detective story, with its growing audience, was worthy of serious attention from literary critics. Although the issue was far from settled in 1932, the fans of the genre were committed and loyal. Fisher's foray into detective fiction could be considered a risk that went beyond the realistic/naturalistic strategies of other Afro-American writers. As a black fiction writer he risked legitimacy in a form not then taken seriously. One wonders, given the sparse attention given to Chester Himes's detective stories later, whether the form is taken seriously today. It is significant that *The Conjure Man Dies* is rarely

---

37. Arthur P. Davis, "Harlem Mysterious," rev. of *The Conjure Man Dies*, *Opportunity* 10 (1932):320.

38. Rev. of *The Conjure Man Dies*, *Time*, 1 August 1932, p. 39.

treated in discussions of novels written by black Americans. In two of the more provocative surveys, for example, Robert Bone's *The Negro Novel in America* and Addison Gayle's *The Way of the New World*, the novel is ignored.

The mystery in *The Conjure Man Dies* turns on the search for the murderer of Dr. N'gana Frimbo, a popular Harlem conjure man and caster of spells. In the opening scene, Dr. John Archer is summoned to examine the corpse of Frimbo. He quickly enlists the aid of his friend and intellectual sparring partner, Perry Dart, one of the few black detectives in the New York Police Department. All five of the suspects were in the room at the time of the victim's death. Because of a coincidence of fingerprints and a stolen handkerchief, Jinx Jenkins—one-half of the comic duo that appeared in the first novel—and Easley Jones, a railroad porter, emerge as the primary suspects.

We learn much later, after Jinx's partner, Bubber, is chased to the basement of Frimbo's house, that Frimbo did not die; still later, we learn that the corpse is that of his assistant. As part of a West African custom, Frimbo is responsible for the proper disposal of the body. This disclosure forces a confrontation scene in which Frimbo begins to interrogate all suspects and witnesses. Unfortunately, this setting also permits the murderer a second chance to murder Frimbo. This time the murderer is successful, though Dart and his men are on hand to promptly capture him.

For most of this highly entertaining book, the personality of Frimbo, like his consultation chambers, is shrouded in darkness. Yet by the end he has emerged as the most interesting character in the tale. He senses that Archer is a man of like interests and equally keen analytical powers. In a lengthy conversation between the two, the conjure man reveals that he is the king of a small West African country. He has abandoned his kingship to learn the lessons of western civilization in the frontier of the American city. Here, despite the racial injustices he has had to suffer, he has managed to finish Harvard and continue deep reading in philosophy and psychology. Frimbo concludes the talk by describing to Archer his faith in an "applied determinism" that is both physical and mental. The combination of these factors gives him extraordinary powers:

> I am a catalyst. I accelerate or retread a reaction without entering into it. This changes the cross currents, so that the coincidences are different from what they would otherwise be. A husband reaches home twenty minutes too soon. A traveler misses his train—and escapes death in a wreck. Simple, is it not? [39]

39. Rudolph Fisher, *The Conjure Man Dies* (New York: Arno Press, 1971), 228

Archer is stunned by Frimbo's revelations and promises another talk, a talk, unfortunately, that will never take place.

Until one learns that Frimbo is the pursued and later the victim, one could regard the Frimbo-Archer encounter as similar to that between Professor Moriarty and Sherlock Holmes in "The Adventure of the Final Problem": two men of equal intellectual power, one a force for good, the other a force of diabolical evil. "What a man!" Archer is forced to confess. Holmes speaks similarly of his rival: "You know my powers, my dear Watson, and yet at the end of three months I was forced to confess that I had at last met an antagonist who was my intellectual equal." By comparison the character of the detective-protagonist—Archer, in this case, is not technically a detective but rather a scientific sleuth—is not developed. These facts seem to ignore one of the early tenets of detective fiction.

In the lengthy introduction to *The Greatest Detective Stories*, Willard Huntington Wright, a.k.a. S. S. Van Dine, suggests that "the most important and original element of the criminal-problem story" is the detective himself. "The life of the book takes place in him, yet the life of the narrative has its being outside of him." [40] In addition to Sir Arthur Conan Doyle's Sherlock Holmes, one thinks of Agatha Christie's Hercule Poirot and of Dashiell Hammett's Sam Spade in this regard.

Aside from Archer's stilted diction, urbane punning, and nimble intellect we know relatively little about the physician. We learn a little of his past from Frimbo. When Archer reluctantly provides the bare outlines of his youth to Frimbo, he suggests that the dull record of his youth is no match for the thrilling account of the African's early life. Yet Frimbo fills in the picture with swift and, apparently, accurate strokes.

> You have omitted the drama my friend. Your father's struggle to educate you, his clinging on to life just to see you complete a college training—which had been denied him; your desperate helplessness, facing the probability of not being able to go on into medicine; the impending alternative of teaching school in some Negro academy; the thrill of discovering help; the rigid economy, to keep the final amount of your debt as low as possible . . . the resentment you feel at this moment against your inability to do what you are mentally equipped to do. If drama is struggle, my friend, your life is a perfect play. [41]

Yet that play never moves beyond outline form. Throughout the book Archer remains the detached scientist with a voice identical to that of the typical Fisher narrator who so often connects and comments on the action

---

40. Willard Wright, "The Great Detective Stories," in *The Art of the Mystery Story*, ed. Howard Haycroft (New York: Biblo and Tannen, 1976), 40.
41. *The Conjure Man Dies*, 224

in the short stories. One senses in both Archer and the short-story narrator a bemused anthropologist watching the streets of Harlem from a third-story brownstone window. With his academic background as well as his love for Harlem cabarets, blues, and jazz, Dr. Fisher was unable in his brief career to synthesize these two seemingly contradictory experiences in one character. Consider the good doctor Archer collecting black jokes and folktales or patting a foot to a song belted out by Ethel Waters at the Savoy while he sips bad gin. It is difficult. It is easier to view him sitting in a large comfortable chair, tastefully aged and positioned near a crackling fire, his own pipe sending forth a pungent odor. On a small table next to the chair would be a small tumbler of cream sherry. The doctor would be reading and alternately chuckling and frowning over the plot intricacies of, say, Dickens's *Bleak House*.

On this last point it is significant that a locale involving secular music, so revealing in the development of other narratives, is missing in *The Conjure Man Dies*. Certainly for the demands of the novel's focus Fisher was correct to keep most of the action close to the building where the first murder was committed. However, another space, a memory described to Archer by Frimbo, is important. Frimbo describes the Malindo, the feast of procreation performed in his father's African kingdom and witnessed by Frimbo when he was a child:

> At the chief's signal, the player of the largest drum stretches his arms high over his head and brings the heels of both hands down hard on the face of his instrument. There is a deep, resounding boom, a sound such as no other instrument has ever produced; as low and resonate as the deepest organ note, as startlingly sudden as an explosion. A prowling cat five miles away will halt and cringe at that sound. The stillness that follows trembles in the memory of it; as that tremor dwindles the drummer strikes again—the cadence is established. Again, again. Slowly, steadily the great drum booms, a measure so large, so stately, so majestic, that all that follows is subordinated to it and partakes of its dignity.[42]

As the ritual proceeds we see the unifying effect of myth and performance; though the setting is not Harlem, the effect is the same as in that supreme moment in "Common Meter." For this story, however, Frimbo is describing a reality that Archer must accept if he is to truly comprehend the complexity of Frimbo. Finally, the close attempt at a developed synthesis is not in the character of Archer but rather in that of Frimbo, despite the fact that the African past as rendered through Frimbo's memory appears over-romanticized.

Perhaps here we can now account for some of the apparent ease of this

42. Ibid., 219.

novel's achievement. The novel blends Fisher's artistic imagination and the scientific method. That is, a full and compelling narrative is developed, but at the same time its resolution depends on the solving of a mystery. That solution is brought about by the same methods a scientific investigator would use to resolve a research problem—observation, experimentation, interpretation, explanation. Physicians might explain it in terms of treating a disease—observation, diagnosis, treatment, prognosis. These steps, as made by Archer and in conjunction with Frimbo's special knowledge, lead toward an explanation of the mystery.

As metaphor, it is significant that Frimbo's concept of "applied determinism," integrating both physical and mental powers, emerges from the shroud of a conjure man's exotica. Still further, his method of explanation—while not discounting intuition, as a great researcher would not—"freed" Dr. Archer to entertain a larger array of possibilities. Though this is not precisely what Fisher meant in his commencement address years earlier when he talked of harmony between science and religion, the novel does demonstrate a resolution between science and religious belief. Intellectually, this novel is the most engaging of Fisher's fiction. Fisher planned at least two sequels to this novel. At the time of his death one was already underway, tentatively titled "Thus Spake the Prophet."[43]

It might be proper here to comment briefly on the novel's adaptation to the stage. The play *The Conjur' Man Dies* was staged as part of the Federal Theater Project and opened 11 March 1936 at Harlem's Lafayette Theater. Hallie Flanagan, author of a study of the project, reports that some eighty-three thousand people viewed the play during its stay at the Lafayette.[44] Later, during the summer, the play ran for five days at Cleveland's Karamu House. Reviews of both productions suggest, as the script shows, that the comic elements and not Frimbo's rich personality were highlighted for the stage.[45] Jinx and Bubber slip dangerously close to minstrelsy, and the religiosity of one of the minor characters is lampooned. Generally, the play stands as a much weaker version of the novel, though popular during its brief runs.

Fisher's last published story, "John Archer's Nose," appeared in the short-

43. John Clark, "Mystery Novel Writer Is Interviewed over the Radio," *Pittsburgh Courier*, 21 January 1933: Schomburg Center Vertical File.
44. Hallie Flanagan, *Arena* (New York: Duell, Sloan and Pearce, 1940), 69. Also see Doris Abramson, *Negro Playwrights in the American Theatre, 1925–1959* (New York: Columbia University Press, 1969), 59–63.
45. Brooks Atkinson, "Harlem Mumbo-Jumbo," rev. of *The Conjur' Man Dies, New York Times*, 12 March 1936, Rudolph Fisher papers/James Weldon Johnson Collection, Yale University Libraries; Glenn Pullen, "Who-Done-It Play Offered by WPA Group," *Cleveland Plain Dealer*, 13 August 1936, p. 10, Archives of Western Reserve Historical Society. Play typescript on microfilm at Arthur A. Schomburg Center for Research in Black Culture, New York Public Library.

lived *Metropolitan* magazine one month after his death. In the opening scene, Dr. Archer relates to Detective Dart how he has failed to save the life of a child because the family, trusting to magic charms, called him in too late. In the middle of a conversation about Afro-American superstitions, the two men are summoned to the scene of a murder. A young man of twenty, Sonny Dewey, has been murdered in his bed, and the story turns on the discovery of the murderer. As in the novel, the possible murderers are limited to those in the Dewey apartment at the time of the death—Sonny's mother, sister, brother, and sister-in-law. As Dart and Archer try to unravel a motive, the finger of guilt points in turn at each member of the family. By the end of the story we must conclude that the mother has taken the life of her son, not to end his hard-living ways, but because he is slowly dying from tuberculosis. Her husband has also died from the disease, and none of her lucky charms and home remedies had been able to save him or help her son. She confesses that she must have lacked faith in her own remedies and therefore made up her mind to kill her son rather than watch him suffer. However, Archer, who has been haunted by a strong odor ever since he entered the Dewey apartment, introduces a new twist, which links the death of the infant to the death of Sonny.

This fast-paced story does not bring the character of Dr. Archer into any sharper focus than the novel; we learn nothing new about his personality or interests. What is of importance is Fisher's elaboration on the subject of superstition and its possible tragic consequences. In the novel, Frimbo's business flourishes because of the faith others have in his powers, though he is powerless to save himself. At the conclusion of this final story, Archer doubts that superstition will ever be stopped. Indeed, he wonders aloud whether any religion is anything more than a collection of superstitions.

Fisher has treated seriously an element of traditional experience used more often than not in American fiction for comic effect. Certainly superstition is treated as such in the play. Critic Darwin Turner in his discussion of black drama from 1920 to 1960 has pointed out such uses in the plays of the 1920s and 1930s: "Negro playwrights of those decades who pictured superstition as a characteristic of the race used it for three purposes: local color, criticism, and comedy. Significantly, however, by associating superstition with the older characters in the plays, they identified it with the past rather than with the future of the race."[46] This is equally true in the fiction of the period. Though we have seen this dynamic at work in Fisher's fiction as it relates to street life—cabarets, dance halls, theaters—we have also seen it as

46. Darwin Turner, "The Negro Dramatist's Image of the Universe, 1920–1960," in *Black Voices*, ed. Abraham Chapman (New York: New American Library, 1968), 682

it related to a fear of the new scientific method and technology. In "Skeeter," an unpublished story, the unemployed main character is in Harlem Hospital awaiting X-rays. The narrator describes the young man's thoughts: "They (x-rays) were mysterious and miraculous contrivances whereby you could see right through everything and everybody. . . . No doubt by turning them on one's head you could see all of one's thoughts, also."[47] The moment is as hilarious and as loaded with science fiction possibilities as the operation scene in Ellison's *Invisible Man*, though the intentions are far less insidious in Fisher's tale. However his stories arrive at the point, for Fisher the challenge of integrating a modifying rural past with the urban present and future was crucial to growth. In his short fiction, the integration is complicated by the disruptive effects of the urban experience on traditional values and institutions such as church and family. In the detective fiction, the emphasis is on critiquing a survivalism of rural life, which can be regressive and tragic. Consistent throughout is Fisher's view on the dangers of self-delusion and provincialism.

Thus, in the two detective stories, Fisher was able to extend his concerns with the effects of urbanization of black America. Also, he was able to add uniquely to the growing series of pieces that focused on the black intellectual (Archer and Dart) as urban hero. This trend has been followed in more recent times by writers as disparate as Ralph Ellison (*Invisible Man*) and Amiri Baraka (*The Dutchman* and *The Slave*).

Fisher also established a solid foundation upon which Chester Himes and Ishmael Reed could develop their black detective novels. Reed's experiments in *Mumbo-Jumbo* and *The Last Days of Louisiana Red* are especially noteworthy here in the way in which the hero, LaBas, utilizes science and hoodoo to unravel mysteries. Chester Himes wrote nine detective novels set in Harlem. The first, *For Love of Imabelle*, appeared first in French under the title *La Reine des Pommes* in 1958. In his autobiographies and in interviews, there was no indication that Himes had read *The Conjure Man Dies*, though he could very well have seen the Karamu House production of the stage adaptation in 1936. On one occasion he related very briefly that he did know of Fisher.[48] At any rate, without attempting to demonstrate influence, one can note significant similarities in their capacities for close description and humor.

*   *   *

47. "Skeeter," typescript in possession of Mrs. Jane Ryder Fisher, pp. 11–12.
48. John A. Williams, "My Man Himes," *Aimstad* 1, ed. Charles Harris (New York: Vintage, 1970), 50.

In March, October, and December of 1934, Fisher underwent operations for a stomach disorder. He rallied after the third one, but only briefly. He died on 26 December 1934 at the Edgecombe Sanitarium, Edgecombe Avenue and 137th Street. Friends were shocked and saddened. Telegrams and condolences poured into the Fisher apartment from all over the country. The one taken at the Western Union Office on the morning of the 27th crystallized the feelings of many:

THE WORLD HAS LOST A GENIUS. YOU HAVE LOST A HUSBAND AND I HAVE LOST A FRIEND. Zora Neale Hurston.[49]

Fisher was buried on 29 December. He was a First Lieutenant in the reserve medical corps of the 369th Infantry, and members of the detachment were in attendance.

In a 1933 radio interview, Fisher responded to a question on whether he intended to write of Harlem exclusively in the future. His answer is important: "I intend to write whatever interests me. But if I should be fortunate enough to become known as Harlem's interpreter, I should be very happy."[50] At a time when the general strategy in black fiction seemed to oscillate too often between a dramatic indictment of a racist society in a strict realist mode and a too facile celebration of black urban life, Dr. Rudolph Fisher kept steadily to the task of probing and exploring. With both affection and a critical eye, he presented a symmetrical portrait of the Afro-American encounter with the modern city. It is Rudolph Fisher's achievement to have given us some of Harlem's possibilities so entertainingly, so carefully and wisely, beyond mere cleverness and glibness, during his short time on this earth.

49. Telegram in possession of Mrs. Fisher.
50. Clark, "Mystery Novel Writer Is Interviewed over the Radio."

# I. THE QUEST

# THE CITY OF REFUGE

Confronted suddenly by daylight, King Solomon Gillis stood dazed and blinking. The railroad station, the long, white-walled corridor, the impassable slot-machine, the terrifying subway train—he felt as if he had been caught up in the jaws of a steam-shovel, jammed together with other helpless lumps of dirt, swept blindly along for a time, and at last abruptly dumped.

There had been strange and terrible sounds: "New York! Penn Terminal—all change!" "Pohter, hyer, pohter, suh?" Shuffle of a thousand soles, clatter of a thousand heels, innumerable echoes. Cracking rifle-shots—no, snapping turnstiles. "Put a nickel in!" "Harlem? Sure. This side—next train." Distant thunder, nearing. The screeching onslaught of the fiery hosts of hell, headlong, breathtaking. Car doors rattling, sliding, banging open. "Say, wha' d'ye think this is, a baggage car?" Heat, oppression, suffocation—eternity—"Hundred 'n turdy-fif' next!" More turnstiles. Jonah emerging from the whale.

Clean air, blue sky, bright sunlight.

Gillis set down his tan cardboard extension case and wiped his black, shining brow. Then slowly, spreadingly, he grinned at what he saw: Negroes at every turn; up and down Lenox Avenue, up and down 135th Street; big, lanky Negroes, short, squat Negroes; black ones, brown ones, yellow ones; men standing idle on the curb, women, bundle-laden, trudging reluctantly homeward, children rattle-trapping about the sidewalks; here and there a white face drifting along, but Negroes predominantly, overwhelmingly everywhere. There was assuredly no doubt of his whereabouts. This was Negro Harlem.

Back in North Carolina Gillis had shot a white man and, with the aid of prayer and an automobile, probably escaped a lynching. Carefully avoiding the railroads, he had reached Washington in safety. For his car a Southwest bootlegger had given him a hundred dollars and directions to Harlem; and so he had come to Harlem.

Ever since a traveling preacher had first told him of the place, King Solomon Gillis had longed to come to Harlem. The Uggams were always talking about it; one of their boys had gone to France in the draft and, returning, had never got any nearer home than Harlem. And there were occasional "colored" newspapers from New York: newspapers that mentioned Negroes without comment, but always spoke of a white person as "So-and-so, white." That was the point. In Harlem, black was white. You had rights that could not be denied you; you had privileges, protected by law. And you had money. Everybody in Harlem had money. It was a land of plenty. Why, had not Mouse Uggam sent back as much as fifty dollars at a time to his people in Waxhaw?

The shooting, therefore, simply catalyzed whatever sluggish mental reaction had been already directing King Solomon's fortunes toward Harlem. The land of plenty was more than that now; it was also the city of refuge.

Casting about for direction, the tall newcomer's glance caught inevitably on the most conspicuous thing in sight, a magnificent figure in blue that stood in the middle of the crossing and blew a whistle and waved great white-gloved hands. The Southern Negro's eyes opened wide; his mouth opened wider. If the inside of New York had mystified him, the outside was amazing him. For there stood a handsome brass-buttoned giant directing the heaviest traffic Gillis had ever seen; halting unnumbered tons of automobiles and trucks and wagons and pushcarts and streetcars; holding them at bay with one hand while he swept similar tons peremptorily on with the other; ruling the wide crossing with supreme self-assurance. And he, too, was a Negro!

Yet most of the vehicles that leaped or crouched at his bidding carried white passengers. One of these overdrove bounds a few feet, and Gillis heard the officer's shrill whistle and gruff reproof, saw the driver's face turn red and his car draw back like a threatened pup. It was beyond belief—impossible. Black might be white, but it could n't be that white!

"Done died an' woke up in Heaven," thought King Solomon, watching, fascinated; and after a while, as if the wonder of it were too great to believe simply by seeing, "Cullud policemans!" he said, half aloud; then repeated over and over, with greater and greater conviction, "Even got cullud policemans—even got cullud—"

"Where y' want to go, big boy?"

Gillis turned. A little, sharp-faced yellow man was addressing him.

"Saw you was a stranger. Thought maybe I could help y' out."

King Solomon located and gratefully extended a slip of paper. "Wha' dis hyeh at, please, suh?"

The other studied it a moment, pushing back his hat and scratching his head. The hat was tall-crowned, unindented brown felt; the head was brown patent-leather, its glistening brush-back flawless save for a suspicious crimpiness near the clean-grazed edges.

"See that second corner? Turn to the left when you get there. Number forty-five's about halfway [down] the block."

"Thank y', suh."

"You from—Massachusetts?"

"No, suh, Nawth Ca'lina."

"Is 'at so? You look like a Northerner. Be with us long?"

"Till I die," grinned the flattered King Solomon.

"Stoppin' there?"

"Reckon I is. Man in Washin'ton 'lowed I'd find lodgin' at dis ad-dress."

"Good enough. If y' don't maybe I can fix y' up. Harlem's pretty crowded. This is me." He proffered a card.

"Thank y', suh," said Gillis, and put the card in his pocket.

The little yellow man watched him plod flat-footedly on down the street, long awkward legs never quite straightened, shouldered extension-case bending him sidewise, wonder upon wonder halting or turning him about. Presently, as he proceeded, a pair of bright green stockings caught and held his attention. Tony, the storekeeper, was crossing the sidewalk with a bushel basket of apples. There was a collision; the apples rolled; Tony exploded; King Solomon apologized. The little yellow man laughed shortly, took out a notebook, and put down the address he had seen on King Solomon's slip of paper.

"Guess you're the shine I been waitin' for," he surmised.

As Gillis, approaching his destination, stopped to rest, a haunting notion grew into an insistent idea. "Dat li'l yaller nigger was a sho' 'nuff gen'man to show me de road. Seem lak I knowed him befo'—" He pondered. That receding brow, that sharp-ridged, spreading nose, that tight upper lip over the two big front teeth, that chinless jaw—He fumbled hurriedly for the card he had not looked at and eagerly made out the name.

"Mouse Uggam, sho' 'nuff! Well, dog-gone!"

II

Uggam sought out Tom Edwards, once a Pullman porter, now prosperous proprietor of a cabaret, and told him:

"Chief, I got him: a baby jess in from the land o'cotton and so dumb he thinks ante bellum's an old woman."

"Where'd you find him?"

"Where you find all the jaybirds when they first hit Harlem—at the subway entrance. This one come up the stairs, batted his eyes once or twice, an' froze to the spot—with his mouth wide open. Sure sign he's from 'way down behind the sun and ripe f' the pluckin'."

Edwards grinned a gold-studded, fat-jowled grin. "Gave him the usual line, I suppose?"

"Did n't miss. An' he fell like a ton o' bricks. 'Course I've got him spotted, but damn 'f I know jess how to switch 'em on to him."

"Get him a job around a store somewhere. Make out you're befriendin' him. Get his confidence."

"Sounds good. Ought to be easy. He's from my state. Maybe I know him or some of his people."

"Make out you do, anyhow. Then tell him some fairy tale that'll switch your trade to him. The cops'll follow the trade. We could even let Froggy flop into some dumb white cop's hands and 'confess' where he got it. See?"

"Chief, you got a head, no lie."

"Don't lose no time. And remember, hereafter, it's better to sacrifice a little than to get squealed on. Never refuse a customer. Give him a little credit. Humor him along till you can get rid of him safe. You don't know what that guy that died may have said; you don't know who's on to you now. And if they get you—I don't know you."

"They won't get *me*," said Uggam.

King Solomon Gillis sat meditating in a room half the size of his hencoop back home, with a single window opening for an airshaft.

An airshaft: cabbage and chitterlings cooking; liver and onions sizzling, sputtering; three player-pianos out-plunking each other; a man and a woman calling each other vile things; a sick, neglected baby wailing; a phonograph broadcasting blues; dishes clacking; a girl crying heartbrokenly; waste noises, waste odors of a score of families, seeking issue through a common channel; pollution from bottom to top—a sewer of sounds and smells.

Contemplating this, King Solomon grinned and breathed, "Dog-gone!" A little later, still gazing into the sewer, he grinned again. "Green stockin's," he said; "loud green!" The sewer gradually grew darker. A window lighted up opposite, revealing a woman in camisole and petticoat, arranging her hair. King Solomon, staring vacantly, shook his head and grinned yet again. "Even got cullud policemans!" he mumbled softly.

# III

Uggam leaned out of the room's one window and spat maliciously into the dinginess of the airshaft. "Damn glad you got him," he commented as Gillis finished his story. "They's a thousand shines in Harlem would change places with you in a minute jess f' the honor of killin' a cracker."

"But I did n't go to do it. 'T was a accident."

"That's the only part to keep secret."

"Know whut dey done? Dey killed five o' Mose Joplin's hawses 'fo he lef'. Put groun' glass in de feed-trough. Sam Cheevers come up on three of 'em one night pizenin' his well. Bleesom beat Crinshaw out o' sixty acres o' lan' an' a year's crops. Dass jess how 't is. Soon 's a nigger make a li'l sump'n he better git to leavin'. An' 'fo long ev'ybody's goin' be lef'!"

"Hope to hell they don't all come here."

The doorbell of the apartment rang. A crescendo of footfalls in the hallway culminated in a sharp rap on Gillis's door. Gillis jumped. Nobody but a policeman would rap like that. Maybe the landlady had been listening and had called the law. It came again, loud, quick, angry. King Solomon prayed that the policeman would be a Negro.

Uggam stepped over and opened the door. King Solomon's apprehensive eyes saw framed therein, instead of a gigantic officer, calling for him, a little blot of a creature, quite black against even the darkness of the hallway, except for a dirty wide-striped silk shirt, collarless, with the sleeves rolled up.

"Ah hahve bill fo' Mr. Gillis." A high, strongly accented Jamaican voice, with its characteristic singsong intonation, interrupted King Solomon's sigh of relief.

"Bill? Bill fo' me? What kin' o' bill?"

"Wan bushel appels. T'ree seventy-fife."

"Apples? I ain' bought no apples." He took the paper and read aloud, laboriously, "Antonio Gabrielli to K. S. Gillis, Doctor—"

"Mr. Gabrielli say, you not pays him, he send policemon."

"What I had to do wid 'is apples?"

"You bumps into him yesterday, no? Scatter appels everywhere—on the sidewalk, in de gutter. Kids pick up an' run away. Others all spoil. So you pays."

Gillis appealed to Uggam. "How 'bout it, Mouse?"

"He's a damn liar. Tony picked up most of 'em; I seen him. Lemme look at that bill—Tony never wrote this thing. This baby's jess playin' you for a sucker."

"Ain' had no apples, ain' payin' fo' none," announced King Solomon, thus prompted. "Did n't have to come to Harlem to git cheated. Plenty o' dat right wha' I come fum."

But the West Indian warmly insisted. "You cahn't do daht, mon. Whaht you t'ink, 'ey? Dis mon loose 'is appels an' 'is money too?"

"What diff'ence it make to you, nigger?"

"Who you call nigger, mon? Ah hahve you understahn'—"

"Oh, well, white folks, den. What all you got t' do wid dis hyeh, anyhow?"

"Mr. Gabrielli send me to collect bill!"

"How I know dat?"

"Do Ah not bring bill? You t'ink Ah steal t'ree dollar, 'ey?"

"Three dollars an' sebenty-fi' cent," corrected Gillis. "Nuther thing: wha' you ever see me befo'? How you know dis is me?"

"Ah see you, sure. Ah help Mr. Gabrielli in de store. When you knocks down de baskette appels, Ah see. Ah follow you. Ah know you comes in dis house."

"Oh, you does? An' how come you know my name an' flat an' room so good? How come dat?"

"Ah fin' out. Sometime Ah brings up here vegetables from de store."

"Humph! Mus' be workin' on shares."

"You pays, 'ey? You pays me or de policemon?"

"Wait a minute," broke in Uggam, who had been thoughtfully contemplating the bill. "Now listen, big shorty. You haul hips on back to Tony. We got your menu all right"—he waved the bill—"but we don't eat your kind o' cookin', see?"

The West Indian flared. "Whaht it is to you, 'ey? You can not mind your own business? Ah hahve not spik to you!"

"No, brother. But this is my friend, an' I'll be john-browned if there's a monkey-chaser in Harlem can gyp him if I know it, see? Bes' think f' you to do is to catch air, toot sweet."

Sensing frustration, the little islander demanded the bill back. Uggam figured he could use the bill himself, maybe. The West Indian hotly persisted; he even menaced. Uggam pocketed the paper and invited him to take it. Wisely enough, the caller preferred to catch air.

When he had gone, King Solomon sought words of thanks.

"Bottle it," said Uggam. "The point is this: I figger you got a job."

"Job? No I ain't! Wha' at?"

"When you show Tony this bill, he'll hit the roof and fire that monk."

"What ef he do?"

"Then you up 'n ask f' the job. He'll be too grateful to refuse. I know Tony some, an' I'll be there to put in a good word. See?"

King Solomon considered this. "Sho' needs a job, but ain' after stealin' none."

"Stealin'? 'T would n't be stealin'. Stealin' 's what that damn monkey-chaser tried to do from you. This would be doin' Tony a favor an' gettin' y'self out o' the barrel. What 's the holdback?"

"What make you keep callin' him monkey-chaser?"

"West Indian. That's another thing. Any time y' can knife a monk, do it. They's too damn many of 'em here. They 're an achin' pain."

"Jess de way white folks feels 'bout niggers."

"Damn that. How 'bout it? Y' want the job?"

"Hm—well—I'd ruther be a policeman."

"Policeman?" Uggam gasped.

"M-hm. Dass all I wants to be, a policeman, so I kin police all the white folks right plumb in jail!"

Uggam said seriously, "Well, y' might work up to that. But it takes time. An' y've got to eat while y're waitin'." He paused to let this penetrate. "Now how 'bout this job at Tony's in the meantime? I should think y'd jump at it."

King Solomon was persuaded.

"Hm—well—reckon I does," he said slowly.

"Now y're tootin'!" Uggam's two big front teeth popped out in a grin of genuine pleasure. "Come on. Let's go."


IV

Spitting blood and crying with rage, the West Indian scrambled to his feet. For a moment he stood in front of the store gesticulating furiously and jabbering shrill threats and unintelligible curses. Then abruptly he stopped and took himself off.

King Solomon Gillis, mildly puzzled, watched him from Tony's doorway. "I jess give him a li'l shove," he said to himself, "an' he roll' clean 'cross de sidewalk." And a little later, disgustedly, "Monkey-chaser!" he grunted, and went back to his sweeping.

"Well, big boy, how y' comin' on?"

Gillis dropped his broom. "Hay-o, Mouse. Wha' you been las' two-three days?"

"Oh, around. Gettin' on all right here? Had any trouble?"

"Deed I ain't—ceptin' jess now I had to throw 'at li'l jigger out."

"Who? The monk?"

"M-hm. He sho' Lawd doan like me in his job. Look like he think I stole it from him, stiddy him tryin' to steal from me. Had to push him down sho' nuff 'fo I could get rid of 'im. Den he run off talkin' Wes' Indi'man an' shakin' his fis' at me."

"Ferget it." Uggam glanced about. "Where's Tony?"

"Boss man? He be back direckly."

"Listen—like to make two or three bucks a day extra?"

"Huh?"

"Two or three dollars a day more 'n what you're gettin' already?"

"Ain' I near 'nuff in jail now?"

"Listen." King Solomon listened. Uggam had n't been in France for nothing. Fact was, in France he'd learned about some valuable French medicine. He'd brought some back with him,—little white pills,—and while in Harlem had found a certain druggist who knew what they were and could supply all he could use. Now there were any number of people who would buy and pay well for as much of this French medicine as Uggam could get. It was good for what ailed them, and they did n't know how to get it except through him. But he had no store in which to set up an agency and hence no single place where his customers could go to get what they wanted. If he had, he could sell three or four times as much as he did.

King Solomon was in a position to help him now, same as he had helped King Solomon. He would leave a dozen packages of the medicine—just small envelopes that could all be carried in a coat pocket—with King Solomon every day. Then he could simply send his customers to King Solomon at Tony's store. They'd make some trifling purchase, slip him a certain coupon which Uggam had given them, and King Solomon would wrap the little envelope of medicine with their purchase. Must n't let Tony catch on, because he might object, and then the whole scheme would go gaflooey. Of course it would n't really be hurting Tony any. Would n't it increase the number of his customers?

Finally, at the end of each day, Uggam would meet King Solomon some place and give him a quarter for each coupon he held. There'd be at least ten or twelve a day—two and a half or three dollars plumb extra! Eighteen or twenty dollars a week.

"Dog-gone!" breathed Gillis.

"Does Tony ever leave you heer alone?"

"M-hm. Jess started dis mawnin'. Doan nobody much come round 'tween ten an' twelve, so he done took to doin' his buyin' right 'long 'bout dat time. Nobody hyeh but me fo' 'n hour or so."

"Good. I'll try to get my folks to come 'round here mostly while Tony's out, see?"

"I doan miss."

Rudolph Fisher

"Sure y' get the idea, now?" Uggam carefully explained it all again. By the time he had finished, King Solomon was wallowing in gratitude.

"Mouse, you sho' is been a friend to me. Why, 'f 't had n' been fo' you—"

"Bottle it," said Uggam. "I'll be round to your room tonight with enough stuff for tomorrer, see? Be sure 'n be there."

"Won't be nowha' else."

"An' remember, this is all jess between you 'n me."

"Nobody else but," vowed King Solomon.

Uggam grinned to himself as he went on his way. "Dumb Oscar! Wonder how much can we make before the cops nab him? French medicine— Humph!"


V

Tony Gabrielli, an oblate Neopolitan of enormous equator, wobbled heavily out of his store and settled himself over a soapbox.

Usually Tony enjoyed sitting out front thus in the evening, when his helper had gone home and his trade was slackest. He liked to watch the little Gabriellis playing over the sidewalk with the little Levys and Johnsons; the trios and quartettes of brightly dressed dark-skinned girls merrily out for a stroll; the slovenly gaited, darker men, who eyed them up and down and commented to each other with an unsuppressed "Hot damn!" or "Oh no, now!"

But tonight Tony was troubled. Something was wrong in the store; something was different since the arrival of King Solomon Gillis. The new man had seemed to prove himself honest and trustworthy, it was true. Tony had tested him, as he always tested a new man, by apparently leaving him alone in charge for two or three mornings. As a matter of fact, the new man was never under more vigilant observation than during these two or three mornings. Tony's store was a modification of the front rooms of his flat and was in direct communication with it by way of a glass-windowed door in the rear. Tony always managed to get back into his flat via the side-street entrance and watch the new man through this unobtrusive glass-windowed door. If anything excited his suspicion, like unwarranted interest in the cash register, he walked unexpectedly out of this door to surprise the offender in the act. Thereafter he would have no more such trouble. But he had not succeeded in seeing King Solomon steal even an apple.

What he had observed, however, was that the number of customers that came into the store during the morning's slack hour had pronouncedly increased in the last few days. Before, there had been three or four. Now there were twelve or fifteen. The mysterious thing about it was that their purchases totaled little more than those of the original three or four.

Yesterday and today Tony had elected to be in the store at the time when, on the other days, he had been out. But Gillis had not been overcharging or short-changing; for when Tony waited on the customers himself—strange faces all—he found that they bought something like a yeast cake or a five-cent loaf of bread. Why should strangers leave their own neighborhoods and repeatedly come to him for a yeast cake or a loaf of bread? They were not new neighbors. New neighbors would have bought more variously and extensively and at different times of day. Living nearby, they would have come in, the men often in shirtsleeves and slippers, the women in kimonos, with boudoir caps covering their lumpy heads. They would have sent in strange children for things like yeast cakes and loaves of bread. And why did not some of them come in at night, when the new helper was off duty?

As for accosting Gillis on suspicion, Tony was too wise for that. Patronage had a queer way of shifting itself in Harlem. You lost your temper and let slip a single "*nègre!*" A week later you sold your business.

Spread over his soapbox, with his pudgy hands clasped on his preposterous paunch, Tony sat and wondered. Two men came up, conspicuous for no other reason than that they were white. They displayed extreme nervousness, looking about as if afraid of being seen; and when one of them spoke to Tony, it was in a husky, toneless, blowing voice, like the sound of a dirty phonograph record.

"Are you Antonio Gabrielli?"

"Yes, sure." Strange behavior for such lusty-looking fellows. He who had spoken unsmilingly winked first one eye then the other, and indicated by a gesture of his head that they should enter the store. His companion looked cautiously up and down the Avenue, while Tony, wondering what ailed them, rolled to his feet and puffingly led the way.

Inside, the spokesman snuffled, gave his shoulder a queer little hunch, and asked, "Can you fix us up, buddy?" The other glanced restlessly about the place as if he were constantly hearing unaccountable noises.

Tony thought he understood clearly now. "Booze, 'ey?" he smiled. "Sorry—I no got."

"Booze? Hell, no!" The voice dwindled to a throaty whisper. "Dope. Coke, milk, dice—anything. Name your price. Got to have it."

"Dope?" Tony was entirely at a loss. "What 's a dis, dope?"

"Aw, lay off, brother. We 're in on this. Here." He handed Tony a piece of paper. "Froggy gave us a coupon. Come on. You can't go wrong."

"I no got," insisted the perplexed Tony; nor could he be budged on that point.

Quite suddenly the manner of both men changed. "All right," said the first angrily, in a voice as robust as his body. "All right, you're clever. You no got. Well, you will get. You'll get twenty years!"

"Twenty year? Whadda you talk?"

"Wait a minute, Mac," said the second caller. "Maybe the wop's on the level. Look here, Tony, we're officers, see? Policemen." He produced a badge. "A couple of weeks ago a guy was brought in dying for the want of a shot, see? Dope—he needed some dope—like this—in his arm. See? Well, we tried to make him tell us where he'd been getting it, but he was too weak. He croaked next day. Evidently he had n't had money enough to buy any more.

"Well, this morning a little nigger that goes by the name of Froggy was brought into the precinct pretty well doped up. When he finally came to, he swore he got the stuff here at your store. Of course, we've just been trying to trick you into giving yourself away, but you don't bite. Now what's your game? Know anything about this?"

Tony understood. "I dunno," he said slowly; and then his own problem, whose contemplation his callers had interrupted, occurred to him. "Sure!" he exclaimed. "Wait. Maybeso I know somet'ing."

"All right. Spill it."

"I got a new man, work-a for me." And he told them what he had noted since King Solomon Gillis came.

"Sounds interesting. Where is this guy?"

"Here in da store—all day."

"Be here to-morrow?"

"Sure. All day."

"All right. We'll drop in tomorrow and give him the eye. Maybe he's our man."

"Sure. Come ten o'clock. I show you," promised Tony.


## VI

Even the oldest and rattiest cabarets in Harlem have sense of shame enough to hide themselves under the ground—for instance, Edwards's. To get into Edwards's you casually enter a dimly lighted corner saloon, apparently— only apparently—a subdued memory of brighter days. What was once the family entrance is now a side entrance for ladies. Supporting yourself against close walls, you crouchingly descend a narrow, twisted staircase un- til, with a final turn, you find yourself in a glaring, long, low basement. In a moment your eyes become accustomed to the haze of tobacco smoke. You see men and women seated at wire-legged, white-topped tables, which are covered with half-empty bottles and glasses; you trace the slow jazz accompaniment you heard as you came down the stairs to a pianist, a cornetist, and a drummer on a little platform at the far end of the room. There is a cleared space from the foot of the stairs, where you are standing, to the platform where this orchestra is mounted, and in it a tall brown girl is swaying from side to side and rhythmically proclaiming that she has the world in a jug and the stopper in her hand. Behind a counter at your left sits a fat, bald, tea-colored Negro, and you wonder if this is Edwards—Edwards, who stands in with the police, with the political bosses, with the importers of wines and worse. A white-vested waiter hustles you to a seat and takes your order. The song's tempo becomes quicker; the drum and the cornet rip out a fanfare, almost drowning the piano; the girl catches up her dress and begins to dance. . . .

Gillis's wondering eyes had been roaming about. They stopped.

"Look, Mouse!" he whispered, "Look a yonder!"

"Look at what?"

"Dog-gone if it ain' de self-same girl?"

"Wha' d' ye mean, self-same girl!"

"Over yonder, wi' de green stockin's. Dass de gal made me knock over dem apples fust day I come to town. 'Member? Been wishin' I could see her ev'y sence."

"What for?" Uggam wondered.

King Solomon grew confidential. "Ain' but two things in dis world, Mouse, I really wants. One is to be a policeman. Been wantin' dat ev'y sence I seen dat cullud traffic cop dat day. Other is to get myse'f a gal lak dat one over yonder!"

"You'll do it," laughed Uggam, "if you live long enough."

"Who dat wid her?"

"How 'n hell do I know?"

"He cullud?"

"Don't look like it. Why? What of it?"

"Hm—nuthin'—"

"How many coupons y' got to-night?"

"Ten." King Solomon handed them over.

"Y' ought to 've slipt 'em to me under the table, but it's all right now, long as we got this table to ourselves. Here's y' medicine for to-morrer."

"Wha'?"

"Reach under the table."

Gillis secured and pocketed the medicine.

"An' here's two-fifty for a good day's work." Uggam passed the money over. Perhaps he grew careless; certainly the passing this time was above the table, in plain sight.

"Thanks, Mouse."

Two white men had been watching Gillis and Uggam from a table nearby. In the tumult of merriment that rewarded the entertainer's most recent and daring effort, one of these men, with a word to the other, came over and took the vacant chair beside Gillis.

"Is your name Gillis?"

" 'T ain' nuthin' else."

Uggam's eyes narrowed.

The white man showed King Solomon a police officer's badge.

"You're wanted for dope-peddling. Will you come along without trouble?"

"Fo' what?"

"Violation of the narcotic law—dope-selling."

"Who—me?"

"Come on, now, lay off that stuff. I saw what happened just now myself." He addressed Uggam. "Do you know this fellow?"

"Nope. Never saw him before tonight."

"Did n't I just see him sell you something?"

"Guess you did. We happened to be sittin' here at the same table and got to talkin'. After a while I says I can't seem to sleep nights, so he offers me sump'n he says 'll make me sleep, all right. I don't know what it is, but he says he uses it himself an' I offers to pay him what it cost him. That's how I come to take it. Guess he's got more in his pocket there now."

The detective reached deftly into the coat pocket of the dumfounded King Solomon and withdrew a packet of envelopes. He tore off a corner of one, emptied a half-dozen tiny white tablets into his palm, and sneered triumphantly. "You'll make a good witness," he told Uggam.

The entertainer was issuing an ultimatum to all sweet mammas who dared to monkey around her loving man. Her audience was absorbed and delighted, with the exception of one couple—the girl with the green stockings and her escort. They sat directly in the line of vision of King Solomon's wide eyes, which, in the calamity that had descended upon him, for the moment saw nothing.

"Are you coming without trouble?"

Mouse Uggam, his friend. Harlem. Land of plenty. City of refuge—city of refuge. If you live long enough—

Consciousness of what was happening between the pair across the room suddenly broke through Gillis's daze like flame through smoke. The man was trying to kiss the girl and she was resisting. Gillis jumped up. The detective, taking the act for an attempt to escape, jumped with him and was quick enough to intercept him. The second officer came at once to his partner's aid, blowing his whistle several times as he came.

People overturned chairs getting out of the way, but nobody ran for the door. It was an old crowd. A fight was a treat; and the tall Negro could fight.

"Judas Priest!"

"Did you see that?"

"Damn!"

White—both white. Five of Mose Joplin's horses. Poisoning a well. A year's crops. Green stockings—white—white—

"That's the time, papa!"

"Do it, big boy!"

"Good night!"

Uggam watched tensely, with one eye on the door. The second cop had blown for help—

Downing one of the detectives a third time and turning to grapple again with the other, Gillis found himself face to face with a uniformed black policeman.

He stopped as if stunned. For a moment he simply stared. Into his mind swept his own words, like a forgotten song suddenly recalled:

"Cullud policemans!"

The officer stood ready, awaiting his rush.

"Even—got—cullud—policemans—"

Very slowly King Solomon's arms relaxed; very slowly he stood erect; and the grin that came over his features had something exultant about it.

# RINGTAIL

I

The pavement flashed like a river in the sun. Over it slowly moved the churches' disgorged multitudes, brilliant, deliberate, proud as a pageant, a tumult of red and blues and greens, oranges, yellows, and browns; from a window above, outrageous, intriguing, like music full of exotic disharmonies; but closer, grating, repellent, like an orchestra tuning up: this big, broad-faced, fawn-colored woman in her wide, floppy leghorn hat with a long cerise ribbon streaming down over its side, and a dress of maize georgette; or that poor scrawny black girl, bareheaded, her patches of hair captured in squares, her beaded cobalt frock, girdled with a sash of scarlet satin. But whether you saw with pleasure or pity, you could have no doubt of the display. Harlem's Seventh Avenue was dressed in its Sunday clothes.

And so was Cyril Sebastian Best. To him this promenade was the crest of the week's wave of pleasure. Here was show and swagger and strut, and in these he knew none could outvie him. Find if you could a suit of tan gabardine that curved in at the waist and flared at the hips so gracefully as his own; try to equal his wide wing-collar, with its polka-dot bow-tie matching the border of the kerchief in his breast pocket, or his heavy straw hat with its terraced crown and thick saucer-shaped brim, or his white buckskin shoes with their pea-green trimmings, or his silver-topped ebony cane. He challenged the Avenue and found no rival to answer.

Cyril Sebastian Best was a British West Indian. From one of the unheard-of islands he had come to Trinidad. From Trinidad, growing weary of coin-diving, he had sailed to Southampton as kitchen boy on a freighter, acquiring en route great skill in dodging the Irish cook's missiles and returning his compliments. From Southampton he had shipped in another freighter for New York under a cook from Barbados, a man who compunctionlessly regarded all flesh as fit for carving; and Cyril had found the blade of his own innate craftiness, though honed to a hair-splitting edge, no match for an un-erringly aimed cleaver. The trip's termination had undoubtedly saved his life; its last twenty four hours he had spent hiding from the cook, and when the ship had cast anchor he had jumped overboard at night, swimming two miles to shore. From those who picked him up exhausted and restored him to bodily comfort he had stolen what he could get and made his way into New York.

There were British West Indians in Harlem who would have told Cyril Sebastian Best flatly to his face that they despised him—that he would not have dared even to address them in the islands; who frequently reproved their American friends for judging all West Indians by the Cyril Sebastian Best standard. There were others who, simply because he was a British West Indian, gathered him to their bosoms in that regardless warmth with which the outsider ever welcomes his like.

Among these latter, the more numerous, Cyril accordingly expanded. His self-esteem, his craftiness, his contentiousness, his acquisitiveness, all be-came virtues. To him self-improvement meant nothing but increasing these virtues, certainly not eliminating or modifying any of them. He became fond of denying that he was "colored," insisting that he was "a British subject," hence by implication unquestionably superior to any merely American Negro. And when two years of contact convinced him that the American Negro was characteristically neither self-esteemed nor crafty nor conten-tious nor acquisitive, in short was quite virtueless, his conscious superiority became downright contempt.

It was with no effort to conceal his personal excellence that Cyril Sebas-tian Best proceeded up Seventh Avenue. All this turnout was but his fitting background, his proper setting; it pleased him for no other reason than it rendered him the more conscious of himself—a diamond surrounded with rhinestones. It did not occur to him as he swung along, flourishing his bright black cane, that any of the frequent frank stares or surreptitious second glances that fell upon him could have any origin other than admiration—envy, of course, as its companion in the cases of the men. That his cocky air could be comic, that the extremeness of his outfit could be ridiculous, that the contrast between his clothes and his complexion could cause a lip to curl—none of these far winds rippled the complacency of his ego. He had studied the fashion books carefully. Like them, he was incontrovertibly correct. Like them, again, he was incontrovertibly British; while these Harlemites were just American Negroes. And then, beyond and above all this, he was Cyril Sebastian Best.

The group of loud-laughing young men near the corner he was approach-ing had no regard for the Sabbath, appreciation for the splendor of Seventh

Avenue, or respect for any particular person who might pass within earshot. Indeed they derived as great a degree of pleasure out of the weekly display as did Cyril Sebastian Best, but of a quite different sort. Instead of joining the procession, they preferred assembling at some point in its course and "giving the crowd the once-over." They enjoyed exchanging loud comments upon the passers-by, the slightest quip provoking shouts of laughter; and they possessed certain stock subtleties which were always sure to elicit merriment, such as the whistled tune of "There she goes, there she goes, all dressed up in her Sunday clothes!" A really pretty girl usually won a surprised "Well, hush my mouth!" while a really pretty ankle always occasioned wild embraces of mock excitement.

An especially favored and carefully reserved trick was for one member of the group to push another into a stroller, the latter accomplice apologizing with elaborate deference, while the victim stood helpless between uncertainty and rage. In Harlem, however, an act of this kind required a modicum of selectivity. The group would never have attempted it on the heavy-set, walnut-visaged gentleman just passing, for all of his suede spats and crimson cravat; but when Cyril Sebastian Best lilted into view the temptation was beyond resistance.

"Push me!" Punch Anderson pleaded of his neighbor. "Not yet, Meg. Wait a minute. Now!"

The impact sent Cyril's cane capering toward the gutter; his hat described progressively narrower circles on the sidewalk; and before Punch could remove his own hat and frame his polite excuse Cyril's fulminant temper flashed. Some would have at least considered the possibility of innocent sincerity; others, wise, would have said nothing, picked up their things, and passed on; but Cyril Sebastian Best reacted only to outraged vanity, and the resultant cloudburst of vituperation staggered even the well-informed Punch Anderson.

"Soft pedal, friend," he protested, grinning. "I'm apologizing, ain't I?"

More damnation. Epithets conceived over kitchen filth; curses born of the sea; worded fetor.

Punch's round-faced grin faded. He deliberately secured the West Indian's hat and cane and without a word handed them to him. Cyril snatched them out of Punch's hand as if from a leper and flung out a parting invective—a gem of obscenity. Punch's sense of humor died.

"Say that again, you black son of a simian, and somebody 'll be holding an inquest over you!"

In the act of raising his hat to his head Cyril said it again. Punch's fist went through the crown of the hat to reach the West Indian's face.

A minute later Cyril, tears streaming, polka-dot kerchief growing rapidly crimson with repeated application, was hurrying through the unbearable stares of gaping promenaders, while in his ears seethed the insult: "Now get the hell out o' here, you ringtail monkey-chaser!"

## II

The entrance of the Rosina wears an expression of unmistakable hauteur and you know it immediately to be one of the most arrogant of apartment houses. You need not stand on the opposite side of the Avenue and observe the disdain with which the Rosina looks down upon her neighbors. You have only to pass between her distinguishing gray-granite pillars with their protective, flanking grille-work and pause for a hesitant moment in the spacious hall beyond: the overimmaculate tiled floors, the stiff, paneled mahogany walls, the frigid lights in their crystalline fixtures, the supercilious palms, all ask you at once who you are and what you want here. To reach the elevator you must make between two lordly, contemptuous wall-mirrors, which silently deride you and show you how out of place you are. If you are sufficiently courageous or obtuse, you gain the elevator and with growing discomfiture await the pleasure of the operator, who is just now occupied at the switchboard, listening in on some conversation that does not concern him. If you are sufficiently unimpressed or imprudent, you grumble or call aloud, and in that case you always eventually take to the stairs. Puff, blow, rage, and be damned. This is the Rosina. Who are you?

What more pleasurable occupation for Cyril Sebastian Best, then, than elevator- and switchboard-operator in the Rosina? If ever there was self-expression, this was it. He was the master of her halls, he was the incarnation of her spirit; in him her attitude became articulate—articulate with a Trinidadian accent, but distinctly intelligible, none the less. There were countless residents and their callers to be laughed at; there were endless silly phone-talks to be tapped at the switchboard; there were great mirrors before which he could be sure of the perfect trimness of his dapper gray-and-black uniform; there were relatively few passengers who absolutely required the use of the elevator, and most of those tipped well and frequently. It was a wonderful job.

Cyril's very conformity with his situation kept him ordinarily in the best of humor, the rendering of good service yielding him a certain satisfaction of his own. It was therefore with a considerable shock that one resident, flatteringly desirous, as she thought, of Cyril's aid in facilitating a connection, heard herself curtly answered, "Ah, tell de outside operator. Whaht you t'ink I keer?"—and that a familiar caller in the Rosina, upon being asked,

"Whaht floor?" and answering pleasantly, "Third, as usual," heard himself rebuked with "As usual! You t'ink I am a mind-reader, 'ey?"

Clearly Cyril Sebastian Best was in no obliging mood to-day.

Nothing amused, nothing even interested him: neither the complexion of the very dark girl who persisted in using too much rouge with an alarmingly cyanotic result, nor the leprously overpowdered nose of the young lady who lived in fifty-nine and "passed" for white in her downtown position. He did not even grin at the pomposity of the big yellow preacher who, instead of purchasing ecclesiastic collars, simply put his lay ones on backward.

Cyril sat before the switchboard brooding, his memory raw with "monkey-chaser" and "ringtail." Now and then a transient spasm of passion contorted his features. In the intervals he was sullen and glum and absorbed in contemplated revenge.

"Cyril! Are n't you ever going to take me up? I'm starving to death!"

He looked up. Hilda Vogel's voice was too sweet, even in dissatisfaction, not to be heeded; and she was too pretty—fair, rougelessly rosy, with dimpled cheeks and elbows. How different from the picture just now in his mind!

Cyril had secret ambitions about Hilda. Like himself, she was foreign— from Bermuda; a far cry, to be sure, from Trinidad, but British just the same. And she was sympathetic. She laughed at his jests, she frankly complimented his neatness, she never froze his pleasantries with silence, nor sneered, nor put on airs. One day, after a week of casual cordialities during their frequent ascents, she had paused for as long as five minutes at her landing to listen to his description of the restaurant he was going to own some day soon. It could n't be meaningless. She saw something in him. Why should n't he have ambitions about her?

"Cyril! How'd you hurt your lip?" she asked in the surprise of discovery as the car mounted.

Merely that she noticed elated him; but he would have bitten the lip off rather than tell her. "I bump' into de door doonsteers."

"Shame on you, Cyril. That's an old one. Do I look as dumb as that?"

He was silent for three floors.

"Goodness! It must have been something terrible. Oh well, if you ignore me—" And she began humming a ditty.

She had never been so personal before. Had his soul not been filled with bitterness, he might have betrayed some of those secret ambitions at once, right there between floors in the elevator. As it was he was content with a saner resolution: he would ask permission to call Wednesday night. He was "off" Wednesdays.

Ringtail                                        21

"You soun' quite happy," he observed, to make an opening, as he slid back the gate at her floor.

"You said it!" she answered gayly, stepping out; and before he could follow his opening her dimples deepened, her eyes twinkled mysteriously, and she added, "I may be in love—you'd never know!" Then she vanished down the hallway with a laugh, while the speechless Cyril wondered what she could mean.

## III

In the flat's largest room a half-dozen young men played poker around a dining-table. A spreading gas-dome of maroon-and-orange stained glass hung over the table, purring softly, confining its whitish halo to the circle of players, and leaving in dimness the several witnesses who peered over their shoulders. One player was startlingly white, with a heavy rash of brown freckles and short kinky red hair. Another was almost black, with the hair of an Indian and the features of a Moor. The rest ranged between.

A phonograph in a corner finished its blatant "If You Don't I Know Who Will," and someone called for the "West Indian Blues."

"That reminds me, Punch," said Meg Minor over his cards. "Remember that monk you hit Sunday?"

"Never hit anybody on Sunday in my life," grinned Punch across the table. "I'm a Christian."

"Punch hit a monk? Good-night! There's gonna be some carvin' done."

"Name your flowers, Punch!"

"'Four Roses' for Punch!"

Meg went on through the comments: "He's an elevator-boy at the Rosina up the Avenue."

"What'd you hit him for, Punch?"

"Deal me threes, Red," requested Punch, oblivious, while Meg told the others what had happened.

"Serves you right for actin' like a bunch of infants," judged Red. "Punch in the Post Office and you supposed to be studyin'—what the hell are you studyin' now, Meg?"

"Serves *us* right? It was the monk that got hit."

"Hmph! D' you think that's the end of it? Show me a monk that won't try to get even and I'll swallow the Woolworth Building."

"Well, we were just feeling kind o' crazy and happened to meet up with that bunch of don't-give-a-kitty kids. It was fun, only—"

"Bet fifteen cents on these four bullets," said Punch.

"Call!"

"Call!"

"You stole the last pot, bluffin'," calculated Eight-Ball, nicknamed for his complexion's resemblance to the pool ball of that number. He tossed a blue chip into the growing pile.

"Have to protect my ante," decided his neighbor, resignedly.

"I'm a dutiful nephew, too," followed Meg.

Punch threw down three aces and a joker and reached for the pile of chips.

"Four bullets sure 'nough!"

"An' I had a full house!"

"The luck o' the Nigrish. Had a straight myself."

"Luck, hell. Them's the four bullets that monk's gonna put into him."

"Right. Get enough for a decent burial, Punch."

"Deal, friend," grinned the unruffled Punch. "I'm up."

"On the level, Punch," resumed Meg, "keep your eyes open. That little ape looks evil to me."

"Aw, he's harmless."

"There ain't no such thing as a harmless monkey-chaser," objected Red. "If you've done anything to him, he'll get you sooner or later. He can't help it—he's just made that way, like a spring."

"I ain't got a thing for a monk to do, anyhow," interjected a spectator. "Hope Marcus Garvey takes 'em all back to Africa with him. He'll sure have a shipload."

Eight-Ball finished riffling the cards and began to distribute them carefully. "You jigs are worse 'n ofays," he accused. "You raise hell about prejudice, and look at you—doin' just what you're raisin' hell over yourselves."

"Maybe so," Red rejoined, "but that don't make me like monks any better."

"What don't you like about 'em?"

"There ain't nothin' I do like about 'em. They're too damn conceited. They're too aggressive. They talk funny. They look funny—I can tell one the minute I see him. They're always startin' an argument an' they always want the last word. An' there's too many of 'em here."

"Yeah," Eight-Ball dryly rejoined. "An' they stick too close together an' get ahead too fast. They put it all over us in too many ways. We could stand 'em pretty well if it was n't for that. Same as ofays an' Jews."

"Aw, can the dumb argument," said Meg. "Open for a nickel."

"Raise a nickel."

"Who was the pretty pink you were dancin' with the other night, Punch?" inquired the observer behind him.

The lethargic Punch came to life. "Boy, was n't she a sheba? And I don't even know her name."

"Sheikin' around some, hey?"

"Nope. My sister Marian introduced me. But I'm so busy looking I don't catch the name, see? When I dance with her she finds out I don't know it and refuses to tell. I ask if I can come to see her and she says nothing doing— would n't think of letting a bird call who did n't even know her name."

"Really got you goin', hey?"

"Damn right, she did. I ask Marian her name afterwards and she won't come across either. Says she's promised not to tell and if I really want to locate the lady nothing 'll stop me. Can y' beat it?"

"Why don't y' bribe Marian?"

"If you can bribe Marian I can be President."

"All right, heavy lover," interpolated Meg impatiently. "You in this game?"

Punch discovered then that he had discarded the three queens he had intended to keep, and had retained a deuce and a fivespot.

"Well, cut me in my neck!" he ejaculated. "Did you see what I did?"

The man behind him laughed. "Boy, you're just startin'," he said. "Wait till you locate the pink!"

*　　*　　*

The gloomy dinginess that dimmed the stuffy little front room of the Rosina's basement flat was offset not so much by the two or three one-bulb lights in surprisingly useless spots as by the glow of the argument, heated to incandescence. Payner, the house-superintendent, whose occupancy of these rooms constituted part of his salary, had not forgotten that he was a naturalized American of twenty years' standing, and no longer fresh from Montserrat; but Barbadian Gradyne had fallen fully into his native word-throttling, and Chester of Jamaica might have been chanting a loud response to prayer in the intervals when the others let his singsong have its say.

"No people become a great people," he now insisted, with his peculiar stressing of unaccented syllables, "except where it dominate. You t'ink de Negro ever dominate America? Pah!"

"Africa," Gradyne lumberingly supported him, "dat de only chance. Teng mo' years, mahn, dis Harl'm be jes' like downg Georgia. Dis a white mahn's country!"

"Back to Africa!" snorted Payner. "Go on back, you b'ys. Me—I doan give a dahm f' all de Garveys an' all de Black Star liners in Hell. I stay right here!"

"You t'ink only for you'self," charged Chester. "You t'ink about you' race an' you see I am right. Garvey is de Moses of his people!"

"Maybeso. But I be dahm' if Moses git any my money. Back to Africa! How de hell I'm goin' back where I never been?"

Neither Gradyne's retaliative cudgel nor Chester's answering thrust achieved its mark, for at the moment Cyril Sebastian Best broke unceremoniously in and announced: "De house is pinch'!"

Like a blast furnace's flame, the argument faded as swiftly as it had flared.

"Where you was raised, boy? Don't you got no manners a-tall?"

Cyril banged the door behind him, stuck out his chest, and strutted across the room. "I tell you whaht I hahve got," he grinned.

"A hell of a nerve," grunted Gradyne.

"An' I tell you whaht I'm goin' get," Cyril proceeded. "I'm goin' get rich an' I'm goin' get married."

"How much you pays, 'ey?" asked Chester.

"Pays? For whaht?"

"For you' licker. You's drunk as hell."

"Den I stays drunk all 'e time. I got de sweetes' woman in de worl', boy—make a preacher lay 'is Bible downg!"

"Who it is?"

"Never min' who is it." But he described Hilda Vogel with all the hyperbole of enthusiasm.

Gradyne inspected him quizzically. "Dat gel mus' got two glass eyes," he grinned.

"Or else you have," Payner amended.

"How you know she care anyt'ing about you?" Chester asked.

"I know." Cyril was positive. "She tell me so dis ahfternoon in de elevator. I been makin' time all along, see? So dis ahfternoon when I get to de top floor I jes' staht to pop de question an' she look at me an' roll 'er eyes like dis, an' say, 'I may be in love!' an' run like hell downg de hall laughin'! Boy, I know!"

Payner and Chester and Gradyne all looked at him with pitying sympathy. Then Chester laughed.

"You cahn't tell anything by that, mahn."

"I cahn't, 'ey? Why not?"

"You had de poor girl too far up in de air!"

IV

"Did you see the awful thing Harriet wore?"

"Did I? Who in the world made it?"

"Noah's grandmother."

"And that King Tut bob—at her age!"

"Maybe she's had monkey glands—"

Cyril, listening in at the switchboard, found it very uninteresting and, leaving off, deigned to take up three passengers who had been waiting for five minutes in the elevator. When he reached the street floor again, the instrument's familiar rattle was calling him back.

"Apartment sixty-one, please."

Something in the masculine voice made Cyril stiffen, something more than the fact that it sought connection with Hilda Vogel's apartment. He plugged in and rang.

"Can I speak to Miss Vogel, please?"

"This is Miss Vogel."

"Miss Hilda Vogel?"

"Yes."

The masculine voice laughed.

"Thought you'd given me the air, did n't you?"

"Who is it, please?" Cyril noted eagerness in Hilda's voice.

"Give you one guess."

"My, you're conceited."

"Got a right to be. I'm taking the queeniest sheba in Harlem to a show tonight, after which we're going to Happy's and get acquainted."

"Indeed? Why tell me about it?"

"You're the sheba."

Hilda laughed. "You don't lose any time, do you, Mr.—Punch?"

"I don't dare, Miss—Hilda."

Cyril, bristling attention, shivered. Despite its different tone, he knew the voice. A hot wave of memory swept congealingly over him; he felt like a raw egg dropped in boiling water.

"How did you find out I was—me?"

"Oho! Now it's your turn to wonder!"

"Tell me."

"Sure—when I see you."

"I think you're horrid."

"Why?"

"Well, I've got to let you come now or I'll die of curiosity."

"Dark eyes, but a bright mind. When do I save your life?"

"Are you sure you want to?"

"Am I talking to you?"

"You don't know a thing about me."

"More 'n you know about me. I looked you up in *Who's Who*!"

"Now you're being horrid again. What did you find?"

"You work in the Model Shop on the Avenue, you live with your ma and pa, and you're too young and innocent to go around with only girls, sheikless and unprotected."

"How do you know I'm sheikless?" Cyril's heart stumbled.

"You're not—now," said the audacious Punch.

The girl gasped. Then, "You did n't find out the most important thing."

"To wit and namely?"

"Where I am from."

"Nope. I'm more interested in where you're going."

"We're—" she hesitated gravely. "I'm—Do you—object to—foreigners?"

It was Punch's gasp. "What?"

"There! You see, I told you you did n't want to come."

"What are you talking about?"

"We're—I'm a Bermudan, you know."

Punch's ringing laugh stabbed the eavesdropping ears. "I thought you were an Eskimo, the way you froze me that night."

"You're not—prejudiced?"

"Who me?" Say, one of the finest boys down at the P.O. is from Bermuda. Always raving about it. Says it's Heaven. Guess he means it's the place angels come from."

She was reassured. "Not angels. Onions."

"I like onions," said Punch.

"What time are you coming?"

"Right away! Now!"

"No. Eight."

"Seven!"

"Well—seven-thirty."

"Right."

"Good-bye."

"Not on your life. So long, Hilda."

"So long, Punch."

"Seven-thirty."

"Seven-thirty."

The lift was full of impatient people audibly complaining of the delay. The only response from the ordinarily defiant Cyril was a terrific banging open and shut of the gates as he let them out, floor by floor. His lips were inverted and pressed tightly together, so that his whole mouth bulged, and his little eyes were reddened between their narrowed lids.

"I may be in love—you'd never know." He had thought she was encouraging him. He would have made sure the next day had there not been too many

people in the car. Fortunately enough, he saw now; for she had been thinking of the ruffian whose blow still rent his spirit, whose words still scalded
his pride: "Now get the hell out o' here, you ringtail—"

He had seen Counselor Absalom. Absalom had said he could n't touch the
case—no witnesses, no money, prolonged litigation. Absalom had n't even
been sympathetic. Street brawls were rather beneath Absalom.

Cyril slammed the top gate to and reversed the controlling lever. As the
car began to drop, something startled him out of his grim abstraction: the
gate was slowly sliding open. It had failed to catch, recoiling under the force
with which he had shut it. Yet the car was moving normally. The safety device whereby motion was possible only when all the gates were shut had
been rendered useless—perhaps by his own violence just now. He released
the lever. The car halted. He pushed the lever down forward. The car ascended. He released it. The car halted again. He pushed the lever down
backward. The car descended. Its movements were entirely unaffected.

Cyril paused, undecided. For a long moment he remained motionless.
Then with a little grunt he rose again and carefully closed the open gate. His
smile as he reached the ground floor was incarnate malevolence, triumphant.


V

Meg Minor was following a frizzly bobbed head and a bright-red sweater up
the Avenue. In the twilight he was n't sure he knew her; but even if he
did n't—he might. Introductions were old stuff. If the spark of attraction
gleamed, blow on it: you might kindle a blaze.

As he crossed a side street an ambulance suddenly leaped from nowhere
and rushed at him with terrifying clangor. He jumped back, the driver swore
loudly, and the machine swept around the corner into the direction Meg was
going.

"Swore like he was sorry he did n't hit me," he grinned to himself. "Must
be out making patients or something. Where's that danger signal I was
pacing?"

The red sweater had stopped in the middle of the next block. So had the
ambulance. When Meg reached the place, a gathering crowd was already
beginning to obstruct passage. Since the sweater had halted, Meg saw no
reason for going on himself, and so, edging as close to it as he could, he
prayed that the forthcoming sight might make the girl faint into his arms.

He paid no attention to the growing buzz about him. There was a long
wait. Then the buzz abruptly hushed and the crowd shifted, opening a lane
to the ambulance. In the shift Meg, squirming still nearer to the red sweater,
found himself on the edge of the lane.

Two men, one in white, came out of the house, bearing a stretcher covered with a blanket. As they passed, Meg, looking, felt his heart trip and his skin tingle. He started forward.

"Punch! For God's sake—"

"Stand back, please!"

"It's Punch Anderson, Doc! What—what—is he—?" Meg pressed after the white coat. "Doc—good Lord, Doc—tell me what happened! He's my buddy, Doc!"

"Tried to hop a moving elevator. Both legs—compound fractures."

Doors slammed. The ambulance made off with a roar and a clamor. Meg stood still. He did not see the bright red sweater beside him or hear the girl asking if his friend would live. He was staring with mingled bewilderment and horror into the resplendent entrance of the Rosina. And, as he stared, the sound of the ambulance gong came back to his ears, peal upon peal, ever more distant, like receding derisive laughter.

# THE SOUTH LINGERS ON

I

Ezekiel Taylor, preacher of the gospel of Jesus Christ, walked slowly along 133rd Street, conspicuously alien. He was little and old and bent. A short, bushy white beard framed his shiny black face and his tieless celluloid collar. A long, greasy, green-black Prince Albert, with lapels frayed and buttons worn through to their metal, hung loosely from his shoulders. His trousers were big and baggy and limp, yet not enough so to hide the dejected bend of his knees.

A little boy noted the beard and gibed, "Hey, Santa Claus! 'Tain't Chris'mas yet!" And the little boy's playmates chorused, "Haw, haw! Lookit the colored Santa Claus!"

"For of such is the kingdom of heaven," mused Ezekiel Taylor. No. The kingdom of Harlem. Children turned into mockers. Satan in the hearts of infants. Harlem—city of the devil—outpost of hell.

Darkness settled, like the gloom in the old preacher's heart; darkness an hour late, for these sinners even tinkered with God's time, substituting their "daylight-saving." Wicked, yes. But sad too, as though they were desperately warding off the inescapable night of sorrow in which they must suffer for their sins. Harlem. What a field! What numberless souls to save!—These very taunting children who knew not even the simplest of the commandments—

But he was old and alone and defeated. The world had called to his best. It had offered money, and they had gone; first the young men whom he had fathered, whom he had brought up from infancy in his little Southern church; then their wives and children, whom they eventually sent for; and finally their parents, loath to leave their shepherd and their dear, decrepit shacks, but dependent and without choice.

"Whyn't y' come to New York?" old Deacon Gassoway had insisted. "Martin and Eli and Jim Lee and his fambly's all up da' now an' doin' fine.

30

We'll all git together an' start a chu'ch of our own, an' you'll still be pastor an' it'll be jes' same as 'twas hyeh." Full of that hope, he had come. But where were they? He had captained his little ship till it sank; he had clung to a splint and been tossed ashore; but the shore was cold, gray, hard and rock-strewn.

He had been in barren places before but God had been there too. Was Harlem then past hope? Was the connection between this place and heaven broken, so that the servant of God went hungry while little children ridiculed? Into his mind, like a reply, crept an old familiar hymn, and he found himself humming it softly:

The Lord will provide,
The Lord will provide,
In some way or 'nother
The Lord will provide.
It may not be in your way,
It may not be in mine,
But yet in His own way
The Lord will provide.

Then suddenly, astonished, he stopped, listening. He had not been singing alone—a chorus of voices somewhere near had caught up his hymn. Its volume was gradually increasing. He looked about for a church. There was none. He covered his deaf ear so that it might not handicap his good one. The song seemed to issue from one of the private houses a little way down the street.

He approached with eager apprehension and stood wonderingly before a long flight of brownstone steps leading to an open entrance. The high first floor of the house, that to which the steps led, was brightly lighted, and the three front windows had their panes covered with colored tissue paper designed to resemble church windows. Strongly, cheeringly the song came out to the listener:

The Lord will provide,
The Lord will provide,
In some way or 'nother,
The Lord will provide.

Ezekiel Taylor hesitated an incredulous moment, then smiling, he mounted the steps and went in.

The Reverend Shackleton Ealey had been inspired to preach the gospel by the draft laws of 1917. He remained in the profession not out of gratitude to its having kept him out of war, but because he found it a far less precarious mode of living than that devoted to poker, blackjack and dice. He was stocky and flat-faced and yellow, with many black freckles and the eyes of a dogfish. And he was clever enough not to conceal his origin, but to make capital out of his conversion from gambler to preacher and to confine himself to those less enlightened groups that thoroughly believed in the possibility of so sudden and complete a transformation.

The inflow of rural folk from the South was therefore fortune, and Reverend Shackleton Ealey spent hours in Pennsylvania station greeting newly arrived migrants, urging them to visit his meeting-place and promising them the satisfaction of "that old-time religion." Many had come—and contributed.

This was prayer-meeting night. Reverend Ealey had his seat on a low platform at the distant end of the double room originally designed for a "parlor." From behind a pulpit-stand improvised out of soap-boxes and covered with calico, he counted his congregation and estimated his profit.

A stranger entered uncertainly, looked about a moment, and took a seat near the door. Reverend Shackleton Ealey appraised him: a little bent-over old man with a bushy white beard and a long Prince Albert coat. Perfect type—fertile soil. He must greet this stranger at the close of the meeting and effusively make him welcome.

But Sister Gassoway was already by the stranger's side, shaking his hand vigorously and with unmistakable joy; and during the next hymn she came over to old man Gassoway and whispered in his ear, whereupon he jumped up wide-eyed, looked around, and made broadly smiling toward the newcomer. Others turned to see, and many, on seeing, began to whisper excitedly into their neighbor's ear and turned to see again. The stranger was occasioning altogether too great a stir. Reverend Ealey decided to pray.

His prayer was a masterpiece. It besought of God protection for His people in a strange and wicked land; it called down His damnation upon those dens of iniquity, the dance halls, the theatres, the cabarets; it berated the poker-sharp, the blackjack player, the dice-roller; it denounced the drunkard, the bootlegger, the dope-peddler; and it ended in a sweeping tirade against the wolf-in-sheep's-clothing, whatever his motive might be.

Another hymn and the meeting came to a close.

The stranger was surrounded before Reverend Ealey could reach him. When finally he approached the old preacher with extended hand and hollow-hearted smile, old man Gassoway was saying:

"Yas, suh, Rev'n Taylor, dass jes' whut we goin' do. Start makin' 'rangements tomorrer. Martin an' Jim Lee's over to Ebeneezer, but dey doan like it 'tall. Says hit's too hifalutin for 'em de way dese Harlem cullud folks wushup; Ain' got no Holy Ghos' in 'em, dass whut. Jes' come in an' set down an' git up an' go out. Never moans, never shouts, never even says 'amen.' Most of us is hyeh, an' we gonna git together an' start us a ch'ch of our own, wid you f' pastor, like we said. Yas, suh. Hyeh's Brother Ealey now. Brother Ealey, dis hyeh's our old preacher Rev'n Taylor. We was jes' tellin him—"

The Reverend Shackleton Ealey had at last a genuine revelation—that the better-yielding half of his flock was on the wing. An old oath of frustration leaped to his lips—"God—" but he managed to bite it in the middle—"bless you, my brother," he growled.

## II

"What makes you think you can cook?"

"Why, brother, I been in the neighborhood o' grub all my life!"

"Humph! Fly bird, you are."

"Pretty near all birds fly, friend."

"Yes—even black birds."

The applicant for the cook's job lost his joviality. "All right. I'm a black bird. You're a half-yaller hound. Step out in the air an' I'll fly down your dam' throat, so I can see if your insides is yaller, too!"

The clerk grinned. "You must do your cooking on the top of your head. Turn around and fly out that door there and see if the 135th Street breeze won't cool you off some. We want a fireless cooker."

With an unmistakable suggestion as to how the clerk might dispose of his job the applicant rolled cloudily out of the employment office. The clerk called "Next!" and Jake Crinshaw, still convulsed with astonishment, nearly lost his turn.

"What kind of work are you looking for, buddy?"

"No purtickler kin', suh. Jes' work, dass all."

"Well, what can you do?"

"Mos' anything, I reckon."

"Drive a car?"

"No suh. Never done dat."

"Wait table?"

"Well, I never is."

"Run elevator?"

"No, suh."

"What have you been doing?"

"Farmin'."

"Farming? Where?"

"Jennin's Landin', Virginia. 'At's wha' all my folks is fum."

"How long you been here?"

"Ain' been hyeh a week yit. Still huntin' work." Jake answered rather apologetically. The questions had been almost hostile.

"Oh—migrant." In the clerk's tone were patronization, some contempt, a little cynical amusement and complete comprehension. "Migrant" meant nothing to Jake; to the clerk it explained everything.

"M-hm. Did you try the office up above—between here and Seventh Avenue? They wanted two dozen laborers for a railroad camp upstate—pay your transportation, board and everything."

"Yas, suh—up there yestiddy, but de man say dey had all dey need. Tole me to try y'all down hyeh."

"M-hm. Well, I'm sorry, but we haven't anything for you this morning. Come in later in the week. Something may turn up."

"Yas, suh. Thank y' suh."

Jake made his discouraged way to the sidewalk and stood contemplating. His blue jumpers were clean and spotless—they had been his Sunday-go-to-meeting ones at home. He wore big, broad, yellow shoes and a shapeless tan felt hat, beneath whose brim the hair was close cut, the neck shaved bare. He was very much dressed up.

The applicant who had preceded him approached. "What'd that yaller dog tell you, bud?"

"Tole me come in later."

"Huh! That's what they all say. Only way for a guy with guts to get anything in this town is to be a bigger crook 'n the next one." He pointed to two well-dressed young men idling on the curb. "See them two? They used to wait on a job where I was chef. Now look at 'em—prosperous! An' how'd they get that way? Hmph! That one's a pimp an' th' other's a pickpocket. Take your choice." And the cynic departed.

But Jake had greater faith in Harlem. Its praises had been sounded too highly—there must be something.

He turned and looked at the signboard that had led him to enter the employment office. It was a wooden blackboard, on which was written in chalk: "Help wanted. All sorts of jobs. If we haven't it, leave your name and we'll find it." The clerk hadn't asked Jake *his* name.

A clanging, shrieking fire engine appeared from nowhere and swept terrifyingly past. It frightened Jake like the first locomotive he had seen as a child. He shrank back against the building. Another engine passed. No more. He felt better. No one minded the engines. No one noticed that he did. Harlem itself was a fire engine.

Jake could read the signs on the buildings across the street: "Harlem

Commercial and Savings Bank"—"Hale and Clark, Real Estate"—"Restaurant and Delicatessen, J. W. Jackson, proprietor"—"The Music Shop"—"John Gilmore, Tonsorial Parlor." He looked up at the buildings. They were menacingly big and tall and close. There were no trees. No ground for trees to grow from. Sidewalks overflowing with children. Streets crammed full of street-cars and automobiles. Noise, hurry, bustle—fire engines.

Jake looked again at the signboard. Help wanted—all sorts. After a while he heaved a great sigh, turned slowly, and slouched wearily on, hoping to catch sight of another employment office with a signboard out front.


## III

It was eleven o'clock at night. Majutah knew that Harry would be waiting on the doorstep downstairs. He knew better than to ring the bell so late—she had warned him. And there was no telephone. Grandmother wouldn't consent to having a telephone in the flat—she thought it would draw lightning. As if every other flat in the house didn't have one, as if lightning would strike all the others and leave theirs unharmed! Grandmother was such a nuisance with her old fogeyisms. If it weren't for her down-home ideas there'd be no trouble getting out now to go to the cabaret with Harry. As it was, Majutah would have to steal down the hall past Grandmother's room in the hope that she would be asleep.

Majutah looked to her attire. The bright red sandals and scarlet stockings, she fancied, made her feet look smaller and her legs bigger. This was desirable, since her black crepe dress, losing in width what style had added to its length, would not permit her to sit comfortably and cross her knees without occasioning ample display of everything below them. Her vanity-case mirror revealed how exactly the long pendant earrings matched her red coral beads and how perfectly becoming the new close bob was, and assured her for the tenth time that Egyptian rouge made her skin look lighter. She was ready.

Into the narrow hallways she tipped, steadying herself against the walls, and slowly approached the outside door at the end. Grandmother's room was the last off the hallway. Majutah reached it, slipped successfully past, and started silently to open the door to freedom.

"Jutie?"

How she hated to be called Jutie! Why couldn't the meddlesome old thing say Madge like everyone else?

"Ma'am?"

"Wha' you goin' dis time o' night?"

"Just downstairs to mail a letter."

"You easin' out mighty quiet, if dat's all you goin' do. Come 'eh. Lemme look at you."

Majutah slipped off her pendants and beads and laid them on the floor. She entered her grandmother's room, standing where the foot of the bed would hide her gay shoes and stockings. Useless precautions. The shrewd old woman inspected her granddaughter a minute in disapproving silence, then asked:

"Well, wha's de letter?"

\*    \*    \*

"Hello Madge," said Harry. "What held you up? You look mad enough to bite bricks."

"I am. Grandmother, of course. She's a pest. Always nosing and meddling. I'm grown, and the money I make supports both of us, and I'm sick of acting like a kid just to please her."

"How'd you manage?"

"I didn't manage. I just gave her a piece of my mind and came on out."

"Musn't hurt the old lady's feelings. It's just her way of looking out for you."

"I don't need any looking out for—or advice either!"

"Excuse me. Which way—Happy's or Edmonds'?"

"Edmonds'—darn it!"

"Right."

\*    \*    \*

It was two o'clock in the morning. Majutah's grandmother closed her Bible and turned down the oil lamp by which she preferred to read it. For a long time she sat thinking of Jutie—and of Harlem, this city of Satan. It was Harlem that had changed Jutie—this great, noisy, heartless, crowded place where you lived under the same roof with a hundred people you never knew; where night was alive and morning dead. It was Harlem—those brazen women with whom Jutie sewed, who swore and shimmied and laughed at the suggestion of going to church. Jutie wore red stockings. Jutie wore dresses that looked like nightgowns. Jutie painted her face and straightened her hair, instead of leaving it as God intended. Jutie—lied—often.

And while Madge laughed at a wanton song, her grandmother knelt by her bed and through the sinful babel of the airshaft, through her own silent tears, prayed to God in heaven for Jutie's lost soul.

IV

"Too much learnin' ain' good f' nobody. When I was her age I couldn' write my own name."

"You can't write much mo' 'n that now. Too much learnin'! Whoever heard o' sich a thing!"

Anna's father, disregarding experience in arguing with his wife, pressed his point. "Sho they's sich a thing as too much learnin'! 'At gal's gittin' so she don't b'lieve nuthin'! Hmph! Didn't she jes' tell me las' night she didn' be-lieve they ever was any Adam an' Eve?"

"Well, I ain' so sho they ever was any myself! An' one thing is certain: If that gal o' mine wants to keep on studyin' an' go up there to that City Col-lege an' learn how to teach school an' be somebody, I'll work my fingers to the bone to help her do it! Now!"

"That ain' what I'm takin' 'bout. You ain' worked no harder 'n I is to help her git this far. Hyeh she is ready to graduate from high school. Think of it— high school! When we come along they didn' even *have* no high schools. Fus' thing y' know she be so far above us we can't reach her with a fence-rail. Then you'll wish you'd a listened to me. What I says is, she done gone far enough."

"Ain' no sich thing as far enough when you wants to go farther. 'Tain' as if it was gonna cost a whole lot. That's the trouble with you cullud folks now. Git so far an' stop—set down—through—don't want no mo'." Her disgust was boundless. "Y' got too much cotton field in you, that's what!"

The father grinned. "They sho' ain' no cotton field in yo' mouth, honey."

"No they ain't. An' they ain' no need o' all this arguin' either, 'cause all that gal's got to do is come in hyeh right now an' put her arms 'roun' yo' neck, an' you'd send her to Europe if she wanted to go!"

"Well, all I says is, when dey gits to denyin' de Bible hit's time to stop 'em."

"Well, all *I* says is, if Cousin Sukie an' yo' no 'count brother, Jonathan, can send their gal all the way from Athens to them Howard's an' pay car-fare an' boa'd an' ev'ything, we can send our gal—"

She broke off as a door slammed. There was a rush, a delightful squeal, and both parents were being smothered in a cyclone of embraces by a wildly jubilant daughter.

"Mummy! Daddy! I won it! I won it!"

"What under the sun—?"

"The scholarship, Mummy! The scholarship!"

"No!"

"Yes I did! I can go to Columbia! I can go to Teacher's College! Isn't it great?"

Anna's mother turned triumphantly to her husband; but he was beaming at his daughter.

"You sho' is yo' daddy's chile. Teacher's College! Why that's wha' I been wantin' you to go all along!"

## V

Rare sight in a close-built, topheavy city—space. A wide open lot, extending along 138th Street almost from Lenox to Seventh Avenue; baring the mangy backs of a long row of 139th Street houses; disclosing their gaping, gasping windows, their shameless strings of half-laundered rags, which gulp up what little air the windows seek to inhale. Occupying the Lenox Avenue end of the lot, the so-called Garvey tabernacle, wide, low, squat, with its stingy little entrance; occupying the other, the church tent where summer camp meetings are held.

*        *        *

Pete and his buddy, Lucky, left their head-to-head game of coon-can as darkness came on. Time to go out—had to save gas. Pete went to the window and looked down at the tent across the street.

"Looks like the side show of a circus. Ever been in?"

"Not me. I'm a preacher's son—got enough o' that stuff when I was a kid and couldn't protect myself."

"Ought to be a pretty good show when some o' them old-time sisters get happy. Too early for the cabarets; let's go in a while, just for the hell of it."

"You sure are hard up for somethin' to do."

"Aw, come on. Somethin' funny's bound to happen. You might even get religion, you dam' bootlegger."

Luck grinned. "Might meet some o' my customers, you mean."

*        *        *

Through the thick, musty heat imprisoned by the canvas shelter a man's voice rose, leading a spiritual. Other voices chimed eagerly in, some high, clear, sweet; some low, mellow, full,—all swelling, rounding out the refrain till it filled the place, so that it seemed the flimsy walls and roof must soon be torn from their moorings and swept aloft with the song:

Where you running sinner?
Where you running I say?
Running from the fire—
You can't cross here!

The preacher stood waiting for the song to melt away. There was a moment of abysmal silence, into which the thousand blasphemies filtering in from outside dropped unheeded.

The preacher was talking in deep, impressive tones. One old patriarch was already supplementing each statement with a matter-of-fact "amen!" of approval.

The preacher was describing hell. He was enumerating without exception the horrors that befall the damned: maddening thirst for the drunkard; for the gambler, insatiable flame, his own greed devouring his soul. The preacher's voice no longer talked—it sang; mournfully at first, monotonously up and down, up and down—a chant in minor mode; then more intensely, more excitedly; now fairly strident.

The amens of approval were no longer matter-of-fact, perfunctory. They were quick, spontaneous, escaping the lips of their own accord; they were frequent and loud and began to come from the edges of the assembly instead of just the front rows. The old man cried, "Help him, Lord!" "Preach the word!" "Glory!" taking no apparent heed of the awfulness of the description and the old women continuously moaned aloud, nodding their bonneted heads, or swaying rhythmically forward and back in their seats.

Suddenly the preacher stopped, leaving the old men and old women still noisy with spiritual momentum. He stood motionless till the last echo of approbation subsided, then repeated the text from which his discourse had taken origin; repeated it in a whisper, lugubrious, hoarse, almost inaudible; "'In—hell—'"—paused, then without warning wildly shrieked, "'*In hell*—'" stopped—returned to his hoarse whisper—"'he lifted up his eyes . . .'"

✳    ✳    ✳

"What the hell you want to leave for?" Pete complained when he and Lucky reached the sidewalk. "That old bird would 'a' coughed up his gizzard in two more minutes. What's the idea?"

"Aw hell—I don't know.—You think that stuff's funny. You laugh at it. I don't, that's all." Lucky hesitated. The urge to speak outweighed the fear of being ridiculed. "Dam' 'f I know what it is—maybe because it makes me think of the old folks or somethin'—but—hell—it just sorter—gets me—"

Lucky turned abruptly away and started off. Pete watched him for a moment with a look that should have been astonished, outraged, incredulous—but wasn't. He overtook him, put an arm about his shoulders, and because he had to say something as they walked on, muttered reassuringly:

"Well—if you ain't the damndest fool—"

# EZEKIEL

It was Ezekiel's first day in Harlem, the Negro colony of New York City. He had arrived the night before, after a long trip north from Waxhaw, Georgia, where the dozen years of his life up to now had been spent. But last night he had been unable to see anything clearly. The enormous Pennsylvania Railroad Station, the multitude of hurrying people, the terrifying subway trains, the heavy traffic of the streets, the glittering clusters of electric lights all had been too much for him to appreciate so suddenly. Last night he had been able only to stare and blink and gasp.

Now, however, the bright sunlight of the calmer morning allowed him somewhat to gather his bearings and observe this strange new place with less bewilderment. Even so, it was still all very much like a mystifying dream.

He was seated on the front stoop of a tall apartment house on 135th Street. His uncle, to whom he had been sent so that he might attend the excellent New York schools, had brought Ezekiel downstairs. He was to wait there on the stoop until his uncle returned. It might be an hour, but Ezekiel musn't go away. If he got lost in Harlem he might never find his way back. Ezekiel had promised faithfully to stay, and so now he sat and looked about him.

Never had he seen so many tall dwellings, side by side, with no elbow-room between. There was only one low building in the whole row, and even that was taller than anybody's house back home. Where were the trees, the grass, the flowers? He looked at the broad concrete sidewalk, at the wide asphalt pavement of the street, with its shining car-tracks down the middle, and wondered if one could dig up the hard level road and plant things and have them grow.

A little way down the street two boys were playing an odd game on the sidewalk. They knelt in turn and went through motions like shooting marbles, only it was not marbles they shot but little round things like checkers. And how they laughed and chattered as they played!

With a curiosity he could not resist, Ezekiel slipped down off his seat on the stoop and slowly moved toward the two boys playing the strange game. Trained as he was to the strictest obedience, he hesitated once or twice as a wave of guilt came over him. He knew he ought to stay on the stoop as his uncle had told him, and once he looked back to be sure that the stoop was still there within his reach. But the new interest conquered his conscience and led him farther away, until in a few moments he found himself standing over the two boys.

He saw now that they were playing with the little round metal caps of soda-pop bottles. The two took turns, kneeling and shooting the caps by flipping out a finger and striking them, sending them sliding in the desired direction. On the sidewalk a number of chalk lines had been drawn to form squares, and the game seemed to depend on how the caps were shot into the squares.

Ezekiel watched a while, his shyness overcoming the constant impulse to ask questions about the game. The two boys at first paid no attention to him, so absorbed were they in the game and each other. The two were evidently the best of friends.

Soon the light one made a winning shot and looked up at Ezekiel with a grin so proud and friendly that the newcomer from the South lost some of his shyness.

"What do you call that game?" he asked.

"Lodi," said the winner promptly. "Ever play it?"

"No," said Ezekiel.

"Got a lodi?" asked the dark boy.

"No," Ezekiel answered. "Wish I had."

"Here," said the first boy. "I'll lend you one." He reached into his pants pocket and extracted a half-dozen bottle-caps. Selecting one which was somewhat battered, he handed it over to the eager and delighted Ezekiel, with the admonition, "But you've got to give it back to me, you know."

"Yes, indeedy," promised Ezekiel.

The two Harlem boys were only too glad to show the stranger how to play. They took pride in their greater knowledge, Ezekiel was an apt and grateful pupil, and three players made a better game than two. Before long they were all having a marvelous time, laughing, shooting, arguing, explaining, shooting and laughing again.

Suddenly there was a clamor of bells directly across the street from where they were playing, then the roar of a mighty engine and an abrupt ear-piercing shriek that frightened Ezekiel almost out of his wits. The game stopped. The other two boys became highly excited.

"Fire!" they shouted. "Wonder where it is?"

Thereupon, before Ezekiel's startled eyes, appeared the most amazing thing he had even seen. Out of the wide entrance of the one low building across the street came a raging, demon-like machine straight toward them. Ezekiel stood rooted to the spot, expecting to be destroyed, but the machine, when halfway to them, turned in some miraculous fashion and started away up the street. It was red and silver in the sun, it had long yellow wooden ladders along its sides and two drivers, one in front and one high on top of the ladder, behind. It seemed as long as the subway train on which Ezekiel had ridden last night, and it made infinitely more speed and noise. Even after it had turned the distant corner and disappeared, the scream of its whistles came back shrill and clear.

Other fire engines soon were heard at a distance and were seen passing the corner where the first had turned. Then the boys noted that people were running toward an invisible point somewhere near that corner, and at that point the clamor of engines seemed quite suddenly to cease. Immediately their excitement became greater.

"It's on the Avenue!—Must be right around the corner!—Come on—Come on!—Let's go!"

Off they sped, the three of them, in the wake of the hook-and-ladder. But as Ezekiel passed the stoop where he had promised his uncle to remain, he halted.

"Come on!" called his new friends, outdistancing him. "Come on, boy! Hurry up!"

For a moment the impulse to follow them was almost too great to resist. Then Ezekiel saw that they were already too far ahead of him now anyway; he could not possibly catch up with them.

Sadly he returned to his stoop and dejectedly resumed his seat. What would they think of him? After they had accepted him as one of them, lent him a lodi, and taught him to play their game, what would they think when he so unaccountably deserted them? It was quite plain what they would think. They would think him a coward. They would never take him back as one of them. They would demand their lodi and never play with him again.

What would be left for him then? Why, he wouldn't dare show his face in the street. He would have to spend all his play-hours indoors, lest he be pointed out to other boys and girls as a coward. Perhaps he wouldn't even dare go to school, after traveling so many miles to do so. His schoolmates would avoid him. No one would associate with a coward. Yes, he would have to spend his time in his uncle's apartment upstairs. Nothing could be more awful—staring down from lonely windows into the street, a dizzy distance below, or staring into the air-shaft, that horrible channel that separated one tall house from the next, a place full of unpleasant noises and odors, one glance into which this morning had been quite enough for him.

Ezekiel felt like crying. Why hadn't he had courage to go on? Was he afraid of being lost? The boys would have shown him the way back—he need not have feared that. Then why hadn't he stuck by them?

A long time he sat there downheartedly, certain that his obedience to his uncle had brought him sorrow. He wondered if his uncle could play lodi. But nobody's uncle would kneel down on a sidewalk to shoot a lodi. Presently he became aware that fire engine noises were again in the air. And in another moment the hook-and-ladder machine reappeared, heading back for its station. As he watched it swing around and slowly back into the engine-house, he wondered what manner of machines these were that could put out a fire so quickly—with ladders.

Then a tremor of fear shot through him as he saw the two boys returning. They would ridicule him, call him coward. They might dare him to fight.

Truly enough, they did laugh when they saw him. But to his great astonishment it was not a laugh of ridicule but of admiration. And when he heard what they said, he heaved a great sigh of relief and joy.

"Boy, you did right," said the darker lad.

"Indeed you did," said the light one. "You've got plenty of sense. It was only a false alarm. Come on—let's play lodi."

# EZEKIEL LEARNS

Within less than a month Ezekiel had become accustomed to the strange sights of the great city. Only a short time ago he would have tingled with fright at the shriek and clamor of fire-machines roaring down his street; would have gaped in awe at the blaring brass bands that so often led proud parades of uniformed societies past his apartment house; would have fled in dismay into the refuge of his own hallway at the occasional riots between oddly excited mobs and grimly determined policemen. But now he took all this for granted, much as if it had been designed for his own entertainment.

For had he not now witnessed all the miracles of greater New York? His uncle, to whom he had recently been sent from Georgia, had taken him downtown on the rumbling subway and shown him the tallest buildings in the world; had even taken him into one, where they entered an elevator that shot upward like a sky-rocket, and from the topmost story, viewed all of Manhattan isle, spreading away below them like a relief map; had taken him then to the famous Aquarium and shown him the most curious creatures of the sea; then out in a boat to the Statue of Liberty, whose raised arm was really a lofty tower which you could climb by a circular staircase; then back to Manhattan and uptown again to the Museum of Natural History, which contained wax figures and mammoth skeletons and mummies thousands of years old. His uncle had further given him a whole day in the enormous Bronx Park Zoo, where he saw in the flesh all the incredible animals that peopled his books. Could Harlem, then, which was merely a part of all this, was indeed merely New York's Negro colony, be expected to show him anything more extraordinary than what he had already seen?

Yet today Harlem did show him such a thing, a thing which he recalled as remarkable long after all the rest had lost its glamor. And oddly enough it was not a thing that happened in the rumbling sub or the rattling el, or in a tall building, a museum or a zoo. It was something that happened within himself, impelling him into action, and showing him for the first time that, stranger though he still was, he could yet meet and solve a problem if he had to. Today Harlem gave him his first glimpse into himself.

He had been playing marbles with four other boys, each, like himself, about a dozen years old. He knew them all by name: Riny, Sam, Spinky, and Fats. But it was Riny whom he liked best, for it was Riny who had invited him to join a game of lodi on his very first day in Harlem, and who had taught him to play and made him feel at ease while he was yet a newcomer. Riny derived his nickname from his appearance, for he possessed that light, freckled skin and rough sandy hair which other dark folk refer to as "riny." On the other hand, it was Spink whom Ezekiel cared for least. For Spink was a loud-mouthed, quarrelsome fellow who always insisted on having his own way and so hated to be opposed or to lose in any contest that he never yielded even the simplest point without some protest or ill-tempered argument.

Such was the case at the moment. Riny had just made an unusually successful shot. Spink promptly objected, insisting that Riny had cheated by shooting from a position nearer than that in which his aggie had previously fallen. But Riny only grinned good-humoredly and said:

"Aw, boy, you're always raising a howl. If you saw I was cheating, why didn't you holler before I shot?"

And he calmly picked up the marbles to which he was entitled.

This so infuriated Spink that for a moment Ezekiel thought there would be a fight. But when Spink saw that he was alone in his accusation and that none of the others was supporting him, he hotly withdrew from the game, proclaiming that he'd be jim-swiggered if he'd play with a crowd that permitted such unfair advantages.

To his chagrin, the others accepted this decision without seeming to mind at all and coolly went on playing without him. Indeed they seemed, if anything, relieved to be rid of him, and this angered him all the more. He stood off to one side looking on sullenly, clearly smoldering in resentment; and it made Ezekiel uncomfortable to see that anyone could be so unnecessarily incensed. He did not understand that what inflamed Spink most was not the loss of the marbles, but the wound to his pride—that nothing stings like being ignored. But he did see that an expression of unbelievable malice was suffusing Spink's thin dark face, an expression so baleful, indeed, that Ezekiel, who was the only one watching, felt as though Spink might at any moment pick up a brick and hurl it into their midst.

A moment later Spink moved away and vanished around the nearby corner; and Ezekiel, seeing the black look which the departing boy threw over his shoulder, instinctively realized that Spink was up to some spiteful mischief. And so Ezekiel was now more apprehensive than ever. The others were wholly absorbed in the game, now silent as they tensely watched a shot, now laughing in honest praise for skill or good-natured derision for failure. But so intensely did Ezekiel watch the corner around which Spink had disappeared that the others had to call his attention whenever his turn arrived.

Suddenly Spink came running back from around the corner, and before anyone knew what had happened he had rejoined the group. A moment later the game stopped as a big fat man, whom they all recognized as the owner of the corner fruit store, came puffing around the same corner apparently in pursuit. He was too fat and awkward to run, but he was doing his best, waddlng hurriedly forward, breathing hard, and bouncing his great paunch before him like a medicine ball.

He reached the staring group of boys and halted, blowing like a steam engine. His black eyes glared.

"Who steala da plum?" he demanded in a gruff and terrible voice. "Who steala da plum?"

He surveyed them uncertainly for a moment. Spink had moved close to Riny. The man's eyes fell upon him. "You—you steala!" he accused and started for Spink.

"No mister!" Spink cried quickly. "Not me—another boy! He just ran past—up that way—honest!" He pointed up the street.

Then Ezekiel saw a curious thing. For he, having been on the lookout, knew that no other boy had just run past, and so he did not look, as did all the others, in the direction in which Spink was pointing. Instead he looked in amazement at Spink who had made the false statement, and so saw what no one else saw: that Spink, with a deft, quick movement, still pointing with one hand, used the other to slip something into Riny's coat pocket.

"No!" bellowed the huckster. "You—you steala! I see! I breaka you' neck—"

"Nobody here took it," Spink insisted, backing off. "We've been playing marbles—haven't we fellows? Sure. Here—search us—we're not afraid. Go on—search us."

"What's a dis—search?" The big man looked from one to another. "I find, I breaka—"

"Go ahead and look in our pockets. We didn't take it. Put your arms up, fellows. Let him look in your pockets!"

Everyone obeyed but Ezekiel, who was for the moment too dumbfounded to move. For now he saw Spink's plan of revenge. Spink had taken the plum himself. That was what he had slipped into Riny's pocket just now. The huckster would find the plum in unsuspecting Riny's pocket, and Riny would take the consequences while Spink looked on in vengeful glee.

The man reached for Fats, who, hands righteously held high, happened to be nearest to him. As he did so Ezekiel started to shout the truth aloud, but something kept him silent. Long afterwards he realized the wisdom of this instinctive silence; for if he had revealed the plum's hiding place, the huckster would have refused to consider how it got there. What would he have cared if someone else *had* put it in Riny's pocket? They were all alike to him, these young rascals, working together, no doubt, and whoever had it would be guilty and must be made an example of to prevent others from doing the same thing. But at the moment Ezekiel was simply obeying the ingrained aversion every boy has to "squealing" on another.

Yet he had to do something, for he was the only one who knew the truth, and Riny, his friend, was in danger. For a moment he stood there, panic-stricken. Only a moment, however. Before the stout vendor had finished feeling roughly through Fats' clothing, Ezekiel found himself doing something he would never have dreamed possible. Quickly he moved toward Riny and Spink, both standing with upraised arms, and thrust himself between them. The huckster was now searching Sam. The other boys' eyes were glued on his great angry form. Ezekiel, with desperate stealth, reached into Riny's coat pocket with one hand, extracted the plum, transferred it behind his back to his other hand, and slipped it into the pocket of Spink. Then he, too, innocently raised both arms high and calmly waited to be searched.

The vendor disgustedly turned from a fruitless search of Sam, whereupon Ezekiel stepped forward and submitted himself. Not to be outdone in a show of innocence, Spink followed Ezekiel's example. Finishing with Ezekiel, the huckster laid hold of Spink's pockets.

Suddenly he became quite motionless, then cried. "Aha!" so fiercely that Spink shrank. Then out of one of Spink's pockets the searcher brought a small, round, purple plum.

"What I tella you!" he shouted triumphantly, and grabbed the thunder-struck Spink before he could wheel and run. Holding the plum in one hand and yanking the howling boy along by the other, he waddled away toward his corner, where stood a tall policeman.

Of course the policeman would only give Spink a thorough scare and turn him loose; or, at the very worst, take him home to his parents and urge proper punishment. But this was not the chief concern of the boys who remained behind. What astonished them was Spink's unbelievable stupidity.

"Why in the world would he tell the man to search when he knew he had the thing in his pocket all along?"

So queried Riny and Sam and Fats and shook their bewildered heads.

But Ezekiel, in the suffusing warmth of a new self-assurance, only grinned and said with town-bred nonchalance:

"Aw forget him. Come on—let's play marbles."

# THE PROMISED LAND

I

At a certain level of the airshaft two songs, issuing from opposite windows, met, mingled minor refrains, and rose together toward Negro Harlem's black sky; two futile prayers which spent themselves like mist ere they reached the roof. The one was a prayer for the love of man, the other a prayer for the love of God: "blues," and a spiritual.

The blues song would have drowned the spiritual had it not labored against a closed window. No such barrier stayed the spiritual. To be sure the singer was old, as her present posture emphasized: shoulders bent round, dim eyes and unsteady hands searching the pages of the Bible on her lap. But her voice was well sustained, and her song was none the less clear because it accompanied her endless thumbing of thin leaves.

Like her eyes and her fingers, her hymn sought comfort, sought while it almost despaired:—

Bow low!—How low mus' I bow?
Bow low!—How low mus' I bow?
Bow low!—How low mus' I bow
To enter in de promis' land?

Presently, as if there came no answer, she interrupted her quest and her song, turned out the gas, and sat back in the darkness to observe the progress of the rent party across the shaft.

A rent party is a public dance given in a private apartment. If, after letting out three of your five rooms to lodgers, your resources are still unequal to your rent, you make up the deficit by means of a rent party. You provide music, your friends provide advertisement, and your guests, by paying admission, provide what your resources lack.

Such a party Mammy now witnessed. Through the window opposite her own she commanded most of one room and a corner of another in the adjacent flat. The window was indeed a screen upon which flashed a motion picture oddly alive and colorful. Boys whose loose trousers were too long for their legs and girls whose tight skirts were too short for theirs hugged each other close, keeping time to the rhythm of hoarsely phonographed blues.

Bright enough dresses, certainly: scarlet and green and glowing purple, rendering dark complexions darker, lending life to pale ones; dresses that, having lost half their volume, put all their color into the rest. Bright enough faces, too: boys wagging their heads and grinning, girls gayly laughing at their jokes.

But such a dance! The camel walk. Everybody "cameling." Had God wanted a man to move like a camel he'd have put a hump in his back. Yet was there any sign of what God wanted in that scene across the shaft? Skins that He had made black bleached brown, brown ones bleached cream-color; hair that He had made long and kinky bobbed short and ironed dead straight. Young girls' arms about boys' shoulders, their own waists tightly clasped; bodies warmly fused, bending to the sensual waves of the "camel." Where was God in that?

Mammy watched as she had often watched before, with a dull wonder that such colossal wickedness should be allowed to prevail. The song that had mingled with hers now filtered through the closed window opposite and came alone to her ears, bringing no reassurance. For all that it plumbed the nadir of woe, was it not a song of sin?

> Lawdy, Lawdy, I can't help but cry an' moan.
> Lawdy, Lawdy, I can't help but cry an' moan.
> My man done gone and lef' me—gone an' lef' me all alone.

One couple swung into view which especially caught Mammy's attention, so completely had it abandoned itself to the dance. Mammy saw with a little quiver of alarm that the boy was her grandson, Sam. Wesley, her other grandson, was also somewhere in that company, and it was Wesley's girl with whom Sam was dancing. If Wesley ever saw Sam dancing like that with Ellie—

In the visible corner of the far room Mammy recognized Wesley's back. Wesley's shoulders, far less mobile than Sam's, were gradually turning as he faced about in the slow measure of the dance. In but a few seconds he would be looking at his cousin through the intervening doorway, would see Sam and Ellie's exaggerated movements, despite the people between. An old and mounting hostility between them would swiftly surge and flare—they would quarrel, perhaps they would fight. Mammy sat up, leaned tensely forward, whispered, "Lawd, have mercy!"

Unlike her earlier prayer, this one was apparently heard, for at that moment the blues halted and the dancing abruptly ceased. The change of partners, however, only momentarily relieved Mammy's qualms. Over her settled a deadly certainty that the clash had been merely postponed. There would be many more dances, one of which would rejoin Ellie and Sam as partners. The later that happened, the higher would everyone's spirits be, the wilder the dancing, and so the quicker and hotter Wesley's resentment. As the new dance began, Mammy grew rapidly surer of what she foresaw. Soon her helplessness and the increasing effort to suppress her excitement welled almost beyond bearing. Her misgiving urged her to do something to prevent this long-deferred crisis; but somehow she could only sit still and look on and pray that this time for once her foresight would prove wrong.

Her apprehension became black emptiness into which memories, rocketwise, soared and burst: rumor of opportunity in the cities of the North—certainty of ruin should rumor prove false; hope of young and old men departing, of women and children gone after them—despair of tranquil homes upheaved, of families ruthlessly scattered; the joy she herself had felt when these two grandsons had finally sent for her—the sorrow of being the last to leave the lopsided old Virginia home.

They were equally dear to Mammy, these two boys, and, until they had come to New York, had been equally fond of each other. They had grown up together, attended the four-months-a-year school together, played hooky, fished, hunted rabbits, and got baptized together; and finally, caught in the epidemic fever of migration that swept the dark-skinned South, they had left home together to find their fortunes in Harlem.

As life had thus brought some to seek wealth, so death, back home, brought others to seek peace; but Mammy had been beckoned toward neither goal, had simply been left quite alone. And rather because there was nothing else to do than because they wanted or needed her, the cousins, Wesley and Sam, had offered to let her housekeep for them in a small flat in the great city.

Scarcely had she got over the shock of underground railroads, of trains overhead, of mountainous buildings where people lived like chickens, before she perceived that the city had done something to Wesley and Sam. They had lost their comradeship, they just managed to tolerate each other, and they compensated for this mere toleration by goading each other persistently with strange, new, malicious jibes:—

"Down-home boy lak you ain' got no business in no city nohow."

"Don' ketch me th'owin' my money 'way on no numbers, though, uh no baseball pool."

"Co'se not. You don' *make* no money. How you go'n' th'ow any 'way?"

Rudolph Fisher

Mammy soon saw what new feature of their life lay at the bottom of this. To Sam, whose hands learned quickly, the city had been kind. Starting as handy man in a garage, he had soon become a mechanic's helper, and now at last was a mechanic with wages of sixty dollars a week. Wesley, always more awkward, had found the city indifferent, and so perforce had become his own boss, washing windows at fifteen cents each. So Harlem, where there was insistent competition to test and reward special skill, and where there was so much more for men to quarrel about and resent, had quickly estranged these two unguarded lads simply by paying the one twice as much as the other; had furnished them thus with taunts that had not been possible back home, and now kept them constantly wounding each other with the heedless cruelty of children—wounds that would one day translate themselves from the spirit into the flesh.

"Ellie? Ellie yo' gal? Whut business you got wid a gal? You could n' buy a gal coffee 'n' a san'wich."

"Reckon you could buy huh champagne an' lobster."

"An' I don' mean maybe."

"Better put some dat money in accident 'nsurance den."

"What you talkin' 'bout?"

"'Cause 'f I ketch you messin' roun' Ellie I'm sho' go'n' turn yo' damper down. An' *I* don' mean maybe."

"Shuh! Listen t' dis boogy. Man, my slowes' move's too fas' f' you."

"Not yo' slowes' move roun' Ellie ain't."

"One my thoughts 'd bust yo' haid wide open."

"Yeah? Well it don't do nuthin' to yo' haid but *swell* it."

Suddenly these remembered mockings leaped out of past into present. As one rudely waked starts up, so Mammy's fear now started out of the stupor of memory. In the room across the airshaft Sam and Wesley were facing each other, the fire of their hostility having driven the onlookers back into an expectant surrounding circle. Mammy saw the boys' lips move, and from their malignant countenances and the dismay on the faces about them she knew that again bitter taunts were being exchanged, this time in company where words quickly kindled action. Hitherto her own presence had always restrained them. Now the only spectators were hoodlums off the street, before whom the boys might well wish to show off, at the same time squaring the urgent account for a hundred bygone insults.

The antagonists stood toe to toe, Sam the more lithe, slightly taller, Wesley broader and heavier. Their lips no longer moved, and Mammy recognized that silent, critical moment in an encounter when the mere forward swaying of a body is enough to free madness.

She jumped up, tried to cry out a warning, achieved but a groan: "Good

Lawd!" Her impotence became frenzy; she cast about wildly for some means of diverting the inevitable. A soft golden glint caught and held her eyes—the gilt edge of the Bible still in her hand, touched to a glow by light from across the way.

The Bible was suddenly divine revelation, an answer. She hesitated only long enough to note Sam's hand creeping toward his coat pocket. "God fo'give me," she breathed; then drew back an arm grown opportunely strong, and hurled the Word with all her might through the pane of the opposite window.

At the crash and jingle of glass she shrank back into the shadow of her own room; yet not so far back as to obscure the picture of her two grandsons, staring limply agape, now at each other, now at the Book at their feet.


II

Mammy asked Ellie point-blank:—

"Which a one my boys you lak sho' nuff?"

And Ellie, a girl of the city, replied with a laugh and a toss of her bob:—

"Both of 'em. Why not?"

They sat in the kitchen of Mammy's three-room flat, of which the parlor served as the boys' bedroom and the third room on the airshaft as Mammy's own. Ellie and a chum occupied a similar apartment, the adjacent one, where the rent party had been given; and Ellie occasionally "ran in," ostensibly anxious to inquire after Mammy, actually hoping to see one of her boys and possibly make a date.

Mammy saw through these visits, of course, and had thought that Ellie's interest was in Wesley. But Ellie's behavior with Sam at the party tinctured this conclusion with doubt. No girl, thought Mammy, who liked one man would behave like that with another—not with both present.

Hence, with characteristic directness, Mammy instituted investigation; and Ellie's side-stepping answer but whetted a suspicion already keen.

"You lak bofe of 'm d' same?"

"I'll say I do."

"Jes' d same?"

"Nothin' different."

"Hmph. Dat mean you don' really lak neither one of 'm, den."

"Oh, yes, I do. Pretty skee sheiks for country jakes."

"Whut you lak 'bout 'm?"

"Well, different things. Sam's crazy and knows how to show a girl a good time, see? Wesley ain't so crazy, but he tries hard and you can depend on him. You wonder about Sam, you know about Wesley. Wesley's better-lookin', too."

"S'posin' you had to choose between 'm. Which a one you take?"

"Oh, Sam. Sam makes twice as much as Wesley."

The casualness of that answer made Mammy wince. To accustom yourself to some things is easy—to subways and "L's," to army-worm traffic, to hard grassless pavements, hot treeless sidewalks, cold distant starless skies; even to a fifth-story roost on the airshaft of a seven-story hencoop. But to accustom yourself to the philosophy of the metropolis, to its ruthless opportunism—that is hard.

"S'posin'," Mammy experimented, "dey bofe made zackly d' same? Which a one you take den?"

The questioning began to irritate Ellie. "Wha' d' y' mean, take? I ain't grabbin' after neither one of 'em, y' know."

"I mean ef day bofe ast you to marry 'm."

"Oh, to *marry* 'em? And both drawin' the same pay? Why, Wesley, by all—" Ellie bit her lip, and withdrew into the cautious neutrality out of which the unexpected contemplation of matrimony had surprised her. "Or—well—either one—I don't know." This old woman was nearer to either boy than was she herself, she remembered. Both the bumpkins spent on her. Why reduce her chances for a good time by making a betraying choice? Play the boobs off against each other, let them both strut their stuff. Maybe a better catch than either would meanwhile gulp your bait. Then you could discard both these poor fish with a laugh. "You know what the song says, Mammy: 'Don't let no one man worry your mind.'"

Mammy looked at Ellie as she might have looked at the armadillo in the zoo—this strange, unbelievable creature who in the spring of her life subjected romance to utility. For Mammy saw that the girl really preferred Wesley to Sam, yet had no apology of word or manner in prospectively renouncing Wesley's character for Sam's superior pay. Young, pretty, live girls like Ellie should have to be told to consider their suitor's pay. With them it ought to be secondary to youth's more compelling absurdities. But here was a slip of a girl who spoke like a thrice-married widow of fifty.

Mammy accepted this as one of the mysteries of city breeding. Having done so, it was easy to prophesy. Ellie's willingness to take equally what Sam and Wesley had to give would be the crux of the boys' antagonism. Wesley claimed right of priority. Neither Ellie nor Sam cared a sneeze for such right. Ellie, city-wise, "liked them both." Into the mould of this situation all of the vague potent bitterness of the boys' recent hatred would be poured, to take definite form. The city had broken the bond between them. The city now fashioned them a bludgeon with which to shatter their common life.

"Listen, daughter. How come you carry on wid Sam lak dat las' night? Did n' you know 't would start trouble?"

"Carry on? Wha' d' y' mean, carry on? I only danced with 'im."

"Dat all? Den whut start d' trouble?"

"Wesley buttin' in, the dumbbell. Why don't somebody tell him something? He ain't down home now. This is New York."

"Uh-huh. Dis is New York. Ḍis is New York. An' ain't New York in God's worl'? Don' New York come under His eyes a-tall?"

This was quite out of Ellie's line. She shrugged and kept still. Mammy's voice, however, grew stronger with her pain.

"New York. Harlem. Thought all along 't was d' las' stop 'fo' Heaven. Canaan hitself. Reg'lar promis' lan'. Well, dat's jes' whut 't is—a promis' lan'. All hit do is promise. Promise money lak growin' on trees—ain' even got d' trees. Promise wuk fo' dem whut want wuk—look at my boy, Wesley. Promise freedom fum d' whi' folks—white man be hyeh to-day, take d' las' penny fo' rent. You know why 't is? You know how come?"

Ellie stared. Mammy got up, stood erect with almost majestic dignity. "Hit's sin. Dat's whut 'tis—sin. My people done fo'got dey God, grabbin' after money. I warn 'm 'fo' dey all lef'. Longin' fo' d' things o' dis worl' an' a-fo'gittin' d' Lawd Jesus. Broke up dey homes in d' country—lef' folks behind sick an' dyin'. So anxious. So scairt all d' money be gone 'fo' dey git hyeh. I tole 'm. Fust seek d' kingdom of God an' His righteousness. But no. Everybody done gone crazy over gittin'. An' hit don' bring nothin' but misery in dis worl' an' hell-fire in eternity. Hit's sin!"

"Soft pedal, Mammy. And hold the sermon, will you?"

"An' dat's another thing." The diminished tone only bared Mammy's intensity. "You-all so scairt o' d' Word o' God. Sam and Wesley done got d' same way sence dey been up hyeh. Seem lak hit make you oncomf'table. Make you squirm. Make you squirm wuss'n 'at low-down dancin' you do. Well, hit oughter. Garment o' righteousness don' b'long on no body o' sin."

Ellie did n't quite get this, but she did n't like the way Mammy was looking at her. "Say, what's the idea?" she inquired.

"Idea?" Mammy grew calm, almost cold; focused her distraction on one problem: "Idea is, you either let *one* my boys alone or let 'em *bofe* alone. You heah? You cain't run wid d' hare an' hunt wid d' hounds. Dis hyeh 'either one' business'll have 'm both at each other's th'oats 'fo' another day. Lawd knows dey'd be better off ef you stayed 'way fum 'm bofe."

At this Ellie flared. "Well, of all the cockeyed nerve! Say, where do you think you get off? D' you s'pose I'm chasin' after your farmer boys?"

Mammy said nothing. It was Ellie's turn to wax loud.

"Pity you old handkerchief-heads would n' stay down South where you belong. First you ask me to state my intentions. Then you tell me I started the argument at the party. Then you preach me a sermon on sin or clothes or somethin'. Then you tell *me* to let *them* alone—as if they did n't pester me dizzy. As if I was *chasin'* them. What are you trying to call me, anyhow? Do you think I'd chase any bozo on earth?"

Mammy did not dream what vile accusation lay in the provincialism "chase." Unaware of what the word meant to Ellie, she commented promptly and bluntly:—

"You sho' ain' chasin' *me*."

Ellie sprang up, furious, inflamed less by the implication than by Mammy's intuitively shrewd analysis. "Why, you dirty old devil—I ought to paste you one! If that's what you think you can all go to hell." She turned and strode hotly away, flinging back a smouldering "Damn you!" The hall door slammed behind her with a bang that jarred the floor.

Mammy stood bewildered a while; presently murmured, "She cuss' me—" Slowly she sank into her chair and looked around at the close kitchen walls; kept repeating, as if to convince herself, "Dat li'l chile—she cuss' me."


## III

The three-room apartment boasted four windows, and on them, following Mammy's request, Wesley agreed to finish his fruitless day.

"I done done d' inside all right," she explained, "but I cain't make d' out-side. I scairt to stick my haid out one o' dese winders. No sense in folks livin' in d' side of a cliff dis-a-way—'cept'n' hit's as near to d' heaven as dey'll ever git again."

Wesley, polishing glass, endeavored to stay the passing light of day with song, but even his song grew dark as the mood of blues settled gradually over it:—

> . . . cain't help but cry an' moan.
> My gal done gone an' lef' me—gone an' lef me all alone.

The words were not without significance. Usually Ellie greeted him with great show of eagerness; comforted him at the end of a poor day when he dropped in for a while before dinner; suggested some means of disposing of the day's return—which, of course, was too small to save. But to-day, after peeping out as usual, she had slammed the door in his face.

"Ellie—wha's a matter?"

Only a diminuendo of angry clicks, receding down her hallway.

Well, it had served him right. He'd been warned about these uppity Northern gals, these "gimme" gals. Always had their hands out, expecting something. Something for nothing. Taxis. Eats. Liquor. Big times. Back home a girl could n't want so much because there was n't so much to want. But here—no effort on his part in spending three days' earnings on Ellie in a single night. No effort on her part to save it, either. And in return a kiss and a promise—a promise to go out again with him some night. Gimme.

Probably sore because he'd started a row at her party last night. Well, was she his gal or was n't she? A kiss. In the city a kiss has many meanings. Maybe she kissed Sam also. Maybe her kisses were a commodity.

He stopped polishing to look down on the street five stories below. Folks look funny at that distance and angle. All look alike. None human. Long thin feet alternately passing each other, arms circling awkwardly outside the feet, heads gliding squatly forward in the midst of arms and legs. People seen on end resemble spiders.

Ellie, maybe, was a spider, and he had been her fly. Having withdrawn his little substance, she now discarded his shell. Sam's turn now. Fly guy, Sam. Ought to swat him. Leave it to Ellie—she'll swat him for sixty bucks a week. Gimme.

"Don' set dey idle, son. Fust thing you know you'll lose yo' holt an' fall."

"Make no diff'unce ef I land on my haid."

"Git th'ough in d' kitchen nex.' Got to git supper. Sam be home tireckly."

"M-hm."

Wesley did the kitchen window and proceeded to Mammy's room. The airshaft was quite dark, so that he had to light the gas jet. He soaped his wet rag and clambered half through, turned, and clamped his heels as usual against the wall beneath the sill, thus leaving both hands free for work. He soaped the outside surface of the pane and, while waiting for it to dry, twisted about to look behind him at Ellie's window. It was still unrepaired; a newspaper covered the jagged opening in the pane. His enlarged shadow fell misshapen on the wall about the window and the jagged opening looked like a wound in his side.

Somewhere beyond the broken window a door banged loudly shut. Soon another, closer door did likewise.

\*　　\*　　\*

Sam shuffled angrily into the kitchen and tossed something back on to the table, where it landed with a thump. Peering over her "specks," Mammy recognized her Bible. She reproved:—

"Don't you know no better 'n to th'ow d' Word of d' Lawd aroun' lak dat? Better learn to keep in near yuh."

"Did n' th'ow it half as fur as you did."

"I th'owed it keep you young fools fum doin' harm. You jes' th'owed it to be th'owin'."

"Da's aw right 'bout doin' harm. Ef I had busted Wesley, he could 'a' gone to d' free hospital. But you busted d' winder. Who go'n' pay fo' dat?"

"Lan'lawd oughter pay fo' it. He charge enough rent."

"Maybe he would, but sump'n done got into Ellie—she raisin' d' devil. 'Clare out she go'n' tell d' lan'lawd you th'owed it—yo' name's wrote in it. Dat mean I have to pay d' bill—lak I pay f' ev'ything else roun' hyeh."

"Dat all she say?"

"No. Say she go'n' have you 'rested fo' disturbin' d' peace. Say sump'n 'bout slander too."

"Humph!"

"Den she slam' d' do' in my face."

"Maybe dat'll help you stay 'way fum 'uh."

"Stay 'way fo' whut?"

"'Cause she ain' got d' love o' God in huh heart, dat's fo' whut. An' neither is you. Hit's a bad combination."

"Ain' lookin' fo' no love o' God. Lookin' fo' Wesley. Wha' he at?"

"Washin' my room winder. Let 'im 'lone."

"I'll let 'im 'lone aw right. I'll th'ow 'im out it."

*　　*　　*

Only Wesley's legs were visible to Sam, entering the room. Wesley was wiping off the frosting of soap that he had allowed to dry on the pane. As he wiped, more of his body appeared through the glass thus made clear, and at last his troubled face. It showed surprise at the presence of Sam, who stood glowering accusation.

"What d' hell you been tellin' Ellie 'bout me?"

Even through intervening glass Wesley's anger was quick to respond. "What d' hell could I tell 'uh bad enough?"

"You been puttin' me in—else she would n' 'a' slam no do' in my face."

"She slam' d' do' in yo' face?"

"Reckon you tole 'uh to do it."

Wesley's anger subsided. He repeated, with something akin to relief, eagerly,—

"Say she slam' d' do' in *yo'* face?"

"Did n' miss it."

Wesley threw back his head and filled the airshaft with loud laughter. To Sam it was galling, derisive, contemptuous laughter, laughter of victory. Anger, epithets, blows he could have exchanged, but laughter found him defenseless. In a hot flush of rage he drew back a foot and kicked viciously at Wesley's legs.

At the moment Wesley had only one leg pressed firmly back against the wall. It was this that received the blow, and the quick sharp pain loosened its grip. In swift effort to catch himself, Wesley snatched at the bottom edge of the lower frame, but with such desperate force that it slid instantly upward, so that his hold was broken by the upper. Grabbing wildly, Sam sprang forward, frightened into contrition—succeeded only in further dislodging his already unbalanced cousin. A brief mad scramble to save him—a futile clawing and slipping of hands—a cry—a moment's incredulous silence—silence that broke with a soft and terrible thud.

Sam shrank back and threw one hand up over his mouth like a child that has heard something forbidden; wheeled, to see Mammy stiff in the doorway, staring with stricken eyes. Hysteria gripped him.

"I did n' do it—I 'clare out 'fo' God, Mammy—" He turned back toward the window; backed off from it, crouching and trembling; faced again toward Mammy. Deprecation gave way to bravado. He whispered sharply, "Ef you tell anybody, I'll—" Then suddenly rushed with insane menace toward her as panic rushed through his brain, reached her, stopped—abruptly collapsed at her feet, shuddering with sobs.

Mammy, roused by a spirit which still hoped in the face of calamity, quickly bent down and shook the crumpled lad with sobering vigor. "Git up, son! Make has'e! Git up! Mammy seen yuh! Seen yuh try to ketch 'im! Make has'e to 'im! Maybe he's on'y hurt!"

The boy raised a countenance wretched with fear and doubt and weakness, but the strength and will in Mammy's eyes brought him to his senses.

"Make has'e, I tell yuh!"

He jumped up, his face still convulsed, and sped toward the outer door and the stairs.


IV

Again Mammy sat by her window, her fingers groping amid the thin leaves of her Bible.

Out of the airshaft sounds came to her, sounds of the land of promise. Noise of a rent party somewhere below from a tiny dwelling that had to be hired out if it was to be dwelt in at all—peculiar feature of a place where your own home was n't your own. Noise of a money quarrel somewhere above, charges, taunts, disputes—fruit of a land where sudden wide differences in work and pay summoned disaster. Noise of sinful singing and danc-

Rudolph Fisher

ing, pastime of Ellie's generation, breed of a city where children cursed and threatened the old and went free.

For Ellie still went her way rejoicing, heedless of what she had precipitated in a passing fit of temper. Sam in a week had forgotten—was with Ellie at this very rent party below. And when the white folks had come to investigate the unfortunate death by violence, Mammy had sworn with stiffened lips it was all an accident.

Into the airshaft crept her old hymn, lifting toward Harlem's black sky:—

Bow low!—How low mus' I bow
To enter in de promis' land?

# GUARDIAN OF THE LAW

Grammie's third-story window commanded the turbulent block. For her dark Harlem's 133rd Street was a stage upon which she looked as from an upper box. It was time now for the hero to enter. An anticipative half-smile on her lively little old face, she waited, looking brightly toward the Seventh Avenue wing. Across her mind comment pursued comment like successive windflaws sweeping the surface of a pool:

"He'll be along presently. Watch those noisy young ones tone down. Yesterday he was jes' like 'em. Yellin'. Fightin'. Rollerskatin' over folks' corns. Stealin' apples off Tony, the peddler. Hookin' rides on trucks and taxis, scarin' the very kinks out my head. Now look—grown. Look like his grandpa that day he won the log-rollin' back home—Watch out, you little monkey you! 'Nother inch and you'd a' been squashed like a persimmon. Devlish young ones—!"

But there was something wrong about that.

"Hmph! Listen at you, you crazy old loon, you. Was they ever a devlisher young one than you fifty years ago? Fight? Done forgot all 'bout the time you bit Zeke Logan's ear half off 'cause he call' you a little yaller weasel. Steal? How 'bout the way you and Peace used to steal Gram Frankie's cider-wine and corn-cakes and puff up with the colic like balloons? Scare yo' folks? 'Member the day you swum Uncle Jake's mare Steppit 'cross the widest part o' Deep Bayou, with yo' laigs drawn up and yo' feet crossed befo' you, same as if you was squattin' in front o' the fireplace? Jes' 'cause that black imp o' Satan, Jesse, up and dared you.— Young ones—"

But the hero had entered.

"Hot you! Hyeh he come!—Swing along, you proud young scamp, you!— Who'd a thought I'd live to see the day—?"

"Hey there, sweetheart!" A young bronze giant in a policeman's uniform had halted directly across the street and was waving cheerily up at her.

Grammie leaned forward, her quick smile answering his merry grin.

"None o' yo' freshness, rookie. I's a lady, if it's any news to you."

"It's my job to look out for ladies, baby. How 'bout a little supper with me tonight?"

"Little is all I get any night, much as you eats."

"Stewed chicken and dumplin's would touch my heart."

"Yo' heart must be in yo' mouth."

"Sho is. Scared I might get corn beef and cabbage."

"Reckon cabbage'd tarnish them brass buttons or sump'm."

"The law demands chicken and dumplin's."

"Go 'long, boy and thank God for whatever you get."

"The law—"

"I'll fan the law with a hickory switch."

"All right, y' gangster. And I'll run you in for killin' an appetite, too." Officer Sam shook a threatening finger, turned and strolled away.

Fine boy. Much of a man. Much more than that no-'count Grip Beasely who lost the appointment Sam won. 'Course every crow thinks her young ones the blackest, but Grip would have been just one more hoodlum in uniform. Couldn't help it—too much Harlem in him. Too smart. Never depending on hard work for anything—always outsmarting somebody. Pulling wires, for instance, while Sam studied. It didn't work, though. Sam passed both tests high up, while Grip fell behind in the written. Of course he got close to Sam on the appointment-list, but Sam got the appointment, was now doing six months' probation; all vacancies were filled and Grip was shut out.

Grip sort of held that against Sam. Though maybe Judy had a lot to do with it, too. Sweet child, Judy, with that red-brown skin and those big black eyes of hers. Little monkey turned Grip down flat and said she was Sam's girl, exclusively. Should have said it before Sam got the appointment, instead of waiting till after. Judy, of course, felt it might make Sam work harder if she withheld her decision till afterwards, but Grip naturally thought she chose Sam just because he got to be a cop.

"I don' trust that Grip—he's go'n' try to make it hard for my chile, sho's you born. Got some smart scheme up his sleeve right now, I know.—Well—guess that chicken's mos' done—time to put in the dumplin's."

Grammie rose, grunting a little with the stiffness of her lame knee, and approached a bureau on top of which lay a box of snuff. It was a small rectangular pasteboard box in one corner of which she had, after her custom, punched a hole with a safety-pin, and by the same device slightly enlarged the aperture to allow the dark brown powder to be shaken out in a thin stream as needed. But as she reached for it now, a sudden sharp pain shot through the lame knee, causing her to catch her weight on the bureau top;

her fingers inadvertently compressed the snuff-box and a jet of brown powder shot across the white bureau-scarf.

"Now jes' look at that," she grumbled. "They's an excuse fo' a pain in the knee, but wastin' snuff and ruinin' linen is tom-foolishness." The pain passed. "Reckon it's a sin to dip snuff anyhow." She picked up the box. "But I likes it."

She returned to the window for a last look at her grandson. Instead of strolling down the street, he had stopped, facing the house on the first floor of which Grip Beasely lived. She saw him stand a moment as if puzzled, then suddenly break for the stoop and dash up the stairs and into the entrance.

"What under the sun—?"

Her bewilderment lasted but briefly.

"Sump'n wrong. That Grip is up to sump'm, sho." She looked about, peered out again toward Beasely's door. "Lemme get out o' hyeh." She caught up an old cloak that quite enveloped her slight form and with amazing agility, hurried out of the apartment and down the hall stairway.

"These chillun'll run me into my grave with their foolishness. I'm go'n' shake that Grip's back teeth loose yet—the imp o' Satan!"

Along and across the street she sped with no sign of a lame knee, up the stoop and into the entrance of the house where Beasely dwelt. On the right of the passage, just within the entrance, was the door to Grip Beasely's flat. Grammie seized the knob, shook it, and stood back impatiently resolute. No answer. She discovered and pushed a button in the door-frame. She waited. Still no answer. The upper panel of the doorway was of glass, not thick plate-glass, but a common frosted window-glass that rattled when the door moved. "Lord help me if I'm right and forgive me if I'm wrong," she breathed, and raised her right foot to the lower edge of the flimsy panel, paused for balance, then thrust vigorously forward, heel first.

There was less crash and clatter than she expected. Through the jagged aperture she negotiated the snap-lock and was quickly inside. The room was unoccupied save by a few mistreated old mock-mahogany pieces of furniture on a gray, worn, dirty carpet, and a battered piano whose key-board grinned evilly at her from a distant dim corner. She halted, cocked her snowy head to one side, peered toward the rear of the apartment. The jangle of glass had drawn no investigation. Far down the obscurity of the narrow hallway, which ran lengthwise from parlor to kitchen, she heard voices and a laugh— an unpleasant, triumphant laugh.

Slowly and cautiously, she started toward that sound, wary of possible ambush from the intermediate rooms opening on the hallway. Deliberately she tip-toed forward, steadying herself with one hand against the wall.

"Mus' got my chile where he can't move—"

The first hall-room door was open, the gray space beyond it lifeless. But now, sharpened by contrast, there came to her perceptions a decided, if intangible, animation somewhere beyond, a definite impression of subdued excitement in one of the rooms further along, somewhat like the far murmur of storm-wind in prairie grass. As she was about to pass the second chamber, the door of which was closed, she heard a chair scrape suddenly against a bare floor. An unexpected close crack of thunder could not have stiffened her to quicker attention.

Close to the door she crouched. The agitation, the voices further down the hall were now ever more decided, and again Grammie heard that laugh. But for the moment she was arrested by the consciousness of something important here in this room at whose closed door she listened. It was very dark. Carefully she reached down feeling for the knob. Her hand encountered a key. The door had been locked from the outside and the key left in. She turned the key slowly, then suddenly threw the door open.

The airshaft-window was wide, and astride its sill, dimly outlined in a gray patch of light was a girl. Her eyes, looking back over her shoulder, were wide with mingled terror and defiance.

"Judy!" went Grammie's sharp whisper. "What you doin', chile?"

"Grammie!"

"Sh! What you doin' in hyeh?"

"How—how'd you get in? Where are they?"

"Who?"

"Grip—Grip and Cawley."

"Cawley?—Who he?"

Judy abandoned the window sill. "Grip's friend.—I was leavin' for your house. Grip came up to our flat and begged me to come see his sister—said she was sick in bed. I did, but his sister wasn't here, and he and this Cawley shut the door and held me in the parlor till Sam came along. They were watchin' for him. When I saw Sam I yelled for him. I didn't know, but that was just what they wanted. They knew they couldn't get him in here any other way. But before Sam realized who yelled, Cawley yanked me away and dragged me down the hall. He put me in here. Said—"

"Sh!—Whisper, chile. Quick—"

"Said if I kept quiet it would just be a joke, but if I didn't it wouldn't. He locked me in. Then I heard 'em all go past down the hall. Grip said, 'No monkey-business, rookie—this thing's loaded.' So I was scared to yell again—Sam would've forgot Grip's gun and got himself shot."

Grammie stepped quickly to the window. Although this was the street floor, the air-well dropped a full story below to the level of the basement. "What was you aimin' to do?"

"Jump to the bottom, go through the cellar, and get help."

"Hmph.—Go on out the front door. Get a police—get all the polices you see—and come a-runnin'."

Before Judy got to the front door, Grammie had traversed the rest of the hall and was outside the room where things were happening. A third time she heard Grip Beasely's laugh. Knowing now what it meant transformed her into the same furious child who, fifty years ago, had bitten Zeke Logan's ear half off. She flung the door wide and stood framed on the threshold, a small, terrible angel of vengeance.

Cawley, his back to the door, was now holding the gun on Sam, who was seated, hands raised, on a chair. Grip was standing beyond Sam, holding a whiskey bottle, and as the door opened, he was growling, "Will you or won't you?"

"What kind o' foolishness is this?" Grammie stepped forward. Cawley turned his head in surprise to look over his shoulder. Grammie's hand shot forward toward that astonished countenance, and suddenly Cawley swore and dropped the gun, as both hands came up to cover his face.

The alert defiance in Officer Sam's eyes had been watching for just this instant's opening. His training as an officer had been brief but sufficient to teach him not to charge a loaded muzzle. Now, however, one of his raised hands quickly smacked the bottle out of Grip's fingers so viciously that it spattered with a wet crash against the wall. The other became a fist which traveled a short distance to reach the point of Beasely's jaw, and in as much as Officer Sam was at the same time lifting his one hundred and ninety pounds off the chair, there was considerable emphasis upon that point.

Cawley, one hand clamped over his face, was groping his way out, Grammie nimbly side-stepped to let him pass. But Beasely was too husky a young animal to be floored by a single blow. His hundred and ninety pounds were more closely packed than Sam's; he was shorter and broader with disproportionately long arms. And he had no physical fear. With Sam's blow he staggered back, shook his head as if in vigorous denial that any such thing had happened, then lunged precipitately forward. The next moment saw him and Officer Sam embracing each other with enthusiasm.

Grammie momentarily ignored them, stooped and picked up the pistol, considered it briefly, and deliberately tossed it into the hallway behind her. Then she stood and beheld the tussle, offering the adversaries' stridor, shuffle, thumps and thwacks such advice and comment as she found indicated:

"Sam, you fool you, turn 'im loose so you can hit 'im. You huggin' 'im like you love 'im. Let him do the huggin'—you hit. —That's better, see? He can outhug you but you can outhit him. —I declare that po' chile look mo' like a gorilla 'n he do like a man. Look out—he'll bite you if he get a chance!—

Now—that's it—that's it—now you got 'im. Tho'w 'im down and sit on 'im. Fine.—You got to bounce up and down on 'im ev'y now and then, y' know, else he'll get his wind back.—'Twon' be long 'fo'—hyeh they is now!"

Here they were indeed, a breathless Judy and two looming envoys of the law, one black, one yellow, both extremely interested.

"The other one went in yonder," said Grammie.

The other one was sought, found, and ungently returned to the scene of major activity, where Officer Sam was explaining:

"Judy yells and I rush in, excited and empty-handed. My bosom-friend, Grip here, has gun a-plenty, see? When I pop in, he's behind me. I start down the hall and he sticks me up from behind. He unloads me. We march down the hall to this back room. Cawley comes up and takes his turn with the gun. I don't get what it's all about till Grip offers me a drink. The idea is to souse me, take my shield and gun, and turn me in. If I don't come around agreeable, I get beaned and the same thing happens anyhow."

"What's it to him?"

"He's in line for my job. I'm still a rookie. If I'm jammed and they break me, he pulls a fast wire and gets in.—So what happens? You'd be surprised. Just as I'm forgettin' there's a rod in the picture and figurin' on a quick dumb move, along comes—"

"A cockaroach."

"Huh?" said everybody.

"A cockaroach," Grammie repeated positively. "Kitchen's right next door, y' see. This cockaroach 'd got on Cawley's collar—right hyeh." She reached up and put her finger on the spot. "Y' all know how cockroaches is. They likes to crawl between things—crazy 'bout cracks and such. So this one crawled right over Cawley's collar and got down between his collar and his neck. Natchelly it itches and natchelly Cawley scratches. And natchelly that takes Cawley's mind off what he was doin', y' see. Sam's lookin' fo' a chance like that. He grabs this Grip hyeh, pulls him 'round between hisself and that Cawley. Cawley can't shoot now 'thout hittin' Grip, y' see. So Sam jes taps this Grip on his chin to stun him a little, so he won' suffer in case he gets hurt—Sam always was a tender-hearted chile—and then shoves him into this Cawley. Natchelly Cawley loses his balance, so Sam can take the gun 'way from him and th'ow it out in the hall. Too bad but he accidentally hit him in the nose doin' it, so he made him go in the kitchen yonder and bathe his face in cold water. And when y'all got hyeh, that Sam was a'kneelin' over Grip tryin' his best to bring him to."

"Well I be dog-goned!" said the yellow cop.

"Mus'n cuss, chile," Grammie reproached him. "Cussin's a sin."

"'Scuse me, ma'am.—But how'd you know all this?"

"Sam jes' now tol' me. Y'see I was passin' by the front do' when Judy run out to get y' all. She tol' me not to come in. Natchelly that made me curious, so in I come. I knowed nuthin' wasn' go'n' hurt me.—But by time I got in back hyeh, seem like ev'ything was over."

"Good boy, Sammy!" commended the black policeman. "That's hoppin' off a tough spot."

Officer Sam looked at Grammie; Grammie looked back at him and with her live eyes dared him to upset her account. And Officer Sam said, "Well, I don' guess he'd 'a' shot the thing off, sho' 'nough."

"If you jump at a guy with a gun, he'll shoot. He can't help it," the black one said.

But now Grip's breath had returned sufficiently for him to protest, "Hey, what kind of lousy frame—?"

"Keep yo' teeth shut," advised the yellow one, "fo' I snatch yo' tongue out."

"This is my house!—He come in here of his own free will, 'cause his gal—"

That was the end of the Beasely defense. The immediately subsequent proceedings kept both Grip and Cawley busy avoiding dismemberment. With no effort to contume Sam's gentleness, the two officers urged the culprits forth.

Grammie, Judy, and Sam brought up the rear. Grammie's foot struck a hard object on the floor. Sam stooped in the darkness and picked up Grip's gun. He said,

"You ought to have this for a souvenir."

"Who me?" Grammie drew away. "Deed, chile, you couldn't pay me to touch one o' them things—I'm scared to death of 'em." Then—"Judy!— bless my soul—I b'lieve my chicken done cooked dry! Come on, chile, less hurry—"

But it hadn't. In a small immaculate kitchen which might have been adequate for Grammie and Judy, but which Sam's magnitude filled to overflowing, supper was under way. "They'll put them birds under the jail," said Sam.

"You Judy," Grammie scolded, as she helped Sam to more chicken and dumplings, "You ought to be 'shamed o' yo'self."

Judy's black eyes twinkled. "Why, Grammie?"

"'Cause you told sump'm that wasn't so."

"When?"

"You promised that Cawley you'd keep quiet if they didn't do nuthin' to Sam. And 'stead o' keepin' quiet, you'd 'a' jumped out that window and busted yo' fool laigs, and walked on yo' hands through the cellar, I reckon, till you got where you could holler fo' help. Only I stopped you.—Now what kind o' keepin' a promise is that?"

66     Rudolph Fisher

Judy and Sam exchanged grins. "Yes, ma'am," Judy said.

"And as fo' you, Sam—look a'hyeh—did you tell 'em any different at the jail-house—'bout that cockaroach?"

"No ma'am," grinned Officer Sam. "Didn' want 'em to think you and Judy would both—uh—uh—"

"You young scamp, if you call me a tain'-so, I'll never make you another chicken-dumplin' as long as you cullud." She eyed him sternly. "You jes' ain' got no sense. Hyeh you is a rookie, on yo' six months' probation, when the boss-men can drop you fo' anything you do. Drop you without givin' no explanation. And you gettin' ready to up and tell 'em that yo' grand-mammy—yo' grandmammy!—had to come along and help you out. Humph!"

"'Twould 'a' been true, wouldn't it?"

"They's a time and place fo' ev'ything. That wasn't no time for the truth."

"But Grammie—" began Judy.

"Hush up!" said Grammie. "When y'all get old as I is, y'all can lie too." She considered this a moment, then added, "But not befo'."

"What I want to know," said Sam, "is what did you hit Cawley with?"

Grammie could masquerade severity no longer. Her bright eyes became those of a mischievous child, she chuckled quite impishly. Into her bosom she reached, withdrew a small pasteboard box, and, exhibiting the hole in its corner, said with relish:

"I squirted his eyes full o' snuff."

# MISS CYNTHIE

For the first time in her life somebody had called her "madam." She had been standing, bewildered but unafraid, while innumerable Red Caps appropriated piece after piece of the baggage arrayed on the platform. Neither her brief seventy years' journey through life nor her long two days' travel northward had dimmed the live brightness of her eyes, which, for all their bewilderment, had accurately selected her own treasures out of the row of luggage and guarded them vigilantly. "These yours, madam?"

The biggest Red Cap of all was smiling at her. He looked for all the world like Doc Crinshaw's oldest son back home. Her little brown face relaxed; she smiled back at him.

"They got to be. You all done took all the others."

He laughed aloud. Then—"Carry 'em for you?"

She contemplated his bulk. "Reckon you can manage it—puny little feller like you?"

Thereupon they were friends. Still grinning broadly, he surrounded himself with her impedimenta, the enormous brown extension-case on one shoulder, the big straw suitcase in the opposite hand, the carpet-bag under one arm. She herself held fast to the umbrella. "Always like to have sump'm in my hand when I walk. Can't never tell when you'll run across a snake."

"There aren't any snakes in the city."

"There's snakes everywhere, chile."

They began the tedious hike up the interminable platform. She was small and quick. Her carriage was surprisingly erect, her gait astonishingly spry. She said:

"You liked to took my breath back yonder, boy, callin' me 'madam.' Back home everybody call me 'Miss Cynthie.' Even their chillun. Black folks, white folks too. 'Miss Cynthie.' Well when you come up with that 'madam' o' yourn, I say to myself, 'Now, I wonder who that chile's a-grinnin' at?

"Madam" stands for mist'ess o' the house, and I sho' ain' mist'ess o' nothin' in this hyeh New York.'"

"Well, you see, we call everybody 'madam.'"

"Everybody?—Hm." The bright eyes twinkled. "Seem like that'd worry me some—if I was a man."

He acknowledged his slip and observed, "I see this isn't your first trip to New York."

"First trip any place, son. First time I been over fifty miles from Waxhaw. Only travelin' I've done is in my head. Ain' seen many places, but I's seen a passel o' people. Reckon places is pretty much alike after people been in 'em awhile."

"Yes, ma'am. I guess that's right."

"You ain' no reg'lar bag-toter, is you?"

"Ma'am?"

"You talk too good."

"Well, I only do this in vacation-time. I'm still in school."

"You is. What you aimin' to be?"

"I'm studying medicine."

"You is?" She beamed. "Aimin' to be a doctor, huh? Thank the Lord for that. That's what I always wanted my David to be. My grandchile hyeh in New York. He's to meet me hyeh now."

"I bet you'll have a great time."

"Mussn't bet, chile. That's sinful. I tole him 'for' he left home, I say, 'Son, you the only one o' the chillun what's got a chance to amount to sump'm. Don't th'ow it away. Be a preacher or a doctor. Work yo' way up and don' stop short. If the Lord don' see fit for you to doctor the soul, then doctor the body. If you don't get to be a reg'lar doctor, be a tooth-doctor. If you jes' can't make that, be a foot-doctor. And if you don' get that fur, be a under-taker. That's the least you must be. That ain' so bad. Keep you acquainted with the house of the Lord. Always mind the house o' the Lord—whatever you do, do like a church-steeple: aim high and go straight.'"

"Did he get to be a doctor?"

"Don' b'lieve he did. Too late startin', I reckon. But he's done succeeded at sump'm. Mus' be at least a undertaker, 'cause he started sendin' the home-folks money, and he come home las' year dressed like Judge Pettiford's boy what went off to school in Virginia. Wouldn't tell none of us 'zackly what he was doin', but he said he wouldn' never be happy till I come and see for my-self. So hyeh I is." Something softened her voice. "His mammy died befo' he knowed her. But he was always sech a good chile—" The something was ap-prehension. "Hope he is a undertaker."

They were mounting a flight of steep stairs leading to an exit-gate, about which clustered a few people still hoping to catch sight of arriving friends. Among these a tall young brown-skinned man in a light grey suit suddenly waved his panama and yelled, "Hey, Miss Cynthie!"

Miss Cynthie stopped, looked up, and waved back with a delighted umbrella. The Red Cap's eyes lifted too. His lower jaw sagged.

"Is that your grandson?"

"It sho' is," she said and distanced him for the rest of the climb. The grandson, with an abandonment that superbly ignored onlookers, folded the little woman in an exultant, smothering embrace. As soon as she could, she pushed him off with breathless mock impatience.

"Go 'way, you fool you. Aimin' to squeeze my soul out my body befo' I can get a look at this place?" She shook herself into the semblance of composure. "Well. You don't look hungry, anyhow."

"Ho-ho! Miss Cynthie in New York! Can y' imagine this? Come on. I'm parked on Eighth Avenue."

The Red Cap delivered the outlandish luggage into a robin's egg blue open Packard with scarlet wheels, accepted the grandson's dollar and smile, and stood watching the car roar away up Eighth Avenue.

Another Red Cap came up. "Got a break, hey, boy?"

"Dave Tappen himself—can you beat that?"

"The old lady hasn't seen the station yet—starin' at him."

"That's not the half of it, bozo. That's Dave Tappen's grandmother. And what do you s'pose she hopes?"

"What?"

"She hopes that Dave has turned out to be a successful undertaker!"

"Undertaker? Undertaker!"

They stared at each other a gaping moment, then doubled up with laughter.

"Look—through there—that's the Chrysler Building. Oh, hellelujah! I meant to bring you up Broadway—"

"David—"

"Ma'am?"

"This hyeh wagon yourn?"

"Nobody else's. Sweet buggy, ain't it?"

"David—you ain't turned out to be one of them moonshiners, is you?"

"Moonshiners—? Moon—Ho! No indeed, Miss Cynthie. I got a better racket 'n that."

"Better which?"

"Game. Business. Pick-up."

"Tell me, David. What is yo' racket?"

"Can't spill it yet, Miss Cynthie. Rather show you. Tomorrow night you'll know the worst. Can you make out till tomorrow night?"

"David, you know I always wanted you to be a doctor, even if 'twasn' nothin' but a foot-doctor. The very leas' I wanted you to be was a undertaker."

"Undertaker! Oh, Miss Cynthie!—with my sunny disposition?"

"Then you ain' even a undertaker?"

"Listen, Miss Cynthie. Just forget 'bout what I am for awhile. Must till tomorrow night. I want you to see for yourself. Tellin' you will spoil it. Now stop askin', you hear?—because I'm not answerin'—I'm surprisin' you. And don't expect anybody you meet to tell you. It'll mess up the whole works. Understand? Now give the big city a break. There's the elevated train going up Columbus Avenue. Ain't that hot stuff?"

Miss Cynthie looked. "Humph!" she said. "Tain' half high as that trestle two mile from Waxhaw."

She thoroughly enjoyed the ride up Central Park West. The stagger lights, the extent of the park, the high, close, kingly buildings, remarkable because their stoves cooled them in summer as well as heated them in winter, all drew nods of mild interest. But what gave her special delight was not these: it was that David's car so effortlessly sped past the headlong drove of vehicles racing northward.

They stopped for a red light; when they started again their machine leaped forward with a triumphant eagerness that drew from her an unsuppressed "Hot you, David! That's it!"

He grinned appreciatively. "Why, you're a regular New Yorker already."

"New York nothin'! I done the same thing fifty years ago—befo' I knowed they was a New York."

"What!"

"'Deed so. Didn' I use to tell you 'bout my young mare, Betty? Chile, I'd hitch Betty up to yo' grandpa's buggy and pass anything on the road. Betty never knowed what another horse's dust smelt like. No 'ndeedy. Shuh, boy, this ain' nothin' new to me. Why that broke-down Fo'd yo uncle Jake's got ain' nothin'—nothin' but a sorry mess. Done got so slow I jes' won' ride in it—I declare I'd rather walk. But this hyeh thing, now, this is right nice." She settled back in complete, complacent comfort, and they sped on, swift and silent.

Suddenly she sat erect with abrupt discovery.

"David—well—bless my soul!"

"What's the matter, Miss Cynthie?"

Then he saw what had caught her attention. They were travelling up Seventh Avenue now, and something was miraculously different. Not the road; that was as broad as ever, wide, white gleaming in the sun. Not the houses; they were lofty still, lordly, disdainful, supercilious. Not the cars; they continued to race impatiently onward, innumerable, precipitate, tumultuous. Something else, something at once obvious and subtle, insistent, pervasive, compelling.

"David—this mus' be Harlem!"

"Good Lord, Miss Cynthie—!"

"Don' use the name of the Lord in vain, David."

"But I mean—gee!—you're no fun at all. You get everything before a guy can tell you."

"You got plenty to tell me, David. But don' nobody need to tell me this. Look a yonder."

Not just a change of complexion. A completely dissimilar atmosphere. Sidewalks teeming with leisurely strollers, at once strangely dark and bright. Boys in white trousers, berets, and green shirts, with slickened black heads and proud swagger. Bareheaded girls in crisp organdie dresses, purple, canary, gay scarlet. And laughter, abandoned strong Negro laughter, some falling full on the ear, some not heard at all, yet sensed—the warm life-breath of the tireless carnival to which Harlem's heart quickens in summer.

"This is it," admitted David. "Get a good eyeful. Here's 125th Street—regular little Broadway. And here's the Alhambra, and up ahead we'll pass the Lafayette."

"What's them?"

"Theatres."

"Theatres? Theatres. Humph! Look, David—is that a colored folks church?" They were passing a fine gray-stone edifice.

"That? Oh. Sure it is. So's this one on this side."

"No! Well, ain' that fine? Splendid big church like that for colored folks."

Taking his cue from this, her first tribute to the city he said, "You ain't seen nothing yet. Wait a minute."

They swung left through a side-street and turned right on a boulevard. "What do you think o' that?" And he pointed to the quarter-million dollar St. Mark's.

"That a colored church, too?"

"'Tain' no white one. And they built it themselves, you know. Nobody's hand-me-down gift."

She heaved a great happy sigh. "Oh, yes, it was a gift, David. It was a gift from on high." Then, "Look a hyeh—which a one you belong to?"

"Me? Why, I don't belong to any—that is, none o' these. Mine's over in another section. Y'see, mine's Baptist. These are all Methodist. See?"

"M—m. Uh-huh. I see."

They circled a square and slipped into a quiet narrow street overlooking a park, stopping before the tallest of the apartment-houses in the single commanding row.

Alighting, Miss Cynthie gave this imposing structure one sidewise, upward glance, and said, "Y'all live like bees in a hive, don't y'?—I boun' the women does all the work, too." A moment later, "So this is a elevator? Feel like I'm glory-bound sho' nuff."

Along a tiled corridor and into David's apartment. Rooms leading into rooms. Luxurious couches, easy-chairs, a brown-walnut grand piano, gay-shaded floor lamps, panelled walls, deep rugs, treacherous glass-wood floors—and a smiling golden-skinned girl in a gingham housedress, approaching with outstretched hands.

"This is Ruth, Miss Cynthie."

"Miss Cynthie!" said Ruth.

They clasped hands. "Been wantin' to see David's girl ever since he first wrote us 'bout her."

"Come—here's your room this way. Here's the bath. Get out of your things and get comfy. You must be worn out with the trip."

"Worn out? Worn out? Shuh. How you gon' get worn out on a train. Now if 'twas a horse, maybe, or Jake's no-count Fo'd—but a train—didn' but one thing bother me on that train."

"What?"

"When the man made them beds down, I jes' couldn' manage to undress same as home. Why, s'posin' sump'm bus' the train open—where'd you be? Naked as a jay-bird in a dew-berry time."

David took in her things and left her to get comfortable. He returned, and Ruth, despite his reassuring embrace, whispered:

"Dave, you can't fool old folks—why don't you go ahead and tell her about yourself? Think of the shock she's going to get—at her age."

David shook his head. "She'll get over the shock if she's there looking on. If we just told her, she'd never understand. We've got to railroad her into it. Then she'll be happy."

"She's nice. But she's got the same ideas as all old folks—"

"Yea—but with her you can change 'em. Specially if everything is really all right. I know her. She's for church and all, but she believes in good times too, if they're right. Why, when I was a kid—" He broke off. "Listen!"

Miss Cynthie's voice came quite distinctly to them, singing a jaunty little rhyme:

> Oh I danced with the gal with the hole in her stockin'
> And her toe kep' a-kickin' and her heel kep' a-knockin'—

> Come up, Jesse, and get a drink o' gin,
> 'Cause you near to heaven as you'll ever get ag'in'.

"She taught me that when I wasn't knee-high to a cricket," David said. Miss Cynthie still sang softly and merrily:

> Then I danced with the gal with the dimple in her cheek,
> And if she'd 'a' kep' a-smilin', I'd 'a' danced for a week—

"God forgive me," prayed Miss Cynthie as she discovered David's purpose the following night. She let him and Ruth lead her, like an early Christian martyr, into the Lafayette Theatre. The blinding glare of the lobby produced a merciful self-anaesthesia, and she entered the sudden dimness of the interior as involuntarily as in a dream. . . .

Attendants outdid each other for Mr. Dave Tappen. She heard him tell them, "Fix us up till we go on," and found herself sitting between Ruth and David in the front row of a lower box. A miraculous device of the devil, a motion-picture that talked, was just ending. At her feet the orchestra was assembling. The motion-picture faded out amid a scattered round of applause. Lights blazed and the orchestra burst into an ungodly rumpus.

She looked out over the seated multitude, scanning row upon row of illumined faces, black faces, white faces, yellow, tan, brown: bald heads, bobbed heads, kinky and straight heads; and upon every countenance, expectancy—scowling expectancy in this case, smiling in that, complacent here, amused there, commentative elsewhere, but everywhere suspense, abeyance, anticipation.

Half a dozen people were ushered down the nearer aisle to reserved seats in the second row. Some of them caught sight of David and Ruth and waved to them. The chairs immediately behind them in the box were being shifted. "Hello, Tap!" Miss Cynthie saw David turn, rise, and shake hands with two men. One of them was large, bald and pink, emanating good cheer; the other short, thin, sallow with thick black hair and a sour mien. Ruth also acknowledged their greeting. "This is my grandmother," David said proudly. "Miss Cynthie, meet my managers, Lou and Lee Goldman." "Pleased to meet you," managed Miss Cynthie. "Great lad, this boy of yours," said Lou Goldman. "Great little partner he's got, too," added Lee. They also settled back expectantly.

"Here we go!"

The curtain rose to reveal a cotton-field at dawn. Pickers in blue denim overalls, bandanas, and wide-brimmed straws, or in gingham aprons and sun-bonnets, were singing as they worked. Their voices, from clearest soprano to richest bass, blended in low concordances, first simply humming a series of harmonies, until, gradually, came words, like figures forming in mist. As the sound grew, the mist cleared, the words came round and full, and the sun rose bringing light as if in answer to the song. The chorus swelled, the radiance grew, the two, as if emanating from a single source, fused their crescendos, till at last they achieved a joint transcendence of tonal and visual brightness.

"Swell opener," said Lee Goldman.

"Ripe," agreed Lou.

David and Ruth arose. "Stay here and enjoy the show, Miss Cynthie. You'll see us again in a minute."

"Go to it, kids," said Lou Goldman

"Yea—burn 'em up." said Lee.

Miss Cynthie hardly noted that she had been left, so absorbed was she in the spectacle. To her, the theatre had always been the antithesis of church. As the one was the refuge of righteousness, so the other was the stronghold of transgression. But this first scene awakened memories, captured and held her attention by offering a blend of truth and novelty. Having thus baited her interest, the show now proceeded to play it like the trout through swift-flowing waters of wickedness. Resist as it might, her mind was caught and drawn into the impious subsequences.

The very music that had just rounded out so majestically now distorted itself into ragtime. The singers came forward and turned to dancers; boys, a crazy, swaying background, threw up their arms and kicked out their legs in a rhythmic jamboree; girls, an agile, brazen foreground, caught their skirts up to their hips and displayed their copper calves, knees, thighs, in shameless, incredible steps. Miss Cynthie turned dismayed eyes upon the audience, to discover that mob of sinners devouring it all with fond satisfaction. Then the dancers separated and with final abandon flung themselves off the stage in both directions.

Lee Goldman commented through the applause, "They work easy, them babies."

"Yea," said Lou. "Savin' the hot stuff for later."

Two black-faced cotton-pickers appropriated the scene, indulging in dialogue that their hearers found uproarious.

"Ah'm tired."

"Ah'm hongry."

"Dis job jes' wears me out."

"Starves me to death."

"Ah'm so tired—you know what Ah'd like to do?"

"What?"

"Ah'd like to go to sleep and dream I was sleepin'."

"What good dat do?"

"Den I could wake up and still be 'sleep."

"Well y'know what Ah'd like to do?"

"No. What?"

"Ah'd like to swaller me a hog and a hen."

"What good dat do?"

"Den Ah'd always be full o' ham and eggs."

"Ham? Shuh. Don't you know a hog has to be smoked 'fo' he's a ham?"

"Well, if I swaller him, he'll have a smoke all around him, won' he?"

Presently Miss Cynthie was smiling like everyone else, but her smile soon fled. For the comics departed, and the dancing girls returned, this time in scant travesties on their earlier voluminous costumes—tiny sun-bonnets perched jauntily on one side of their glistening bobs, bandanas reduced to scarlet neck ribbons, waists mere brassieres, skirts mere gingham sashes.

And now Miss Cynthie's whole body stiffened with a new and surpassing shock; her bright eyes first widened with unbelief, then slowly grew dull with misery. In the midst of a sudden great volley of applause her grandson had broken through that bevy of agile wantons and begun to sing.

He too was dressed as a cotton-picker, but a Beau Brummel among cotton pickers; his hat bore a pleated green band, his bandana was silk, his overalls blue satin, his shoes black patent leather. His eyes flashed, his teeth gleamed, his body swayed, his arms waved, his words came fast and clear. As he sang, his companions danced a concerted tap, uniformly wild, ecstatic. When he stopped singing, he himself began to dance, and without sacrificing crispness of execution, seemed to absorb into himself every measure of the energy which the girls, now merely standing off and swaying, had relinquished.

"Look at that boy go," said Lee Goldman.

"He ain't started yet," said Lou.

But surrounding comment, Dave's virtuosity, the eager enthusiasm of the audience were all alike lost on Miss Cynthie. She sat with stricken eyes watching this boy whom she'd raised from a babe, taught right from wrong, brought up in the church, and endowed with her prayers, this child whom she had dreamed of seeing a preacher, a regular doctor, a tooth-doctor, a foot-doctor, at the very least an undertaker—sat watching him disport himself for the benefit of a sinsick, flesh-hungry mob of lost souls, not one of whom knew or cared to know the loving kindness of God; sat watching a David she'd never foreseen, turned tool of the devil, disciple of lust, unholy prince among sinners.

For a long time she sat there watching with wretched eyes, saw portrayed on the stage David's arrival in Harlem, his escape from "old friends" who tried to dupe him; saw him working as a trap-drummer in a night-club, where he fell in love with Ruth, a dancer; not the gentle Ruth Miss Cynthie knew, but a wild and shameless young savage who danced like seven devils—in only a girdle and breast-plates; saw the two of them join in a song-and-dance act that eventually made them Broadway headliners, an act presented *in toto* as the pre-finale of this show. And not any of the melodies, not any of the sketches, not all the comic philosophy of the tired-and-hungry duo, gave her figure a moment's relaxation or brightened the dull defeat in her staring eyes. She sat apart, alone in the box, the symbol, the epitome of supreme failure. Let the rest of the theatre be riotous, clamoring for more and more of Dave Tappen, "Tap," the greatest tapster of all time, idol of uptown and downtown New York. For her, they were lauding simply an exhibition of sin which centered about her David.

"This'll run a year on Broadway," said Lee Goldman.

"Then we'll take it to Paris."

Encores and curtains with Ruth, and at last David came out on the stage alone. The clamor dwindled. And now he did something quite unfamiliar to even the most consistent of his followers. Softly, delicately, he begun to tap a routine designed to fit a particular song. When he had established the rhythm, he began to sing the song:

> Oh I danced with the gal with the hole in her stockin'
> And her toe kep' a-kickin' and her heel kep' a-knockin'—
>
> Come up, Jesse, and get a drink o' gin,
> 'Cause you near to the heaven as you'll ever get ag'in'—

As he danced and sang this song, frequently smiling across at Miss Cynthie, a visible change transformed her. She leaned forward incredulously, listened intently, then settled back in limp wonder. Her bewildered eyes turned on the crowd, on those serried rows of shriftless sinners. And she found in their faces now an overwhelming curious thing: a grin, a universal grin, a gleeful and sinless grin such as not the nakedest chorus in the performance had produced. In a few seconds, with her own song, David had dwarfed into unimportance, wiped off their faces, swept out of their minds every trace of what had seemed to be sin; had reduced it all to mere trivial detail and revealed these revelers as a crowd of children, enjoying the guileless antics of another child. And Miss Cynthie whispered:

"Bless my soul! They didn' mean nothin' . . . They jes' didn' see no harm in it—"

> Then I danced with the gal with the dimple in her cheek,
> And if she'd 'a' kep' a-smilin', I'd 'a' danced for week—
> "Come up, Jesse—"

The crowd laughed, clapped their hands, whistled. Someone threw David a bright yellow flower. "From Broadway!"

He caught the flower. A hush fell. He said:

"I'm really happy tonight, folks. Y'see this flower? Means success, don't it? Well, listen. The one who is really responsible for my success is here tonight with me. Now what do you think o' that?"

The hush deepened.

"Y'know folks, I'm sump'm like Adam—I never had no mother. But I've got a grandmother. Down home everybody calls her Miss Cynthie. And everybody loves her. Take that song I just did for you. Miss Cynthie taught me that when I wasn't knee-high to a cricket. But that wasn't all she taught me. Far back as I can remember, she used to always say one thing: Son, do like a church steeple—aim high and go straight. And for doin' it—" he grinned, contemplating the flower—"I get this."

He strode across to the edge of the stage that touched Miss Cynthie's box. He held up the flower.

"So y'see, folks, this isn't mine. It's really Miss Cynthie's." He leaned over to hand it to her. Miss Cynthie's last trace of doubt was swept away. She drew a deep breath of revelation; her bewilderment vanished, her redoubtable composure returned, her eyes lighted up; and no one but David, still holding the flower toward her, heard her sharply whispered reprimand:

"Keep it, you fool. Where's yo' manners—givin' 'way what somebody give you?"

David grinned:

"Take it, tyro. What you tryin' to do—crab my act?"

Thereupon, Miss Cynthie, smiling at him with bright, meaningful eyes, leaned over without rising from her chair, jerked a tiny twig off the stem of the flower, then sat decisively back, resolutely folding her arms, with only a leaf in her hand.

"This'll do me," she said.

The finale didn't matter. People filed out of the theatre. Miss Cynthie sat awaiting her children, her foot absently patting time to the orchestra's jazz recessional. Perhaps she was thinking, "God moves in a mysterious way," but her lips were unquestionably forming the words:

> —danced with the gal—hole in her stockin'—
> —toe kep' a-kickin'—heel kep' a-knockin'.

Rudolph Fisher

# II. THE NEW LAND

# HIGH YALLER

The timekeeper's venomous whistle killed the ball in its flight, halfway to the basket. There was a triumphant bedlam. From the walls of Manhattan Casino impatient multitudes swarmed on to the immense floor, congratulating, consoling, gibing; pouring endlessly from the surrounding terrace, like long restrained torrents at last transcending a dam; sweeping tumultuously in from all sides, till the dance floor sank beneath a sounding flood of dark-skinned people, submerged to its furthest corners save the distant platform that gave the orchestra refuge, like a raft. A sudden blare of music cut the uproar. The turbulence gradually ordered itself into dense, crawling currents, sluggish as jammed traffic, while the din of voices at length reluctantly surrendered to the rhythmic swish-swash of shuffling feet.

Looking down from a balcony on that dark mass of heads, close together as buckshot, Evelyn Brown wondered how they all managed to enjoy it. Why must they always follow a basket-ball game with a dance?—the one pleasurable enough, the other mob-torture, she knew.

"Game?" challenged MacLoed.

She couldn't refuse her escort, of course. "If you are."

They descended and struck out like swimmers in the sea. MacLoed surrounded her as closely as a lifesaver. She knew that he had to, but she hated it—this mere hugging to music, this acute consciousness of her partner's body. The air was vile—hot, full of breath and choking perfume. You were forever avoiding, colliding, marking time on the same spot. So insulating was the crush that you might sway for several minutes near a familiar couple, even recognize their voices, yet catch only the merest glimpse of their vanishing faces.

Something of the sort was happening now. Evelyn heard someone say her name, and the mordant intonation with the succeeding spiteful snatch-phrases made her forget the physical unpleasantness of the moment.

"Evelyn Brown?—Hmph!—got yellow fever—I know better—color struck, I tell you—girls she goes around with—all lily whites—even the fellows—Mac to-day—pass for white anywhere—Jeff, Rickmond, Stanley Hall, all of 'em—You? Shoot! You don't count—you're crazy 'bout high yallers anyhow."

The words were engulfed. Evelyn had not needed to look. Mayme Jackson's voice was unmistakable.

The dance number ended on an unresolved, interrogative chord that set off an explosion of applause. Jay Martin, who had just been defending Evelyn against Mayme's charge, spied the former's fluff of fair hair through several intervening thicknesses of straight and straightened black, and, dragging Mayme by the arm, he made for the other couple.

"Now say what you said about Evelyn!" he dared Mayme, mock-maliciously, quite unaware that Evelyn already knew.

"Sweetest old thing in the world," came Mayme's tranquil purr.

"Rake in the chips," gasped Jay. "Your pot." He addressed Evelyn. "How about the next wrestle?"

There was a ready exchange of partners. The orchestra struck up an air from a popular Negro comedy: "Yaller Gal's Gone Out o' Style." Soon the two couples were urged apart in increasingly divergent currents.

"Black sea," commented Jay.

But Evelyn was thoughtful. "Jay?"

"Nobody else."

"I heard what Mayme said."

"You did? Aw, heck—don't pay any attention to that kid. She's a nut."

"I'm not so sure she isn't right, Jay."

"Right? About what?"

"I've been thinking over my best friends. They're practically all 'passing' fair. Any one of them could pass—for a foreigner, anyway."

"Me, for instance," he grinned. "Prince Woogy-boogy of Abyssinia."

"I'm afraid you prove the rule."

He was serious. "Well, what of it?"

"Oh, I don't mean I've done it intentionally. I never realized it till just now. But, just as Mayme says, it looks bad."

"Hang what Mayme says. She's kind o' gone on yaller men, herself. See the way she melted into Mac's shirtfront? Hung round his neck like a chest-protector. Didn't drape herself over *me* that way."

"Jay! You're as bad as she is."

"That's what she said."

"What do you mean?"

"Claims I fall only for pinks."

"Oh. I didn't mean that."

"Neither did she. Point is, there aren't any more dark girls. Skin bleach and rouge have wiped out the strain. The blacks have turned sealskin, the sealskins are high-brown, the high-browns are all yaller, and the yallers are pink. How's a bird going to fall for what ain't?"

They jazzed on a while in noisy silence. Evelyn's tone was surprisingly bitter when at last she spoke again:

"I wish I looked like Mayme." Astonished, Jay stared at her as she went on: "A washerwoman can make half a million dollars turning dark skins light. Why doesn't someone learn how to turn light skins dark?"

And now, in addition to staring, he saw her: the averted blue eyes, the fine lips about to quiver, the delicate, high-bridged nose, the white cheeks, colorless save for the faintest touch, the incredible tawny, yellow-flecked, scintillant hair,—an almost crystalline creature, as odd in this dark company as a single sapphire in jet. He was quick to comprehend. "I know a corner— let's sit out the rest," he suggested.

When they achieved their place in a far end of the terrace, the orchestra was outdoing itself in the encore. One of its members sang through a megaphone in a smoky, halt-talking voice:

Oh Miss Pink thought she knew her stuff,
But Miss High Brown has called her bluff.

When the encore ended, the dancer demanded yet another. The rasp of syncopation and the ceaseless stridor of soles mingled, rose about the two refugees, seeming to wall them in, so that presently they felt alone together.

"Jay, can you imagine what it's like to be colored and look white?"

He tried to be trivial. "Very convenient at times, I should think."

"But oftener unbearable. That song—imagine—everyone looking at you— laughing at you. And Mayme Jackson—'yellow fever'! Can I help it?—Jeff— Rickmond—Stanley Hall—yes, they're light. But what can I do? I like the others. I'd be glad to go places with them. But they positively avoid me."

"I don't, Ev."

"No, you don't, Jay." But her bitterness recaptured her. "Oh, I've heard them talking: 'There goes Evelyn Brown—queen of the lily-whites—nothing brown about her but her name'!" A swiftly matured determination rendered her suddenly so grim that it seemed, fragile as she was, something about her must break. "Jay, no one's going to accuse me of jim-crowing again!"

"Shucks. What do you care as long as you don't mean to?"

"I'm not only not going to mean to. I'm not going to. I'm going to see to it that I don't."

"What the deuce—by cutting your gang?"

"No. By cultivating the others."

"Oh."

"Jay—will you help me?"

"Help you? Sure. How?"

"Come to see me oftener."

"Good night! Don't you see enough of me at the office every day?"

"Come oftener. Take me places when you're not too broke. Rush me!"

He grinned as he perceived her purpose. "Doggone good stunt!" he said slowly, with increasingly enthusiastic approval. "Blessed if I wouldn't like to see you put it over, Ev. It'll show Mayme something, anyhow."

"It'll show me something, too."

"You? What?"

She was about to answer when a sharp, indecent epithet rent the wall of noise that had until then isolated them. Looking involuntarily up, Jay saw two youngsters, quarreling vituperatively. They were too close to be ignored, and, since dancing was at its height, no one else was about.

"Excuse me a second," he said, rising before Evelyn could protest. The pair were but a few feet away. The evident aggressor was a hard-looking little black youth of indefinite age,—perhaps sixteen actual years, plus the accumulated bonus of worldly wisdom which New York pays its children. He grew worse, word by word. Approaching, Jay spoke sharply, in a low voice so that Evelyn might not hear:

"Cut out that gutter-talk, boy!"

"Aw, go to hell!"

Jay stopped, less amazed than aggravated. He knew his Harlem adolescent, but he was not quite sure what to do with it. Meanwhile he was being advised: "This is a horse-race, big boy. No jackasses allowed!"

He seized the lad firmly by the shoulder and said, "Son, if you don't cover that garbage-trap of yours——" but the boy flung away and defied him in a phrase both loud and ugly. Thoroughly angered, Jay clapped one hand over the offending mouth and, catching the youngster around the waist with the other, forcibly propelled him through a tangle of empty, spindle-legged chairs to a place where two big policemen, one black and one red, were complacently watching the dancers. Here he released him with "Now—talk."

The boy scowled with wrath and impotence. So outraged in the street, he would have found a stone to throw. Now only a retaliative speech was left him, and the nearness of the law attenuated even that:

"Aw 'ight! Showin' off before 'at ole 'fay gal, huh? Aw 'ight, y' pink-chaser. Ah'm goan put y' both in." And he sidled darkly off, pulling at his disadjusted collar.

Evelyn, out of earshot, followed it all with her eyes. "Mac wouldn't have done that," she mused as she saw Jay turn from the boy and start back toward her. "Mac would have pretended he didn't hear." And before Jay reached her, she had decided something: "I certainly like Jay Martin. He's so—white."

## II

Over 134th Street's sidewalks between Fifth and Lenox Avenues Jay Martin's roller-skates had rattled and whirred in the days when that was the northern boundary of Negro Harlem. He had grown as the colony grew, and now he could just recall the time when his father, a pioneer preacher, had been forever warning him never to cross Lenox Avenue and never to go beyond 135th Street; a time when no Negroes lived on or near Seventh Avenue and when it would have been almost suicidal for one to appear unarmed on Irish Eighth.

School had been a succession of fist-fights with white boys who called him nigger, until, when he reached the upper grades, the colored boys began to outnumber the white; from that time until high school, pitched battles superseded individual contests, and he ran home bruised less often. His high school record had been good, and his father, anxious to make a physician of him, had sent him on to college. At the end of his third year, however, the looming draft menace, combined with the chance of a commission in the army, had urged him into a training camp at Des Moines.

He had gone to France as a lieutenant. When he returned, unharmed, he found his father fatally ill and his mother helpless. Further study out of the question, he had taken his opportunity with a Negro real estate firm, and for five years now he had been actively concerned in black Harlem's extension, the spread whose beginnings his earlier years had witnessed.

About Evelyn, of course, there had been hypothesis:

"Looks mighty funny to me when a woman Jennie Brown's color has a yaller-headed young one white as Evelyn."

"Daddy was white, so I understan'."

"Huh. An' her mammy, too, mos' likely. 'At's de way dese rich white folks do. Comes a wile oat dey doan want, dey ups an' give it to one de servants— to adopt."

"Oh, I dunno. How come she couldn't been married to some white man 'nuther? Dey's plenty sich, right hyeh in Harlem."

"Plenty whut? Plenty common law, maybe. You know d' ain' no se'f-respectin' white man gonna—"

"Well, doan make no diff'nce. Cain' none of us go but so fur back in our fam'ly hist'ry 'fo we stops. An' doan nobody have t' ask us why we stops. We jes' stops. Evelyn's a good girl. Smart—works regular an' makes mo' out o' dem real estate niggers 'n she'd ever make in Miss Ann's kitchen. Bad 's her mother's asthma's gittin', no tellin' whut they'd do if 'twasn't f' Evelyn's job an' dem two women lodgers."

"Oh, I ain' sayin' nuthin' 'gins 'em. Only seem like to me—dey's a white man in de woodpile somewha'."

Her own singularity had become conscious early in Evelyn's life. There crept often into her mind of late an old, persistent recollection. She and Sookie Johnson, seven-year-old playmates, had been playing jacks on the front stoop. There arose a dispute as to whose turn it was. Sookie owned the ball and Evelyn the jacks; neither would surrender her possession to the other, and the game was deadlocked. Whereupon, the spiteful Sookie had resorted to abuse:

"Y' ole yaller thing, you! My mother say y' cain't 'speck nuthin' f'm yaller niggers nohow!"

Evelyn had thrown the jacks into Sookie's face and run heartbroken to her mother. Why didn't she have kinky hair and dark brown skin like Sookie's? "Why, honey, you're beautiful," her mother had comforted her. "Folks'll call you names long as you live. They're just jealous, that's all."

Thus fortified, Evelyn had come to maturity, finding her mother's prophecy ever and again true. "They're just jealous" was but a fortification, however; within it Evelyn's spirit was still vulnerable, and she knew that under constant fire this stronghold could not stand forever. Mayme Jackson's thrust-in-the-back culminated what Sookie's sneer had begun. Evelyn felt her mother's defence crumbling rapidly and alarmingly, and her appeal to Jay Martin was a rather desperate effort to establish a defence of her own.

They sat now in the front room of her flat; a room too full of mock-mahogany furniture about to collapse; a room with gas light and a tacked-down carpet, with flower-figured wall-paper and a marble-topped walnut table in one corner, bearing a big brown morocco-bound Bible.

"Jay, will you?"

"Remember the time I pulled your hair in Sunday-School?"

"I'm going to pull your ears if you don't answer me!"

"Did you say something?"

"You make me tired."

"Aw, for Pete's sake, Ev, I can't take you to that dump."

"Have the last two weeks frozen your nerve?"

"No—but—"

"Well, this isn't like the others, you know. This is a colored place."

"But why go there? Let's go to Broadway's or Happy's."

"No. I want to see something new. Why isn't Hank's decent, anyway? It can't be any worse than the Hole in the Wall."

"Much worse. Regular rat-trap. No gentleman would take a lady—"

"You flatter us. Let's don't be a gentleman and lady tonight. I want to see the rat-trap."

"Why, Ev, the place was raided only last week!"

"You can't scare me that way. If it was it'll be all the safer this week."

"Lord! You girls know it all."

"I don't know anything about Hank's."

"But I'm trying to tell you—"

"Seeing is believing."

"There's nothing to see."

She introduced strategy. "All right. I guess Mac won't be so hard to persuade."

"Ev—please—for Pete's sake don't let anybody take you to that—"

"Jay, I'd really hate to have to go with anybody but you." He was growing helpless. "Just the tiniest peep into the place, Jay. We won't stay—cross my liver."

"Your mother wouldn't like it."

"Come here." She led him by the arm down the long hallway to the dining-room, where her mother was sewing.

"You may go any place you please, if you go with Jay," smiled Mrs. Brown.

*　　*　　*

Hank's, at first glance, presented nothing unique: a sedate old house in an elderly row of houses with high entrances, several steps above the sidewalk; houses that had once been private, but now, trapped in an extending matrix of business, stoically accepted their fates as real estate offices, printing shops and law rooms. Here and there a card peeped around the corner of a window and whispered, "Rooms"; but not the most suspicious eye would have associated those timid invitations with the bold vertical electric sign projecting over the doorway of the one lighted building in the row. Great letters, one above another, blazed the world "Café"; smaller horizontal ones across the top read "Hank's," and others across the bottom "Cabaret."

"This doesn't look so bad," commented Evelyn as they approached. "Police station right in the same block."

"Yes—convenient."

Several men stood about on the sidewalk, smoking and talking. One of these, a white man, looked sharply at Jay and Evelyn as they mounted the steps and entered.

"Why, this is like any restaurant," said Evelyn. "Just a lot of tables and folks eating."

"Only a blind," explained Jay. "The real thing is downstairs."

A dinner-coated attendant came toward them. "I'm sorry. Everything's gone in the cabaret. Would you care to wait a few minutes?"

Jay, eager for an excuse to flee, looked at Evelyn; but the blue eyes said, "Please," and he nodded. "Very well."

"This way, then."

They were led up a narrow flight of padded stairs, along a carpeted hallway with several mysterious closed doors on either side, and finally into a little room near the end. Against one wall of the room was a table with two chairs, and against the opposite a flat couch with two or three cushions. Curtains draped the one window, facing the door. The table was bare except for a small lamp, with a parchment shade of orange and black, yielding a warm, dim light.

"M—m!" exclaimed Evelyn. "Cozy!"

"We can serve you here if you like," suggested the attendant.

"No, thanks," Jay answered quickly. "We'll wait."

The attendant seemed to hesitate a moment. Then, "All right," he said. "I'll let you know as soon as there's space in the cabaret." He went out and closed the door.

Evelyn was alive with interest. "Spiffy, isn't it?" She sat down on one of the chairs and looked about. "Couldn't get lost, could you?"

Jay thoughtfully took the other chair.

"You might," he said absently.

"What are you talking about? Goodness, what a lot of fun you're having!"

"I don't like this, that's a fact."

"What's wrong?"

Jay looked and noted that the door locked from within. He went over to the window, pulled the shade aside a crack, and made out the skeleton of a fire-escape in the darkness outside.

"Oh, nothing," he said, returning to his seat. "Not a thing."

"Heavens, you give me the shivers! What is it?"

He was not eager to answer. "I'm not sure but—I believe—that bird thinks you're ofay."

"White? What difference would that make?"

"Well, I'll tell you, Ev. This place, like some you already know about, has a mixed patronage, see? Part jigs, part ofays. That's perfectly all right as long as the jigs keep to their own parties and the ofays to theirs. But as soon as they begin to come mixed, trouble starts. The colored men don't like to see white men with colored women and the white men don't like to see colored men with white women. So the management avoids it. I don't believe that house-man was telling the truth when he said there was no room in the cabaret. It's too early in the evening and it's not a busy night. Fact is, the place is probably half full of ofays, and he figured that if we went down there together some drunk would get fly and I'd bounce him on the nose and right away there'd be a hullabaloo. So he took a chance that maybe we were more interested in each other than in the cabaret anyhow, and sidetracked us off up here."

"But he said he'd let us know—"

"Of course. He thought we'd be tickled silly to be in one of these rooms alone; but after I refused to be served up here, what else could he say? I don't think he has any more idea of coming back than Jack Johnson."

"Then what does he expect you to do?"

"Get tired waiting and beat it."

"Oh." A depressed silence. Then a tragic diminuendo: "Lord, what a misfit I am!"

He was contrite at once. "I'm a bum. I shouldn't have told you. I don't know—maybe I'm wrong. We're here so let's wait awhile and see."

"Jay, if only I were one thing or the other! You can't imagine—"

He absolutely could not answer. From somewhere below a thin strain drifted to their ears, like a snicker: "Yaller Gal's Gone Out o' Style."

Jay rose. "Let's breeze. That shine isn't coming back."

"All right. I'm sorry to be such a nuisance."

"You're not the nuisance. It's—folks."

They went down the soft-carpeted hallway. Strange, low sounds behind the closed doors seemed to hush apprehensively as they approached and revive after they passed. Once a shrill laugh was abruptly cut off as if by a stifling hand. There was a thick atmosphere of suppression, a sense of unspoken fears and half-drawn breaths and whispers.

As they reached the head of the padded stairs they saw someone hurrying up and drew aside to let him pass. It was a youth in a white coat, bent on some errand. He looked at them as he went by. They resumed their course and proceeded down the stairs; but the boy halted in his, and turned to look again. Immediately, he left off his errand, and waiting until he heard the front door close behind them, retraversed the staircase. A minute later he was on the sidewalk talking in an undertone to the white man who had so sharply observed Evelyn and Jay when they entered, and who now stood smoking still, following their departure with his eyes.

"Ah know 'at sucker," scowled the little black youth. "Collects rents f'

Hale an' Barker. See 'at 'fay wid 'im? Seen 'im pick 'uh up pre' near two weeks ago at Manhattan Casino."

The white man puffed a minute, while the boy looked up at him, side-long, expectant. "Hale and Barker, huh?—Hmph! All right, Shorty. I'll keep my eye on 'im. If you're on, I'll fix y' up as usual."

"'At's the time papa." And the boy too stood eyeing the disappearing pair, an imp of malice and satisfaction.


## III

A young man leaned nonchalantly on the high foot of Jay's wooden bed, grinning goodnaturedly at him; a young man who looked exactly like Jay, feature for feature, with one important exception: his skin was white.

"Who in hell are you?" asked Jay.

"What you would be if you could," came the prompt, pleasant response.

"Liar."

"Straight stuff, brother. Think of the heights you might rise to if you were I."

"Hell!" grunted Jay.

"Eventually, of course. But I mean meanwhile. Why, now you'd be in a big firm downtown, on your way to wealth. Or you might be a practicing physician—your old man could have kept you out of the draft."

"Oh, well, I'm not doing so worse."

"No, nor so better. And then there's Evelyn."

"What about Evelyn? Why, I wouldn't even know her."

"You'd know somebody like her. Don't kid yourself, boy. You like 'em pink. Remember Paris?"

"You lie like a bookmaker. I like 'em intelligent. If they happen to be bright on the outside, too, why of course, I don't bar 'em."

"No—of course not." The sarcastic caller paused a thoughtful moment. "I've got a jawful of advice for you, old-timer."

"Swallow it and choke."

"Now listen. Don't you get to liking Evelyn, see. She's too damned white."

"What of it?"

"Be yourself, son. You ask me that, after these last two weeks?"

Jay reached up and wiped a mosquito from his forehead and smacked at another singing into his ear. They irritated him. "I'll like whoever I damn please!" he flared.

"Don't get high, now," soothed the other. "I'm only warning you. Pull up on the emergency before something hits you. That girl's too fair for comfort."

"But I like her."

The other disregarded this. "You're too dark, buddy. You're ultra-violet anyhow, alone. Beside her you become absolute black—invisible. The lady couldn't see you with an arc-lamp."

"Shucks! Evelyn doesn't care."

"You're wrong there. She does. She can't help it. But she doesn't want to, so she tries hard to make herself believe she doesn't. She takes up with you, tells herself how much she likes you, invites all sorts of embarrassments upon both of you. She might even marry you. It's like taking bad medicine she thinks she's got to take and telling herself it's sweet. She figures it's better to gulp it down than to sip it, and it's better to say it's sweet than to make faces."

"Well, maybe. But I'm just conceited enough to think she likes me."

"Of course she does. I'm not talking about you. I'm talking about your color. If you were I, now, she'd jump at you."

"Humph! I don't see her jumping at MacLoed."

"Mac isn't either of us, buddy. He hasn't got a thing but his looks, and Evelyn's too wise to fall for that alone."

"There are others."

"None who can make her forget what she's trying to do. She thinks it's a sort of duty to be colored, so she's going to make a thorough job of it—do it up brown, you might say. See? The only man that could unscramble her would be a real white man. She's not going to compromise."

"You're too deep for me. But I don't believe she cares about the color of a fellow's skin."

"You don't? Well, stay away from her anyhow."

"How come?"

"To save her feelings. Every time you two go out together you're in torture. Everybody stares at you—jigs and ofays both. You've tried it now for two weeks. What's happened? The first night you went to Coney Island and nearly got yourself mobbed. A couple of days later you went into an ice-cream parlor on 125th Street, a place where Evelyn goes anytime she likes, and the proprietor had the nerve to tell you *your* presence hurt his business. Then how about that crowd of jigs on the subway? And last night, when you wanted to get up and punch that shine waiter in the ear because he gave Evelyn the once over and then rolled his eyes at you behind her back, as much as to say 'Oh boy! How I envy you!'—and she looking at him all the time in the mirror! Tonight caps it all. You go out to enjoy yourself in a 'colored' place, and get jim-crowed by a man of your own color who's afraid to let the two of you be seen. Do you think Evelyn enjoys a string of things like that?"

"She enjoys 'em as much as I do."

"But it isn't the same. When people look at you, it's just with surprise. All their look says is, 'Wonder what that nigger is doing with a white woman?' But when they look at her, it's with contempt. They say, 'Humph! What a cheap drab she must be to tag around with a nigger!' No matter whether it's true or not. Do you suppose she enjoys being looked at like that?"

Jay was silent. Sounds came from the street below into his open window; an empty Coney Island bus, rumbling, clattering, shrieking, eager to get in before daybreak; gay singing of a joy-riding chorus, swelling, consummating, dying away; the night-clear whistle of a lone, late straggler—"Yaller Gal's Gone Out o' Style."

"What do you expect me to do about it?" he finally asked.

"Ease out. See less and less of her. When you breeze away for your vacation, forget to write."

"Simple, ain't it?"

"Quite." The devil straightened up. "And now that that's settled, suppose you go to sleep for awhile."

"Suppose you go to hell," suggested Jay glumly.

"With pleasure. See you again."

Jay closed his smarting eyes. His caller departed into the clothespress or the hall or up the airshaft, he wasn't sure where; he knew only that when again he looked about, he was alone.

Evelyn Brown, too, lay in bed, debating with a visitor—a sophisticated young woman who sat familiarly on the edge of the counterpane and hugged her knees as she talked, and who might have been Evelyn over again, save for a certain bearing of self-assurance which the latter entirely lacked.

"Well, you've tried it," said the visitor. "See what a mess you've made of it."

"I wish you'd let me alone."

"I think too much of you, dear. And you're thinking too much of Jay. Surely the last two weeks have shown you how impossible that is."

"Two weeks isn't a long enough test."

"Quite long enough. The only place you and Jay could be happy together would be on a desert island that nobody could find. You can't go to a single place together without sooner or later wishing the ground would swallow you."

"Oh, I'd get hardened to it."

"Would that be happiness? And even if you did, he wouldn't. You don't think he enjoys all this, do you?"

"No, I suppose not."

"No. And don't think he's dumb enough to put himself into it for life, either."

"He cares enough to, I think."

"Then you've got to care enough not to let him."

"How?"

"Drop him."

"I can't."

"You must. Don't you see now why you lily-whites seek each other? It's self-protection. Whether you do it consciously or not, you're really trying to prevent painful embarrassment."

"But I can't just shut myself away from everyone who happens to be a little darker than I am. If I did it before I didn't realize it, and I wasn't to blame. But if I do it now, intentionally, I'm just drawing the color-line, and that wouldn't be right. What can I do?"

Her visitor smiled. "Do? Get out. Pass. What else?"

"That's impossible. There's mother. Wherever I'd go I'd have to take her, and she couldn't pass for anything but American Negro—"

Her protest was drowned in her visitor's laughter. It was harsh, strident laughter, like the suddenly stifled outburst she'd heard at Hank's that night. It was long, loud laughter that left the visitor breathless, panting pitiably.

Of a sudden Evelyn sat upright, fearfully aware that the laughter of her dream had merged into something real and close. She listened a moment. It was her mother in the next room. Asthma again.

She met both the women lodgers in the hall, frightened; helpless.

"Did you hear her?"

Shortly Evelyn hurried from her mother's room, leaving the two women with her. She slipt on as little as she dared and sped out to get a physician.

A half hour passed before she returned with one. She noted a bright light in the front room and hastened to it, thinking the two women had taken her mother there for air; but she found only two of them, huddled together on the sofa, shivering in their bathrobes, with something close to panic in their eyes.


IV

Jimmy MacLoed, red-eyed, stretchy, disconsolate, and broke, all the event of a prolonged and fatal night of stud-poker, got up at noon-time, dressed, and strolled languidly into the street, wondering from whom he could bum four bits for breakfast. At the corner of 135th Street and the Avenue he encountered Jay Martin, hurrying to lunch. This was luck, for Jay always had bucks.

"See me go for breakfast?" he asked.

"No," grinned Jay, "but I'll add it to the five I'm by you already."

Dick's lunchroom seemed to have been designed so that the two waitresses could serve everybody without moving from where they stood. You could pass from the little front door to your stool before the counter without colliding with someone only when there was no one else there. Many a patron had unexpectedly thrust his knife further into his mouth than he intended because some damn fool, rushing out, squeezed between him and the wall. But one of the waitresses was pretty; and the ham with your eggs was cut thick, not shaved; and the French fried potatoes were really French fried, not boiled ones warmed over in grease. Jay and MacLoed considered themselves lucky to find two of the dozen stools still unoccupied.

They gave their orders and rested their elbows on the counter while the waitress that wasn't pretty threw down some pewter implements before them.

"Too bad about Evelyn's old lady, huh?" said MacLoed.

Jay became grave. "Too bad about Evelyn."

"Evelyn? Wha' d' y' mean?"

"Nobody's seen her since the funeral."

"No? Only three days. Maybe she's gone off for a rest."

"Didn't leave any notice at the office."

"Think she went dippy and jumped in the river or somethin'?"

"No. But I think she's jumped out of Harlem."

"You mean—passin'?"

"I don't know. The last time I saw her she was sick enough to do anything. Those two women roomers wouldn't stay in the house another night. None of her friends would either, even after her mother was safe in the undertaker's. She had three rotten days of it, except when my mother was there. Nobody much went to the funeral. I sent the only flowers. Next day, my mother went around to see how she was making out and found nobody home.—There hasn't been, since."

"Didn't leave word with nobody, huh?"

"Nope."

" 'S funny. 'D she have any relations?"

"Nope."

"Hm! Then that's what she's doin' all right."

"Passing?"

"Yea." Mac contemplated the ham and eggs that the homely waitress had just slid between his elbows. "Don't blame her. I'd do the same thing if I didn't have so damn much brownskin family."

"Why?"

"Why?—Why not? Wouldn't you?"

"Be white if I could?" Jay paid the waitress. "I don't know."

"The hell you don't. What would you be afraid of? Meetin' somebody? Hell! Don't see 'em. If they jump you, freeze 'em.—But you'd never meet anybody you knew. S'posin' you looked white and didn't have anything to stop you, what would be the hold-back?"

Jay chewed a minute thoughtfully. Then he looked at MacLoed as if wondering whether he was worth a reply. Finally he answered:

"Kids."

"Kids?" Mac ingested this with two pieces of the real French fried potatoes well swabbed in ham gravy. "You mean you might get married and have a little pickaninny to account for, huh? Well, you could get out o' that all right. Just tell her she'd been runnin' around with a nigger and quit."

Jay knew MacLoed too well to be shocked. "You might not want to quit," he said. "You might like her. Or you might have a conscience."

"Humph! Conscience and kids. Old stuff, buddy."

"And even if your scheme worked with a man who was passing, it wouldn't with a woman. She couldn't tell her white husband he'd been running around with a colored girl. That wouldn't explain the pickaninny."

"No.—The woman catches hell both ways, don't she?"

"It's a damned shame." Jay was speaking rather to himself than to MacLoed. "I know. I took her—places. That girl was white—as white as anybody could be. Lord only knows what she'll be now."

Three or four men had come in, standing in what little space they could find and reading the menu signs while they awaited seats. No one paid any particular attention to one of these who was "ofay." White patrons were not infrequent in Dick's. This one had moved close enough to Jay to hear his last statement. He touched him on the shoulder. As Jay turned the white man drew aside his coat, and Jay glimpsed a badge. When the officer motioned him to step outside, there was nothing else to do, and with an "Excuse me a minute, Mac—be right back," he preceded the other to the sidewalk.

Outside, Jay asked, "What's the idea?"

"Didn't want to start a row in that dump. Somebody might 'a had a gun."

"What's the idea?"

"Let's walk down this way." Jay knew better than to refuse, though "this way" led toward the police station. "So you think it's a damned shame, do you? Well, I think it's a damned shame, too."

"What the devil are you talking about?"

"Come down out o' that tree, son. I'm talking about you and the white girl you picked up at Manhattan Casino a while back. You y'self said just now she's white. That about settles it."

"White? Why, I only meant—"

"I heard you. You said 'white'. White's white, ain't it?"

Presently: "What's the charge?"

"Don't play dumb, bud. There's been too damn much of this thing goin' on here. We're goin' to stop it."

Suddenly Jay Martin laughed.

The two walked on in silence.

## V

From a point in the wide, deep balcony's dimness, Jay followed the quick-shifting scenes; not those on the screen at which he stared, but others, flashing out from his mind.

Coney Island. He and Evelyn arm in arm, inconsequent, hilarious, eating sticky popcorn out of the same bag, dipping in at the same time, gaily disputing the last piece. Their laughter suddenly chilled by an intentionally audible remark: "Look at that white girl with a nigger." A half-dozen lowering rowdies. Evelyn urging him away. People staring.

An ice-cream parlor. A rackety mechanical piano, tables with white tops and dappled wire legs; outside 125th Street traffic shadowing past; Evelyn and he, wilted with the heat, waiting a couple of eternities for a waitress; he finally looking about impatiently, beckoning to one, who leers through him. The proprietor. "Of course we don't mind serving the lady, sir; but while we can't actually refuse, why—er—frankly your presence is unprofitable to us, sir." People staring.

The subway. He and Evelyn in a corner of the car. Above the rattle and bump of doors and clang of signal-gong, wild laughter, coarse, loud. Different. Negro laughter. Headlong into the car, stumbling over one another, a group of hilarious young colored people. Men contesting seats with women, and winning; women flouncing defiantly down on the men's knees. Conscious of the attention attracted by their loudness; pleased with it. Train starting, accelerating. Train-din rising. Negro-noise rising through and above it, like sharp pain through and above dull ache. "Oh, you high yaller!" Evelyn ashamed. People staring.

Finally a back room in the police station. Two or three red-faced ruffians in brass-buttoned uniforms, sneering, menacing, quite like those Coney Island rowdies. Himself, outraged, at bay, demanding to know on just what score he was there. Surly accusation, hot denial, scalding epithet—flame. A blow. Swift, violent struggle. "Now mebbe y'll leave white women alone!"

Emptiness. After a time release; release raw with bodily anguish, raw with the recurrent sting of that cover-all charge of policemen, "resisting an officer."

What an enormity, blackness! From the demons and ogres and ravens of fairy tales on; storm-clouds, eclipses, night, the valley of the shadow, gloom, hell. White, the standard of goodness and perfection. Christ himself, white. All the angels. Imagine a black angel! A black angel with a flat nose and thick lips, laughing loudly. The devil! Standards, of course; but beneath the standards, what? An instinctive shrinking from the dark? He'd seen a little white child run in terror from his father once, the first black man the child had ever seen. Instinctive? He looked about. All this balcony full of fellow creatures instinctively shrinking from him. No help for it? Awful idea. Unbearable.

A general murmur of amusement refocussed his attention for a moment on the screen. Two chubby infants sat side by side on a doorstep; the one shiny black, with a head full of kinks and eyes of twinkling midnight; the other white, with eyes of gray and the noonday sun in its hair; both dimpled and grinning and happy. Kids. Old stuff, buddy. Evelyn—would she dare?

The thoughts that gathered and throbbed like an abscess were suddenly incised. Off to one side, a row or two ahead, he had caught sight of an oddly familiar face. The dimness seemed to lift mockingly, so that he should have no doubt. Evelyn, like an answer. Different, but—Evelyn. The attitude of the young man beside her was that of an escort, and something in his profile, in the fairness of his hair and skin, discernible even through the dusk, marked him to the staring Jay as unmistakably white. Watching with quickened pulse Jay saw the young man's hand move forward over Evelyn's arm, lying on the elbow-rest between them; move forward till it reached her own hand, which turned palm-upward to clasp it. Saw one white hand close firmly over the other.

He rose abruptly and made his way past stubborn knees to the aisle. The orchestra struck up a popular bit of Negro jazz. It fell on his ears like a guffaw: the familiar refrain of "Yaller Gal's Gone Out o' Style."

# DUST

The long, low, black-and-silver roadster overtook a small clutter of cars waiting at a town crossing, snorted impatiently once or twice, and settled into a grumbling, disgusted purr. The people in the other cars stared, conferred among themselves, and stared again.

Pard grinned at the girl beside him. "Kills 'em to see us in a car like this. Know what they're saying?"

Billie smiled back. "Of course. 'Why, my *dear*, they're *colored*.'"

"No," said Pard. "One word: 'Niggers!' Leaves 'em speechless.—Look at that barmaid in the flivver—can't get her mouth shut."

The signal changed, the cars moved forward. Pard said:

"Now, damn it, eat niggers' dust."

Easily the mighty motor swept them in and out past car after car till they were far in the lead.

"Too bad," said Billie.

"What?"

"There isn't any dust."

With open country and a rolling straight-away they settled down to an even forty. A warm breeze sang round the windshield, ruffling the brown girl's hair with gentle fingers—glossy black hair which the low sun touched to a glow. She looked thoughtfully out over the Connecticut landscape. Wide meadows swept past or stretched gently away, lifting into distant hills; the hills dodged behind one another, and the sun dodged behind the high hills. She looked at the proud dark face of her companion, still grim with the joy of outstripping the white folks.

"Horrible thing, prejudice," she said. "Does you all up. Puffs you all out of shape."

"Not if you have a safety-valve. This buggy's mine. Take anything on the road. Only fun fays give me."

"It's such bitter fun."

"Deep, though. Satisfying. If hating's their game, I can hate right along with 'em. They hate me—sure. But I out-hate 'em. I hate 'em so much I like it."

"No. You like covering them with dust."

"Sure."

"Even when there isn't any dust."

*   *   *

A sudden, loud, almost articulate warning cried startlingly out behind them. Pard instinctively swung over, and a bright yellow sport coupe, of a make as powerful as his own roadster, eased effortlessly past. The interval between the two cars widened rapidly; the other motor's abrupt guffaw dwindled to a receding chuckle.

"Billie, did you see that?"

"He's doing sixty."

"The license-plate, I mean."

"Green and white."

"Georgia."

"Georgia?"

"Georgia—the dirty—"

"Lord protect us now," prayed Billie, knowing what was coming.

"Lord protect him," Pard corrected, his face again grimly bitter. "Hold fast."

His foot went down on the gas; the roadster jumped forward like a cruelly spurred horse, then laid back its ears and flattened itself out in a wild, head-long, heedless run.

Already the car ahead was lost around a left bend in the road. Pard took the bend blindly on its inside margin at fifty miles an hour, while Billie closed her eyes. When she looked again the yellow machine was vanishing to the right at the end of a half-mile straight-away. This they clipped off at seventy, taking the next curve, which was luckily shallow, at fifty-five.

The other car re-appeared; the interval had merely been maintained, not diminished. But the road now chose to climb the low ground-rises rather than side-step them so that, save for occasional depressions, it was now visible straight ahead for two miles. And it was clear.

The yellow sport-coupe, unaware of pursuit, maintained its even sixty. Pard's speedometer passed seventy-five. As his fifteen-mile-an-hour advantage devoured the stretch between him and his object, his lips formed rancorous words:

Dust

"No damn cracker—do that to me . . . die first . . ."

Billie yelled, "If you mean that, let me out!"

"Lyncher. . . . Atta baby—go get 'im—Red-necked hill-billy. . . . Ought to run him off the road anyhow—every cracker less is a nigger more. . . . Listen. . . ."

As they drew nearer, the other engine's voice came back to them no longer a derisive chuckle but a deepening, desperate snarl.

"Holler, damn it. Holler and burn—like a black man down in Georgia—"

"Let up, Pard! Sharp curve ahead—"

The Georgia car, now a mere hundred yards in the lead, was slowing around the turn. Pard took the limit of approach before his foot sought the brake; his tires screeched in a straight skid, protesting the sudden change.

The sound seemed definitely to warn the yellow coupe of hostile approach from behind, whereupon it flung off the turn and engaged the next stretch in deadly earnest. This again was long long straight highway, flatter than the other and flanked on either side by low, broad pasture-lands level with the road.

"Here we go," said Pard. Billie hung on, praying. The engine roared insanely, the wind whipped harshly past, swiftly, steadily the lead diminished. Perhaps three-quarters of a mile remained of the stretch when Pard, looking beyond the Georgia car ahead, saw the road split in a fork.

"Got to beat him to that fork. Next town's coming."

"And some cars, maybe," said Billie, thanking God for clear roads thus far.

"Come on, baby!" Pard jammed his foot down and held hard with both hands.

Billie squeezed her lids together. The stridor of the yellow car grew, beat painfully in her ears. "Bye-bye, cracker!" An irresistible impulse forced the girl's eyes open to observe impending disaster: Either car was flinging itself precipitately at the fork, Pard's roadster now a length ahead, to the left; both took the left bend of the fork; when, fifty yards ahead, a third car came out of a blind left intersection and stopped dead halfway across the road, startled to a standstill by the mad onrushing pair.

Both jammed on brakes, Pard bearing right, directly into his competitor's path. The latter swung off the road with a crash into the grassy triangle between the two bends of the fork, managing by the grace of heaven and consummate skill not to flip upside down. Either car came to a standstill, Pard's fifty yards up the highway, the other in the middle of the field.

Billie was trembling. "Pard—go back—he must be hurt—"

No question now of hatred. Pard wheeled and drove back through the grass to the coupe. As they stopped, the yellow door opened, the driver backed stiffly out, and turned to present to their astonished eyes as black a face as ever came out of Georgia.

A deep breath all around. Then, "Are you—hurt?" Billie managed; and, "I'm sorry," from Pard—"I'll pay for any damage—"

A far hill covered the face of the sun, like a hand concealing a grin.

# THE BACKSLIDER

The meeting-house had once been a dwelling, no better, no worse than all the other houses in the row. It had dressed like them in curtains of lace, in half-drawn shades, in soft, seductive, crimson-shaded lights. But now, transfigured into a church, it wore the saintlier garb of a proper convert: an uncompromising halo from a globe-light over the doorway; windows stained with tissue-paper, red and green in squares. Its very voice had changed, no longer crooning balmy blues but shouting hallelujahs. If the Lord dwelt anywhere in Negro Harlem, surely He dwelt in this place.

So thought Ebenezer Grimes. Eben knew he had sinned and felt like it. He stood irresolute, staring fearfully up at the three narrow first-floor windows, mustering courage to mount the front steps, open the door and go in. But the halo glared at him balefully. The tissue-paper of red and green curled and shrank from its window-edges, leaving clear corners to transmit merciless slashes of yellow light. Surely not only the Lord was in this place, but His wrath as well.

Eben weighed the issues; compared these unmistakably divine manifestations with the terrors of Hell-fire; contrasted the momentary shame of public repentance with the eternal tortures of the damned. There could be but one decision, but, even so, it was with fear and trembling that he went up the steps into the halo, slowly pushed open the door and turned backwards into the meeting-room, pretending thereby to close the door the more carefully.

No sooner had he crept into a chair than he sensed surrounding tension. Prayer-meeting had not begun, and ordinarily there would have been noise— chairs scraping, feet shuffling, ripple of voices, splashes of laughter. But tonight there was heavy silence. Sister Gassoway over in the corner, big, shiny and round, would have been gyrating as usual on her perilous pedestal of a chair, diffusing cheer, bouncing with full-bosomed merriment. Tonight she was as ominously still as a large, billowy storm-cloud. Brother Hezekiah

Mosby, sexton, usher and chorister, would have been busily flitting about like a worrisome little black fly, grinning, whispering, buzzing useless greetings, questions, confidences. Tonight he sat on the front row alone, silent, with folded arms. Beyond all these Eben recognized the most dismaying sign—not one of the saints turned to greet him, not one called the customary welcome, not one gave any indication of being so much as aware of his presence. Eben's heart dropped out of his chest. They knew. All of them knew.

Now Senior Deacon Crutchfield, assistant to the absent shepherd, mounted the low platform at the end of the room. Eben had only admiration for Deacon Crutchfield. He was a magnificent man, big, hearty, bass-voiced, with an engaging smile and a painfully powerful hand-shake. Eben longed for the power to squeeze a hand as did Deacon Crutchfield. And, incredibly enough, only two years ago Deacon Crutchfield had been, in his own words, a rat in the gutter, a thief in the night, a poor lost soul who had never even heard of the mercy of God. From rat in the gutter to Senior Deacon in two years—there was a career!

Eben contrasted himself—brought up, down home, in church from infancy; Sunday-school as far back as he could recall; finally conversion and baptism, years of faithful attendance; but now, in New York, instead of advancing to high office, miserably falling from grace, a sinful backslider.

"Let us read the word of the Lord," rumbled the voice of Deacon Crutchfield, who scowled straight at Eben with a light in his eyes curiously like the halo over the entrance. Eben heard the psalmist's distant thunder, nearing: "'But the ungodly are like the chaff which the wind driveth away. Therefore the ungodly shall not stand in the judgment, nor the sinners in the congregation of the righteous. For the Lord knoweth the way of the righteous, but the way of the ungodly shall perish.'" Here Deacon Crutchfield turned too many pages, but read on with triumphant satisfaction: "'Let the sinners be consumed out of the earth, and let the wicked be no more! Bless thou the Lord, O my soul. Praise ye the Lord.'" Then in the vibrant quiet followed: "Brother Mosby, lead us in prayer." The deacon sat down.

No one will deny that public praying is a decidedly difficult accomplishment. It demands rare capabilities—unusual range of voice, accurate appraisal of the occasion, an appearance of having completely forgotten the audience—which is, of course, impossible—and ability to sound spontaneous even when everybody knows the prayer by heart. It demands, in short, technique.

In this particular art, Christendom has probably never seen the peer of Brother Hezekiah Mosby. His repertoire was inexhaustible and displayed the most extraordinary versatility; he could pop up and pray on an instant's notice at meeting, banquet or wake, and always with the proper wail or shout or moan or sing-song; you had but to hear his prayer to know the occasion.

Never had Eben heard Brother Hezekiah pray as he prayed tonight. He addressed God by at least three dozen different designations, obviating any possible failure of connection. In a sonorous voice that soared and sank like shifting diapasons, he called down the punishment of Heaven to humble the heads of the wicked. He omitted no competent agent of vengeance—"Thy divinable wrath—terrible right hand—revengeable angel—diluvient thunder and lightning—the resuming fire by night and the fumigant sword by day—" Nor did he neglect any worthy object of destruction—"liar—thief—gambler—contamerating drunkard—bootlegger—politician—" Abruptly he halted, surprising his accompanying chorus of amens and glorys, which clamored on for a moment, unable to cease so suddenly. Then, resuming, in a soft, weepy tremolo: "If there do be one amongst us which are unworthy of Thy mercy"—he rose to a passionate roar—"cast out the hypocrite, the *backslider* like the seven devils of old!"

The end of the prayer was submerged beneath a tide of approving cries.

There was a lull, a moment of calm ere the final deluge broke. Deacon Crutchfield rose, as also did Eben's pulse-rate.

"Brothers an' sisters, this bein' the reg'lar monthly business meetin', it becomes our duty to take up certain matters. We will leave the best till the last and take up the painfullest first.

"It comes to our ears on good authority that our former brother Ebenezer Grimes has been seen on two occasions comin' out of one of Harlem's worst dens of iniquity, the Rodent cabaret." Silence with an occasional rustle. "Both times was after midnight." Silence, save for Eben's heart-beats. "And both times our former brother was unquestionably drunk." Silence intact. Deacon Crutchfield's flashing eyes now engaged Eben's reluctant, shifting ones. The awful question leaped forth: "Young man, is these things true?"

Eben had planned to pray aloud, to confess his sins in his prayer, to plead for pardon. But after Brother Hezekiah's masterpiece, any effort of his would have been puny. Now, transfixed with this challenge of Deacon Crutchfield, the backslider was rendered speechless. He groaned as if the question had been a spear.

"Our former brother seems to have nothing to say. What is yo' pleasure?"

Brother Hezekiah popped up. "It are my painful duty, brothers 'n' sisters, to relate that this hyer same young man up and took communion Sunday!" There was a horrified gasp of unbelief, especially from those who had seen him take it. To share communion after sinning—unforgivable! "Tha'fo', I move you, Brother Senior Deacon, that this onworthy young man's name be hencefo'th an' fo'ever struck off'n our church roll!"

Eben jumped up in a panic. They were putting him out of church. A dozen protests stuck in his throat. Hell-fire—eternal damnation—putting him out of church—

He sank weakly back, unable to state a defense. Some one objected—called for a vote. They were voting. Voting on him. Ten ayes, for putting him out. Ten noes, opposed. A tie, thank the Lord. There was hope now. Maybe Deacon Crutchfield would save him. He tried to beseech the Senior Deacon with his eyes, but the Senior Deacon was uttering terrible, righteous, decisive words:

"In case of a tie like this, brothers and sisters, it becomes the duty of the moderator, which is yo' humble servant, to cast his vote. Shall we strike this name off from our rolls?" An instant's exquisite uncertainty. Then, "The Lord bids me vote 'aye'!"

After a blurred, stunned moment, Eben rose and stumbled out.

\*    \*    \*

Whither may that man go on whom God has turned His back? To the Devil, sooner or later. It happens in Harlem, as elsewhere, that God and the Devil are neighbors—it is but the briefest step from the One to the other. And so, five minutes after his excommunication, Ebenezer Grimes was in the Rodent.

The Rodent is, of course, nothing but a transformed cellar—not too much transformed. It is very exclusive in its membership; no habitué is expected to have retained any vestige of good reputation, and those are its special favorites whose occupations are unknown or unmentioned. Its transient guests, therefore, are naturally people of excellent repute, who, attracted by its unconcealed vices, get a far more violent "kick" out of its smoky closeness, its wire-legged chairs, its three-piece, slow-jazz orchestra than ever they get out of the velvet pomp and splendor of more carefully disguised cellars. The Rodent has, in short, successfully capitalized its bad name. You simply can't plan a wicked night and leave the Rodent out.

To this place Eben had first been introduced as the unwitting victim of one of its regular practitioners in good standing, a certain "Spider" Webb, who anesthetized the "jay-bird" with gin and successfully extracted his pay-envelop. The second time, Eben returned to see if any one had found his lost pay-envelop. He didn't discover the envelop, but he did discover Lil. Lil was the entertainer. He told her it really didn't matter anyhow—she was worth a

The Backslider                                                    105 dozen envelops. Rather intrigued by this brand-new line, she spent half an hour with him, just to see how green and grimy they could come. Then, warning him to keep better company than Spider Webb, if he didn't want to lose all of his envelops, she tanked him up on corn and sent him staggering blissfully homeward.

This, then, was Eben's third call at the Rodent. It was dismally early. There was a waiter or two about. A bareheaded girl sat brooding at a table. Stripped of its song and smoke and laughter, the squat little room was as desolate as an empty coal-bin. To Eben the impish silhouettes on the walls became hunched, clubfooted menaces, and on the bare little platform, naked of its orchestra, Deacon Crutchfield might have been standing, pronouncing final sentence.

He dropped into a chair. The girl saw him, rose and came over to his table. "Hello, Eben."

He looked up. It was Lil. "Evenin', Miss Lil."

"You're early tonight."

"No place else to go."

She caught his tone, his limpness. "What's the grand tragedy?"

"Nothin'."

"Liar." She sat down. "Come on, spill it. Help take my mind off my own troubles."

"You in trouble too?"

"Never out. What is it, bucks?"

"No'm. Church."

"Church? For the love o' cream cheese!"

"'Tain' no mystery," he said. "Somebody seen me both times I was hyeh. Seen me come out drunk. Dass all."

"That's all? Well, for cryin' out loud—what's the grand larceny? What if they did see you?"

"Oh—dey put me out o' church."

"Just for getting soaked a coupla times?"

"Uh-huh."

"Why, the hypocrites!" And then she promptly and whole-heartedly threw herself into his problem. After a moment's ponderous thought she exclaimed: "Why, it's easy! It's a cinch! What kind of a church is this?"

"Baptis'."

"Huh. Bogus, you mean. Well, now, all you've got to do is find yourself another kind of church, see? One that's not so tight—one with a broader mind."

To Eben churches were of three classes, Baptist, Methodist and others. "Methodist?" he ventured.

"Naw. They're just like the Baptist—horn-rimmed. Get yourself into a regular kind with a long name, like Episcolopian or Utilitarian or something. They don't care what you do."

"How come you know so much 'bout 'em?"

She contemplated his curious eyes, his clean brown skin, his carefully parted, not too kinky hair. Then she contemplated the table top. "Well," she said presently, and Eben caught in her eyes shadows of tragedy older than his, "I don't usually brag about it, but my old man was a preacher ages ago. Not the fly kind they got nowadays, though. Nothing synthetic about him; real genuine stuff, vintage of 1850."

"Yea? He got a church now?"

"Nope. He's got a harp. Say, I know just the joint for you—Saint Augustine's, over by Morningside heights. Boy, that's some swell dump, no perjury."

Eben stared with more interest than understanding.

"Know what I'm goan do?" he said, coming to.

"Something dumb, I bet."

"Sent me straight to de Devil, didn' dey? All right, den. I'm goin'!"

"Halt, friend. You've arrived."

"All my life I been tryin' to do right. Seem like doin' right never was doin' nothin' but what you didn' want to do. Ev'ybody else doin' different. Ev'ybody doin' wrong—but me. Ev'ybody happy but me. Couldn' go fishin' Sundays down home, 'count o' Sunday-school or church. Couldn' steal peaches, couldn' fight, couldn' dance, couldn' do nothin' wuth doin' thout bein' scared o' missin' Heaven. Now 'tain' no need to worry 'bout Heaven—ain' goan git da' nohow. I kin dance all I dog-gone please! I kin cuss! Hot dam', I kin cuss! I kin fight—git even wid folks what does me wrong. Dat lil yaller slew-face booger what stole my pay-envelop—I'm goan git 'im an' knock 'im from amazin' grace to a floatin' opportunity! Dey put me out? Well, dey done me a favor! I'm free—free as a dog-gone bird! An' I'm goan act like it too—you watch!"

"Take it slow and easy, cuckoo. Birds can be caged, you know."

He grew silent but no less intense. Before he'd had time to say a word, they'd voted on him. Ten ayes. Ten noes. Senior Deacon Crutchfield—had he, then, never done wrong? Yes—he'd had *his* fun *first*. But it wasn't Deacon Crutchfield who'd sent him to Hell. "The Lord bids me vote 'aye.'" The Lord—the Lord . . .

Eben's head suddenly fell on his arms.

\*       \*       \*

The Backslider          107

"Snap out of it, bozo. We'll have spectators in a minute."

Eben exposed a bitter countenance. "Is dey put you out o' church too?"

"'Tisn't what they've put me out of. It's what they're going to put me in."

"What's 'at?"

"Jail."

"Jail! Wha' fo'?"

"Debts." Eben sat up and gaped. "Cops'll be here any minute now. Sweet mamma'll have some escort, big boy. Liveried, what I mean. Lucky at that. A private room in prison beats a clothes-press in a flat and costs less." She sighed, prodigiously sardonic: "Hey-hey—bring on the bright brass buttons."

It did not occur to Lil that Eben, evergreen though he undoubtedly was, would think of taking her half-jest literally. But he did, and not without reason. Down home Eben had seen men sent beyond jail for less than debt.

Slowly inspiration came, yielding a simple solution. He could save Lil and vindicate himself—if he acted quickly enough.

*　　*　　*

Ebenezer Grimes walked rapidly, in quest of a chance to steal. The only concern, then, was time; the only danger delay. He reached the corner of the avenue and turned out of the side street's darkness into the glow of lighted shop-windows. Now he proceeded more deliberately, looking carefully into the shops, noting those which were closed and dark—a Universal Grocery, a clothing store, a real estate office, a barber shop. He went up to the window of the barber shop, intently peered into the dimness. On the ledge in front of the wall mirror gleamed a silver and porcelain cash-register. If he could get into the rear of the place, he could reach that cash-register and empty it. The grocery, on investigation, presented a cash-register too. The others looked lean and barren. Two chances. He must get around back somehow.

Above the foundation of shops rose several layers of apartments, and between the shops at intervals gaped the narrow apartment-house entrances. One of these was beside the grocery, and into it Eben slipped. Eagerly he traversed the hallway, only to find that it ended blindly, without any door, and with only a ground-glass window, firmly nailed down. He came back and mounted the hall stairs that led to the flats above. At the rear of each floor's hallway he sought the window corresponding to the first. The second, third and fourth were immovable. The fifth went up with a bang. To Eben's satisfaction it opened on the balcony of a fire-escape.

With no notion of how rare a thing a full cash-register is, and quite unaware of his own futility, the new disciple of Satan awkwardly clambered through the window and began to scuffle none too quietly down the iron skeleton.

He was negotiating his second story, creeping past a kitchen which shared its balcony with the corresponding hall, when he observed that, of the few lighted windows above, one was just beyond the balcony rail. He halted and saw, too, that it was open. Then his new patron disclosed to his eyes, on the near edge of a bureau, a large, flat patent-leather purse, such as·many women insist on carrying under the arm.

"Amazin' grace!" he whispered. "Ain't dis sump'n?"

Without looking into the darkness below, he measured the distance from the balcony rail to the nearer edge of the window and decided to acquire the purse. He got over the rail and holding to it with one hand, leaned out as far as he could. The room was apparently empty. A half-minute later he had his prize and was scrambling back over the rail the way he had come.

Up the fire-escape he made his way, back through the still open window.

He dived down the stairs, still holding the purse in his hand. In the hall-way below he brought up short, guiltily facing a man whose approach he had not heard. The purse was still in plain sight—the man's gaze upon it. In the same moment that Eben saw the uselessness of hiding it, he recognized Spider Webb, the man who had caused his pay-envelop so strangely to disappear. Webb now recognized him also, and took a surprised step backward.

"You needn' run," grunted Eben. "Ain' got time to git you now. But next time we meets, when I git thoo you ain' goan be fit fo' hog-fodder."

He slipped the purse under his coat and brushed swiftly past.

"Not so good," thought Spider Webb. He wheeled and, unobserved, followed Eben down the street. Eben turned the corner, but was not ten yards beyond it before Spider was pointing him out to a black policeman at the curb.

"Say, Ben, see that black bird there?"

"With both eyes."

"Step after him and find out what he's doin' with a woman's pocketbook. My guess is he snatched it. See?"

"Snatched a woman's pocketbook, huh? Where's the woman?"

"Never mind—get *him* first—before he fades."

"Right." At a rapid stride the officer made after Eben. Half-way down the block Eben cast a glance behind, saw the uniform approaching. He did not know that the officer was pursuing him, but he did know distance was desirable and that, in any case, Lil's security depended on his speed. He began to run. The policeman began to run too.

Eben reached the Rodent's door and, too frightened to look back, plunged in. The officer was almost at his heels, intent now on making an arrest. Somehow in the precipitous descent Eben's feet managed to keep ahead of the rest of him. His momentum carried him headlong past two or three startled rounders who had come in during his absence, and landed him squarely in the center of the floor and the middle of one of Lil's songs.

Lil herself was well-nigh mowed down. "For the love o'——"

"Hyeh—take it—quick!" gasped Eben, thrusting out the purse.

There was, perhaps, but one person in the room whose respirations were normal. That one said:

"Well, if it ain't Big Ben, the cream o' the force! What's the idea chasin' my friend around? He don't need exercise."

The policeman pointed at the purse with his night-stick. "He snatched that off a woman."

Lil rescued the purse from Eben's infirm grasp. "Oh, he did, did he? Where?"

"Up on the avenue."

"You see him do it?"

"No—Spider Webb did."

"That yellow insect? Why, if he saw Saint Peter at the gates of Heaven he'd swear he was chargin' admission. You believe him?"

"Sorry this is friend o' yourn; but there's the bag, y' see."

"Certainly. Right in mamma's arms, where it belongs."

"Yours?"

"I didn't say your grandpa's."

"Why—but what's this bird doin' with it, then?"

"Be your age. I sent him for it, of course."

"Well—what was he runnin' for?"

"Because I told him to hurry, Sherlock."

The gendarme grinned and scratched his head. "Well, I'll be—'scuse me. I'm goin' to run that Spider Webb in for lyin', sure as I got a badge."

"If you don't, you hadn't ought to have no badge."

The officer left. Eben was limp as a mop. Lil dragged him to a corner and dropped him across a chair. The few spectators, fully recovered, were now intent on their own concerns.

"What's the bright notion?" demanded Lil.

"Didn' you say dey was goan put you in jail fo' debt?"

It took a good deal to amaze Lil, but this did it. Sixty seconds went by before she could ask, "Do you want to take it back now or later?"

"Take it back?"

"You ain't blind."

"You doan want it?"

"Listen, darkness." Lil's tone was not unkind. "Mamma plays with lots o' things, including fire. But mamma doesn't play with hot stuff, see? And she'd feel lots better if you didn't either. Take it back."

After a moment she got up and went to resume her song. Eben sat in a daze. He felt as if he'd poured kerosene on a fire and the fire had promptly gone out. As if he'd jumped off a bridge and landed back on the bridge again. Deacon Crutchfield's awful "Aye!" Lil's cold "Take it back." Forsaken by God and denied by the Devil. Lost.

Presently he, too, got up and crossed the floor. Then, without God or Devil, with only a purse full of money, he made his way up the stairs and out into the pitiless night.

Standing by the piano, Lil watched him disappear. "The poor sap would-a gone to jail for me," she wonderingly mused. "Phil, there's the kind of a bozo I'd—I'd join church for, no perjury."

*    *    *

Precisely how he returned the purse Eben never remembered. One thing he knew—somehow he got it back. It was two hours after he left the Rodent before he performed a clearly conscious act.

He would not have been jolted out of his stupor then had he not walked headlong into a crowd; and the impact of his blind collision was not nearly so reviving as the retaliative thrusts of comment from those whom he had bumped.

He found himself standing at the edge of a thick group of people, chiefly men in collarless shirts which bloused loosely over their belts; a few women, some in kimonos, their hair tightly twisted in knots. Through the middle of this crowd an open space ran across the sidewalk, beginning at the steps of a brightly lighted house and ending at the curb. As if in anticipation of a procession, every one craned his neck to keep this pathway in view, and Eben, craning, saw that at the curb end of the lane some sort of vehicle was backed up. He wondered about it. A moving-van? Too small; too late at night. An ambulance, then? That would explain the interest and excitement. Some one hurt, no doubt—about to be brought out on a stretcher. He craned still further. Strange sort of an ambulance—two vertical rails of shining brass; between them a rear entrance so narrow it made either wall look a foot thick; two or three steps below.

"Dog-gone!" he exclaimed. "One dem patrol-wagons!"

"Naw!" grunted a bystander. "Baby-carriage."

"Who dey after?"

"That's what we're all waitin' to see, Oscar."

Eben was wide awake now. With an interest arising out of his own narrow escape from arrest, he pursued his questioning in the face of every discouragement. Laboriously he learned that the police were making a raid; that a raid was a legalized rampage upon blind pigs and gambling dens; that a blind pig was a place where you could buy bootleg liquor if you were wealthy enough; yes, that Harlem as a whole might be considered a prolific sow without eyes; but that the police rarely bestirred themselves save where bootleg and blackjack were wed; that everybody found in any such establishment was placed under arrest, lined up and marched out into the wagon; finally, that in the present case the next would be a third and last wagonload, hence the close attention—the ringleaders always came out last, having proved the hardest to find.

There came now a stir and a hush. All eyes focused on the door of the house, a half-dozen steps above the sidewalk. A lone policeman stepped through the glowing doorway, a majestic silhouette, slowly descended the stairs and waved the crowd back with his stick. The crowd, of course, paid him no attention. Then the moment's lull broke into a murmur, and the doorway grew dark with heads—more policemen than Eben had ever seen at one time, roughly ushering out a fagged line of captives. Down the steps they passed in file, this one bareheaded, that one's hat hiding his eyes, this one coatless, that one's ears deep in his collar; some erect, some slouching, some requiring support.

Eben somehow envied them. They were at least loyal to their sins. A phrase of the old folks came to him: "It's mighty hard to be a loyal soldier." His own case came before him—he had been dishonorably discharged from one army. All right—he had joined another. And now, having lost his very first fight, he was on the point of deserting. Why, he belonged in that very line of prisoners filing past; that was his army now.

Out of such wry delirium rose a crazy urge to join them.

Eben wriggled through the crowd, which was now too absorbed in the panorama to resent his jostling; reached the edge of the lane. As he did so, the last of the prisoners descended the steps and approached. Eben, rather mad, taut, half intent on slipping into line behind this last man, of a sudden fell back as abruptly as if an officer had turned and clubbed him. It seemed to him that he shrieked, but his cry was the phantom of a whisper:

"Senior Deacon Crutchfield! 'Mazin' grace!"

His wide eyes watched the senior deacon pass, saw him reach the curb, mount the steps of the patrol-wagon, suffer a policeman to push him none too gently, stoop, disappear within.

Senior Deacon Crutchfield! The patrol-wagon roared and was gone. Senior Deacon Crutchfield! The crowd had melted away. Senior Deacon Crutchfield—gambler—bootlegger—hypocrite.

It took time for this to register. Eben wandered slowly along, trying to grasp what he had seen. Deep-rooted memories of old folks' words rose again to his rescue.

Hypocrite, hypocrite God despise
Always tellin' dem Christian lies.

Why—then it hadn't been God Who'd put him out of church; it had been Senior Deacon Crutchfield—nobody else. A hypocrite whom God despised.

Eben halted, confronting revelation: "I ain' never been forsook a-tall. 'Twas jess dem narrer-minded niggers—an' dat hypocrite a-blamin' it on de Lawd!"

He heaved a sigh of tremendous relief and grew interested in his whereabouts. Looking up, he discovered moonlight. And not a hundred yards away rose the spire of Saint Augustine's.

For a long time he gazed upon it as upon some lofty aim. "I did backslide on de Lawd," he penitently confessed, "but"—he grinned with the joy of redemption—"now 'm goan backslide on de Devil."

"Wonder," he added presently, "wonder ef Lil would backslide too."

# FIRE BY NIGHT

"For the cloud of the Lord was upon the tabernacle by day, and fire was on it by night."

L enox Avenue arises in a park, flaunts a brief splendor, dies and is buried in
a dump. From 110th Street it marches proudly northward with the broad
grandeur of a boulevard. Fatal pride. Within half a dozen blocks comes sudden hopeless calamity—a street-car line slips in from a side street, stealthily
as from ambush, and with a whir, a rising roar, a crash, deals the highway its
death-blow. Splits its spine. Ugly, cheap little shops attack it, cluster like
scavenging vermin about it. Trucks crush blindly, brutally over it, subway
eats wormily into it. Waste clutters over it, odors fume up from it, sewer-
mouths gape like wounds in its back. Swift changes of complexion come—
pallor—grayness—lividity. Then, less than a mile beyond its start, the Avenue turns quite black.

So might you feel, coming unwarned into this part of the colony. You
shudder a little, perhaps, sensing more than merely a change of color; and
rightly, for these sudden dark faces belong not to Negroes, simply, but to a
distinct group of Negroes, mentioned even by their own as "bad." These are
they whom police respect most and have learned it is best not to bother.
These are the heirs of those who protected the colony in its infancy by their
skill with pistols and knives and fists.

To be sure, there is little need of them now; the colony is mature and competent in ways beyond those of steel and flesh. But these "bad" Negroes lin-
ger yet, spending their heritage on each other, on dickties, the high-toned
hated ones, or on 'fays, the indiscreet whites. They live in that forbidding
strip whose western edge is black Lenox Avenue, whose northern end is the
dump. Alien enough by day, this tameless corner of Negro Harlem is transformed by night into a quivering wilderness. Here strange songs ring, and
queer cries sound, and life stumbles blindly toward death.

114

On one side of the Avenue, just beyond its change of color, you see this morning a triad of small frame houses, burned well toward the ground. What flame has left undone above, flood has accomplished below. Roofs and attics are a wretched steaming crush of ash and charcoal, while the unburned lower walls are thoroughly drenched and dripping still.

Even yesterday, ere last night's disaster, the triad looked miserable enough. They huddled together in the middle of the block, as if trapped between the brownstone walls approaching on either hand; as if caught and squeezed ever tighter and tighter till they cracked and puckered and caved. Roofs were sunken, windows stared vacantly, clapboards were wry and colorless.

Like a brace to save the three from collapse, a flat sign stretched across their front. "The Club," said the sign defensively. Beneath it a doorway opened at street level, and beyond this the three ground floors were thrown into one large, low-ceilinged room. Green-covered pool-tables squatted in rows, green-shaded drop-lamps showered light on them. Men stood beside them, chalking their cues, or leaned far over them, making hard shots; men in vests and silk-striped shirt-sleeves; big men with brown felts pushed back from their brows, small men with caps yanked down over one eye; mostly young men, war vets, consciously hard, the most worldy-wise and the most heedless Negroes on earth.

As evening advanced the Club grew more crowded; toward midnight the room was alive. Pool-balls clicked and chunked into pockets, cue-handles thump-thumped the floor for reracking. There was rough kidding and rougher replying and curses and laughter through smoke.

A narrow platform ran along one wall, bearing occasional stools for spectators. On one of these hunched Rusty Pride, watching the whole affair glumly; watching it all with a self-disgust unrelieved by this place or these men.

"Me"—he mused—"I'm that eight-ball there. Black all over but one spot. God knows what, inside. Watch it now. Three times he's tried it for that side pocket. Easy shot. Soft shot. But it won't go in. It's me. Shoot, fool. What you wastin' time for squintin' and squirmin'? It won't go in. Shoot, I tell you. See? Hit the cushion and hopped. What's I tell you? Like my old man, tryin' to shoot me into a hole. Hmph! That's good. My old man shootin' pool. Imagine. A Baptist preacher shootin' pool. That's good."

Some one came near. "Let's go, Rusty. Last table's comin' up."

"Nothin' doin'," Rusty refused briefly.

"Spot you ten. Hundred points for two bits."

"No." Curt, briefer still.

"The hell with you, then." The speaker grinned and departed.

More musing. "The old man shooting me into a hole. Wild. Well, what of it? Who's tame in this man's town? Me—his son—disgracing him. Hmph. Did I ask to be his son? Join church. Church. Niggers prancing—raising hell and calling it religion. What does it matter what you call it? Or where you raise it? It's hell, that's all. Blues—spirituals. Shimmy in a dance-hall—shout in a church. Religion. Join church. Acknowledge God—or else get out and find Him. That's what he said. Well, I got out. Nearly a year ago I got out. What did I find? Hell. Plenty of hell. That's all. God? He don't bother getting in people's way."

Some one else came up. "Come on, pool-shark. I'm yo' bait."

Rusty might have been deaf.

The challenger insisted. "Snap out of it, biggy, and get yo'self licked."

Rusty gave him a silent, virulent scowl; the challenger shrugged and passed on.

The eight-ball touched another and shied off as if alarmed at the contact. "Me again. Meeting Roma Lee today. Her of all people in this part of Harlem." One of those chance meetings from which he forever shrank. She had squealed a delightful recognition—run to him and thrown her arms about him there on the street, hugged him on Lenox Avenue where always he felt people's eyes. Impulsive kid, Roma.

"Rusty, for goodness' sake! Where did you come from?"

"Nowhere much." Shabby. No collar. Coat turned up to hide his bare neck. Shoes like old boxing-gloves. Baggy knees—sacks.

"But you must've been away. Nobody's seen you for a year."

"Been running on the railroad. Canada." Rag of a coat—both pockets ripped out at the corners. Hide 'em with your thumbs, fool. Two days' beard—chin like a brush.

"Gee, but it's good to see you! Going to the dance tonight? . . . Didn't know about it—the So-and-So's supper-dance? . . . Then when are you coming round? . . . Married—me? Lord—who'd be goose enough? Waiting for you, silly."

Laughing at him. Well—but was she? Used to care some. Might yet. What of that moonlight sail? Wide Hudson—shore lights—a nook astern—jazz laughing somewhere ahead, white wake laughing behind. Something today in her eyes, something incredulous, pained, anxious, coming with a gleam instead of a twinkle. Laughing at him? Or shuddering? Or maybe crying a little underneath? Jackass!

Rusty withdrew himself from meditation with an effort. It was as though he were a well into which he himself had fallen, floundered a while, almost drowned. Many times in places like this he had fallen into the well, tripping usually over the memory of his father's final dictum. Now as before he reached in and pulled himself out with a tug.

Just as he emerged, a little black figure rushed past him, catching his eye—a little cinder of a man with bare, crinkly scalp, shriveled face and uncovered ashen forearms. He had come in from the street on this midwinter night in an undershirt and trousers, and he sped past as if he'd been thrown. As if he'd been thrown at Turpin, the proprietor, who sat behind an iron cage in one back corner of the Club. Turpin, too, saw the flying cinder coming. His hand reached under the shelf on which he'd been leaning. The little man brought up in front of the cage. Only the nearest heard or cared what he said, and of these Rusty happened to be one.

"You sell my brother dat gin today?"

Turpin's hand, holding a pistol, came from beneath the shelf and rested upon its surface. Turpin, small, compact, cool and hard, looked the questioner up and down. "Talk sense, Chinaman," he advised.

"Well, you done kilt 'im."

Turpin grinned. "How often do you take it, friend?"

"Sole 'im bad gin, you did. Pizen gin. Now he's daid. Went blind, he did. Went blind, doubled up 'n' died."

"You sho' takes it calm."

"I could tell d' police ef'n I felt lak it. I could tell 'em you sole my brother pizen fo' licker and kilt 'im daid. Tell 'em you sole 'im bad gin."

"They's no sich thing as bad gin. All gin is good."

"Twouldn' do no good. Know whut dey'd say? Dey'd say any fool nigger whut drinks pizen licker's too dumb t' live anyhow."

"An' they'd be right."                    ·

"Aw right—dey'd be right. An' y'know whut I say? I say any chinch whut sells pizen licker's too low-down t' live. An' I'm right—dead right."

Turpin still caressed the gun. "Which means which?" he inquired with some deference.

"I see yo' gun. An' I ain' no fool." For a moment the accuser hesitated, as though, having confirmed his suspicion about the sale, he had no idea what to do next; as though something unforeseen, Turpin's gun, perhaps, prevented what otherwise would have occurred.

The doubt passed quickly. "Killin' you won't help none nohow," the little man contemplated. "But I got t' pay you fo' dat licker. You ain' been paid fo' it yit."

"Remarks," smiled Turpin pleasantly.

"I ain' no fool." The other spoke with a sort of meditative menace. He stiffened with quick decision now. "But ef'n you got mo' pizen licker to sell, sell it fas', you hyeh? 'Cause sumpin' tells me you ain' goan be sellin' it long."

Rusty listened beyond the first few words not because such scenes were strange to him, but because this one was different. In company like this some one was always accusing somebody of something, but the accuser was usually drunk. This man was certainly sober. Usually the words of the offended one were loud, befuddled and heedless. This man's words, though breathless, were low, clear and deliberate. The usual plaintiff would have libeled the defendant's several ancestors one by one; would have dared the defendant, ever more loudly, to raise and point his gun; would have invited him outside his cage and promised to carve him like a turkey. This little shrunken fellow, however, displayed no swagger, no bravado. He was agitated, indeed, but cool; threatening, but intensely quiet; was not loud nor invective, nor especially self-assured; attracted hence no great attention. But Rusty, watching, had the impression that every word was weighed, as though some other spirit than his own was using this little man's body. His gin-dead brother's spirit, perhaps.

Rusty snorted at this hypothesis as he'd snorted at his others. The snort plunged him back into the well. Acknowledge God. Everything that met his eyes at the moment denied God. Everything argued Hell. Turpin might have been Satan himself, surveying his cavorting imps, and enjoying especially the acute torture of this particular rum-scorched soul.

The cinder-man departed. Well, Turpin wasn't overcareful about the quality of his gin. He made it himself. Up-stairs in that blank-looking attic were tin cans full of alcohol. Rows of them. Occasionally Turpin boasted of them, and of the gin he made. It might be good alcohol he put into it; it might not. Turpin took the word of those from whom he got it, too ignorant to do otherwise, too unscrupulous to care. An honest moonshiner, a good business man, even, would at least have protected his clients. Not Turpin. Gin was gin—a gallon of alcohol, a gallon of water, a little extract of juniper—gin.

So Rusty brooded, ill with revolt, with revolt against his revolt. Beasts like Turpin and the rest of these thugs. If he, Rusty Pride, were that little shine, do you know what he would do?

He'd manage to get up-stairs to that alcohol—by way of the next roof maybe. Get to that alcohol and dump it all over the place. Then he'd set fire to it—and pray that Turpin, the thick little brute, would try to save it and would get trapped while trying.

Pray. Hmph. "Now I lay me . . . And look at me now. The old man must be pretty lonesome living there all by himself. His own fault, though. Oh, Lord, I want to go home! No, I'm hanged if I do."

A third challenger approached. "Well, blacker'n me, how 'bout pushin' a few around? You been takin' up room long enough."

It was Stud Samson, Turpin's partner, a creature whom Rusty never looked upon without revulsion. His coarse granular skin was dingy yellow and scarred, and the only facial expression of which he was capable was inevitably a grimace. Even at rest his features described a leer, and this never changed save into a spreading, snaggle-toothed distortion. His whole squat head, you could suppose, had been fashioned of yellow clay by a sculptor who, in a fit of disgust, had seized chin and forehead between angry palms and compressed them with all his might.

Rusty, already on edge with his thoughts, found himself summoned now out of the most turbulent reflections by Stud Samson's hoarse derision, to gaze upon that ugly face and hear its equally ugly hint. He had an impulse to get up and bury his fist in Samson's face; to smash it, shattering thus by proxy the evil it symbolized. The habit of repression turned this impulse into sarcasm. With an unpardonable look and scalding effrontery, Rusty said:

"Go get your face lifted."

Now of ordinary kidding the coproprietor of the Club was able to take his share. You could criticize his taste in gals, for example, or his taste in ties—if you grinned. You might even get away with "slipping" him "in the dozens," reminding him with impunity of his wooden-legged uncle or his grandmammy's cross-eyed cousin. If you grinned. There is in Harlem a term which signifies the last straw, the maddening limit, the one thing that won't be tolerated. It is expressed in the phrase "my cup runneth over" and is shortened to the one word "cup." Any contemptuous reference to Stud Samson's face was Stud Samson's cup. Rusty had made such a reference; and Rusty had not grinned.

For a moment the Stud's face did seem to lift, to straighten out, to untwist; then it tightened into a knot, like a coiled spring suddenly released. "Say that ag'in an' I'll lift yo' jaw," came rasping out of the knot.

Rusty was in a complying mood. "I said," he repeated, unruffled, "to go try and get your face lifted. And while you're about it, you might have 'em straighten your hair."

Between this stimulus and Stud's reaction there was an appreciable latent period. Rusty had time to imagine the insult boring through Samson's thick head to his brain, then down and out to his muscles. The expected lunge came. Rusty in his chair on the platform, with his back against the wall, simply drew his knees up to his chin as Stud rushed and suddenly straightened his legs. Some seconds later Stud crawled dazedly out from under the nearest pool-table.

"The fall of Samson!" commented a wag, and Stud, looking about, realized that the bystanders considered the joke on him. It is difficult at once to encounter a husky enemy and a dozen shouts of laughter. Stud Samson knew no fear like that of appearing ridiculous. The attitude of the onlookers, therefore, though it enraged him the more, yet tended to check his impending rush. Crouching a little, his arms hanging ape-like, he stood still and leered about him, and probably no one really knew whether he was trying to smile or to frown.

Nor did most of them ever find out, for in that moment of doubt a door banged open and some one rushed in with news. It was news that commanded attention. Players pulled up as they sighted their shots, arrested by the first word. Cues about to rap on the floor or mark off points overhead halted promptly just where they were, while those who held them gave ear. Within five seconds a single loud voice had taken the place of thirty.

"Gravy, you boogies! Yassuh! Le's go! Gravy an' I doan mean maybe! Keep yo' red flannel shirts on now. I'm tellin' you fas' as I kin. Dat dickty dance what I'm checkin' coats fuh at d' New Casino is 'bout to break up in a row. Three drunks tried to bust in. I lef' 'em fightin'. Rich niggers, packed up fo' cabaret parties. 'Tain' two blocks away—all y' got to do is mix in an' grab it. Dey's fat rolls cryin' fo' a home!"

"Listen to d' man!" . . . "Gravy, he say!" . . . "Le's go f'm hych!" . . . "Hot dam', baby!" . . . "Git on d' gravy-train!"

Within a few moments the Club was miraculously empty. Only Rusty, Turpin and a player or two remained. Even Turpin's partner, Stud Samson, had departed with the marauders.

Rusty had at first no thought of joining them. His own melancholia had enshrouded him like mist. Even his upsetting of Stud had been instinctively defensive, and he had seemed to be observing himself as in a dream. Visionary likewise had been the dance announcement and the responding babel and hubbub. But as action and noise had blurred his surroundings and driven him into himself, so now unusual quiet rendered them clear and drew him out. He got up, looked about him, realized that excitement had just tramped out of the door. Excitement had become Rusty's tonic and dope; he never denied himself a dose. With a grin of anticipation he adjusted his cap, hunched up his collar and went trudging out of the Club.

A figure, surprised by the suddenness of his exit, shrank into an adjacent doorway as he turned up the street. Managing purposely to walk near this doorway, Rusty peered warily in as he passed. The eyes that met his glared through the shadow with a sort of subdued madness. They belonged to the cinder-man, who just now had uttered a smoldering threat to the sneering Turpin.

Rusty, hurrying on, found himself muttering: "Pizen gin—blind—doubled up 'n' died—you ain' been paid fo' it yet."

Between Lenox and Seventh Avenues lives Harlem's middle class, flanked on the east by rats, by dickties on the west. Accordingly, those who are middle in station are more or less middle in territory. This central strip is in truth the colony's backbone. Here live its laborers, haulers, truck-drivers, carpenters, chauffeurs, mechanics; here live its steady, dependable, year-around wage-earners, family providers. Its businesses fringe and invest this strip and subsist largely upon it. But those who own the businesses and the strip have moved across Seventh avenue, occupying the so-called private houses of the dickty upper two hundreds. When they move, they move west-ward and northward: Edgecombe, St. Nicholas, Morningside; even River-side Drive will be reached one day.

This is middle ground—there are other plots like it, but none approach-ing it in extent. Accordingly, here Harlem's one tradition, the church, has its firmest foundation; and most of the remnant that still fears God will be found in these mountains of flats.

Here too, in occasional private houses, still reside many of those who min-ister to this class. Of these none is more widely known or loved than Zach-ary Pride, Rusty's father. "Daddy Pride" the children of his parish call him, while to their parents he is "The Rev'm." He is seventy years old, and his dark face is lined, his soft hair is white as a halo. But he has the bearing of one who has braved a thousand indignities, and in his face are a courage and faith undisturbed by the jazz all about him. He has knelt by a sick-bed and made God hear through the wild liquor party overhead. He has gone into a cellar when police declined and settled a clamorous argument. He believes in a God who can see and hear and a church that can teach and serve. The doctors of divinity in Harlem call him "a preacher of the old school."

They smile at his disregard of the proprieties; for instance, that cross on his church steeple. Every one knows that a Baptist church has no business with a cross on its steeple. It isn't proper. When Zachary Pride's congrega-tion purchased this building, which had been an Episcopal mission, the first thing they should have done was to take down the cross. It had never even occurred to Zachary Pride to take down the cross.

His is a small gray church on a side street, not far from Lenox Avenue; and while it stands humble between the lofty dwellings on either side, it yet sends its spire and its criticized cross far above them.

This particular prayer-meeting night service had held later than usual, and the elderly shepherd was left unwontedly weary of mind. There had been fi-nancial questions to settle; coal was running low in the bins though ever so high on the bills; the notes on the newly installed organ promised to require far more than one rally; there was a leak in the roof and a spreading area of discoloration on the ceiling over the choir—plaster might drop in the middle of an anthem next Sunday if repairs were delayed; a dozen members on the sick-list were badly in need of help, and the sick-fund would be spread too thin if all received equal share. Then there was the problem of

Fire by Night

young folks—sin contagious as smallpox. Old members came with their burdens to him—he must help old Sister Mosby find the father of her grand-daughter's coming baby; he must testify in court to the character of Len Wiggin's boy, the dupe of some thieving jail-dodgers; he must find jobs for a dozen derelict sons. . . .

Tonight, as usual, Zachary Pride was the last to leave. The church was near Lenox Avenue, but his house was a hundred yards away toward Seventh, on the opposite side of the street. Here he had lived since the church was bought years ago from white Christians for whom the region was growing altogether too dark. This house had been a home then. Sarah, his wife, and three bright youngsters had made it a home in those days. The children grew up—romped to bed one night and woke up the next morning grown. Jessie went out to a party against his persuasion—he refused to coerce—and caught cold. She never recovered. The War and the draft came along and swept the two boys off to sea. Zachary junior never came back, and his mother went—to find him. Russell—Rusty—returned unharmed, but not the same lad that had left—a swaggering, regardless, worldly-wise Rusty, who boasted acquaintance with Hell and the Devil, but laughed at God and religion.

The old preacher prayed for two years about it and finally reached a decision. There had been no quarrel, no unpleasant preface, no stern denunciation. The father had met his son at breakfast one morning—Rusty had been out all night—and had spoken quietly and earnestly.

"Son, you don't seem to like it here. You squirm under my eye—you chafe. You even laugh at my faith. Why not be free? You're twenty-three. Leave. Find God for yourself; and when you have found Him, come back."

It had cost something, that experiment; it had taken the faith of Abraham. All the old man's fleeing hopes had sought refuge in this boy.

Zachary Pride entered his house. The door closed behind him—a hollow sound. He had let the two upper floors to a couple who'd agreed to cook and clean for him. He was a roomer and boarder in his own home.

Yet never a moment did he doubt that Rusty would sometime return. He simply could not believe that his life would be stripped of this last little sweetness. All that made the place bearable to him was the thought of the boy's coming back, living here, free of that devil-born restlessness. He would marry some fine girl, perhaps; the house would again be a home. Some girl like Roma Lee, clear-eyed and impulsively honest.

It was Roma's aunt and uncle who rented the upper floors of the house, and with them Roma spent much of her time. She always asked about Rusty. Where was he? When would he be back? Nor was she merely being polite. Roma's questions were as genuine now as they had been a dozen years ago when she had asked Daddy Pride in Sunday-school if there really was a special nigger Heaven. She still called him "Daddy Pride," even.

He smiled and wished that it might really be Roma whom his son would choose. And after a while he knelt by his bed and prayed the prayer he'd prayed every night for a year:

"Reveal Thyself unto my boy, and in Thine own time bring him again to me; and let him be an example unto many that grope as the blind in darkness."

And at the moment of his prayer one man was threatening another with destruction for selling his brother bad gin; another was rushing to a pick-pocket gang to herald a profit-sharing rough-house; and the suppliant's own son was upsetting an adversary by implanting both feet in his chest.

*    *    *

Harlem knows no dance-hall more elegant than the New Casino, which has looked upon crowds of every kind in their moments of greatest pretension. The Barbers' Ball, the Jumpsteady Club, the Dirty Dozen, the Backbiters—all hold forth in the New Casino two or three times a year. But, although this place is situated in the dictydom west of Seventh Avenue, only once has it been honored by the presence of the So-and-So Club, and the memory of what happened then is this lofty society's cup. Never will the So-and-So's Supper Dansant take place again in the Casino.

Had you arrived a half-hour before midnight, you could not have believed possible the storm that later broke. A magnificent liveried attendant stood at the curb in front of the door. Above him an elongated canopy extended from the sidewalk edge to the entrance. With utmost deference the attendant opened door after door of cab or limousine and out stepped handsome, dark-skinned blades, sharply arrayed in black and white, turning to hand down gorgeous women in bright-colored wraps or fur cloaks. From a brilliant mirror-walled foyer they ascended lateral stairways, railed with palms. Above they found a smaller lobby with a coat-checking room on either side. Wraps were left here, ladies' on one side, gentlemen's on the other; company then rejoined, and arm in arm stepped into the spacious ballroom.

And gasped. Only the So-and-So's could transform the Casino like this. There were no walls, but palisades of palms and banks of flowers. One guest braved his wife's glares to remark that it was the biggest funeral he'd ever seen; and later that night added grimly, "I told you so." There was no orchestra, but matchless music from somewhere behind the palms. There were no benches, but cushions thrown carelessly here and there on the plant tubs and a casual group of easy chairs in the center amid tubbed orange-trees. Above all, there was no glaring light; just a floor lamp or two in the central group and a shadowy glow from amid the palms, soft as the saxophone crooning the drowsy melody of a waltz. It was indeed to be a night of nights; the punch was full of promise; and the dancers' spirits and heads and feet grew rapidly light together.

In the lobby, near the ballroom door, sat members of the So-and-So dance committee, checking off names of invited guests on a list as they arrived. It was nearly midnight when three rather unsteady lads presented themselves to the committee—a tall, lanky yellow boy whose features were spattered with brown freckles as if he'd been sprayed with hot grease; a big-shouldered black fellow with a broad, flat face and a protrusive underlip; and a short, stocky, noisy, belligerent young man who unanimously elected himself spokesman. Each of the three had in him six drinks and an equal number of devils. They had decided that the rent party which they'd been attending considerably cramped their style. They had further concluded that the So-and-So's stomp-down would be just about their speed. They had plenty of jack for their admission, they thought, and a decided taste for shimmying with sweet yaller gals. And so they walked past the liveried one at the entrance, stumbled upstairs and approached what appeared to be ticket-sellers, asking the price of admission.

But the So-and-So's represented an aristocracy too young to be very generous, and the strangers' questions, with their absence of evening dress, betrayed them at once as Philistines.

"Private dance," said the chairman shortly.

This should have been sufficient dismissal; but a real hard Negro around six drinks. . . .

"Listen, mistuh. Is anybody ast you what kind o' dance dis is?"

"You can't come in without an invitation."

The spokesman, unheeding, turned to his companions. "Did I ast him what kind o' dance dis was?"

"We don't care what kind o' dance hit is."

Reassured, the spokesman turned back. I ain't ast you what kind o' dance dis was, mistuh. I *know* what kind o' dance *dis* is. Dis is a dickty dance, dis is. Rich uppity boogies. Plenty bucks. Doctors, lawyers and undertakers, what I mean, with nothin' but sweet an' pretty pinks. When dey leave hyeh dey go to a cabaret and stay all night. Big-time niggers, see? Well, we're big-time niggers, too. Me, I'm a doctor myself, see? An' my boy hyeh, he's a lawyer, he is. An' my other boy theh, he's a undertaker. And what we want to know ain't what kind o' dance dis is. What we want to know is how much does we put up to git in."

Another member of the committee interceded. "You'll have to go, boys. We don't sell tickets."

The intruder turned red eyes to this new opponent, looking him up and down. "Listen, mistuh. Is anybody ast you anything? Is dey? Huh? An' nobody talkin' to you. I'm talkin' to my doctor friend hyeh. I know dis nigger, I do. Him an' I used to hop bells in de same hotel, we did. Now he doan know me. Dass all right, too. I ain' astin' im fo' nothin' but info'mation. He doan need yo' help. He kin talk, dumb as he is. He ain' been a dicty all his life."

The doctor began to realize why it would have been better to sacrifice appearances and have policemen at the door. He tried a bluff. "Call that officer inside there, Jim," he said.

"Yea, call 'im," growled the trespasser. "Tell 'im to bring his dice an' licker wid' 'im, too."

The chairman was desperate. "We've told you we aren't selling tickets!"

The contentious one grew calm, seeing the subject in a possible new light. "You doan sell no tickets!"

"No!"

"Nobody doan pay to go in?"

"No!"

"Well, ain't dat nice? Le's go, you niggers. Hit's free!"

"Free?"

"No 'tain't."

"Sho, 'tis. Didn' y' jess hyeh' im say 'twas free?"

The trio started for the door. The second committeeman caught the leader by the arm. The leader halted.

"Go on in," urged his companions. "What you stop fuh?"

"Mistuh, listen," arbitrated the intercepted one. "Doan you go gittin' so bran'-new, see? You's second-hand, an' you has been worn, an' you sho kin be worn ag'in."

"That way out," said the So-and-So, giving the other a little shove.

"Mistuh, I ain't lookin' f' no trouble. Bud de las' man whut put his hand on my arm like dat is got his haid bound up like a Hindu."

So saying, the invader attempted to jostle past, but his obstacle stood firm. Followed a bit of a scuffle, the sharp crack of a blow to the face, and promptly a barroom battle was under way. The intruders were in that state of half-anesthesia where senses are dulled but actions are violent. Blows meant nothing to them, and, even sober, they would have enjoyed a fracas. The two committeemen were soon disposed of.

Guests near the door rushed to their aid, demanding explanations. The answers were hard fists that hurt, while furious attempts at self-defense served merely to spread the commotion. Dickties dance well but fight poorly. Within three minutes men were engaged in the rumpus who had no idea why they were fighting nor whom they were supposed to strike, and who even if they had, would not have known in the least how to make their blows tell.

The rough-looking lad in charge of the men's coat-room rushed out and down the stairs.

"Riot up yonder," he breathed to the doorman. "Stay put. I'll git d' cops quick."

And the dressed-up doorman, who had no thirst for battle, stayed very decidedly put, although he wondered mistily why the checker had not sped toward the police-station instead of the Club.

*   *   *

By a small, velvet-hung, unobtrusive doorway, the ladies' dressing-room was directly accessible to the ballroom; and, since the scantiest attire requires yet much attention, the traffic through this doorway was not inconsiderable. There were mirrors about this dressing-room, and comfortable wicker settees; there was a thick, soft carpet on the floor, and the arrangement was such that a second inside door joined this room with the ladies' coat-room, making it unnecessary for one to go out into the lobby to get one's wraps.

Roma Lee, a fresh little creature of rose and tan, bright with the thrill of her first big party, had slipped into this dressing-room to resurvey herself in a mirror. Nothing could have been more reassuring than what she saw—glossy black bob quite innocent of irons, dark eyes dancing, white teeth flashing, slim waist stressed by a filmy frock that gathered and flared at the hips.

Sally Epps, a scrawny, speckled, cream-colored girl with long skinny arms, unbelievably thin legs and enormous feet, who thoroughly enjoyed being colored and habitually wallowed in Harlemisms, came limping and grunting into the room behind Roma and kicked off both slippers.

"Great head o' the church, but them things burn! After this I'm wearin' nothin' but galoshes. Oh, baby, what a carpet! Spread out feet, and radiate. Ladies, here's your original red-hot mama—right from ankles down. Bet this pair o' feet'd make a pan o' water bubble."

"They'd make a *tub* of water bubble, dear," smiled an observer, whose companion sniffed agreement.

Sally grinned and flopped into a chair as the disapproving pair went out, leaving her and Roma alone.

"Say, sweet and pretty, don't believe all that mirror tells you. Mirrors are the smoothest liars on earth. Fact is, you've got bad hair and a nose that was melted and thrown at you, and your knees are perfect strangers; while I, if you only notice, have the form of Venus de Nigro and a strawberry-shortcake complexion."

Roma came and sat on the arm of her friend's chair. "Sally, you're horribly colored and an awful goose."

"Hold on, flapper! Don't tell me I got web-feet."

"Hush and listen. Who do you think I saw today?"

"Adam and Eve fightin' over a fig-leaf."

"Rusty."

"Rusty Pride?"

"Rusty Pride."

"Where's that no-'count tramp been?"

"He isn't a tramp. He's been running on the railroad to Canada all this time."

"Bootleggin', I bet. If there ever was a shine that was jail-house bound—"

"Sally!"

Sally stopped and stared. Stared from unbelief to wonder and from wonder to conviction.

"Romie, how long've you been likin' that triflin' scamp?"

"Liking him? Me? Don't be a nut. It was on Daddy Pride's account. You know Aunt Min sort of takes care of Daddy Pride since she rented most of his house. He's been worrying lately—wants Rusty home again. He's such a darling old man—I hate to see him so unhappy. I 'd heard some of the boys say Rusty hung out around that Club place down on Lenox Avenue. So today I walked down that way to see if I could see him. Just curiosity. And I did."

"You did? And what of it?"

"That's all. I just saw him. It fell rather flat. I spoke to him, tried to show him I was glad to see him and all. Didn't seem to brighten him much. He looked as though he needed somebody to take care of him."

"How'd you like to have the job?"

"Oh, Sally, I hate to see him look like that!" Roma caught herself up and added, "I hate to see anybody look like that."

"Anybody. Of course. Well, ain't this sumpin' to print in the papers?"

"What do you mean?"

"I mean, baby, wasn't it just too sweet of you to think so much of the Rev'm Daddy Pride? That's what I mean. He'll certainly appreciate it. Such a darling old man! Well, can y' imagine this?"

Sally's ironic laugh halted at the sudden shrill yell of a woman. Both girls stopped to listen. The dance-music had broken off, and in its place came strange, startling sounds; first muffled, shuffling, breathing noises, swelling steadily into a crescendo more and more unmistakably evil; then cracks, thumps, claps, thuds against a continuous laborious stridor, growing by seconds, broken by half-oaths and shouts.

Sally jumped up and ran to the door that led to the dancing floor, drew the velvet draperies aside. "Great Gordon gin, it's a fight, Romie! If it ain't, I'm a Chinaman. Look!"

Well might they look. A crowd mobbed about the main doorway; people at the edges craning their necks; people rushing up from the far corners of the room; signs of a violent scramble at the entrance; certainty of a clamorous battle beyond it; people watching as the focus spread, now falling back from the central turbulence, now closing in anew.

Sally turned suddenly, made a dive for her discarded slippers. The tumult grew. "Romie, you wearin' your fur coat? Me too. We got to get 'em. Hear that fool woman holler somebody was stealin' coats? In two minutes this room'll be a bargain-counter."

They were across the carpet and at the inner door of the coat-room, calling to the girl in charge. There was no girl in charge. Without waiting to determine her whereabouts, Sally got the lower movable half of the door open and crawled under the shelf over which wraps were normally delivered. Roma followed.

"Did you see where they put yours when they took it? Mine's—here it is! Sweet three hundred berries, come to your mama. Find it? Grab it—here come the harpies!"

The "harpies" had indeed come, had come in a drove: girls who had saved for two years to buy seal wraps; wives who had wheedled for months to get a caracal like Mrs. Jones'; women who had undertaken payment for their Persian lambs by instalments and feared now to lose the entire bargain—all came rushing at once into the dressing-room, each elbowing, shouldering her way through the rest, attempting to get to the racks of cloaks. The inner door, its lower half already swinging open, presented no barrier at all; they swarmed under it, over it, through it, in among the rows of coats, which dangled untouched on their hangers; they grabbed and jerked and discarded and chattered; they quarreled and tussled and wept.

The outer door of the coat-room, through which guests' wraps were received on arrival, opened into the lobby, and so commanded the scene of the original scrimmage. Sally and Roma had by now reached this outer door, just beyond which riot raged. They found themselves thus between fighting, cursing men on one hand and hysterical women on the other; danger of physical injury beyond the door, scarcely less danger this side of it.

Sally kept saying, "Can you imagine this?" Roma was scared and silent. Ere they could decide either to stay or flee, a woman came rushing toward them.

Rudolph Fisher

"That's my coat!" she cried, seizing Sally's wrap and giving it a tug. "That's my coat! Take it off!"

"It won't be nobody's coat in a minute," observed Sally. "Get away. Shoo! Go chase yourself."

"Mine, I say! I'd know it in a million!"

"Lady, it'll be your funeral if you tear it." But the frantic claimant fell to yanking and dragging, and Sally became very busy defending not only her wrap but herself.

Another woman had already spied Roma and was coming toward her with speed. One look and Roma made up her uncertain mind, ducked quickly under the door-shelf and out into the lobby.

She was now on the rim of the major fracas, which showed no sign of abating. She did not know, of course, that two dozen of those engaged were deliberately keeping up the tumult, slipping their hands into dress-suit pockets at every opportunity. She edged along the wall toward the head of the stairs, watching them wrestle, hardly knowing what she herself was doing. Then somewhere in the chaos of features she caught sight of Rusty Pride's face. He was grinning as he grasped and held a dickty in a close embrace. The dickty wriggled and twisted and bucked; Rusty rode him as a buster rides a broncho, just held on and squeezed and grinned. Then Roma, staring, saw something shoot up into the air over Rusty—a chair in the hands of another dickty, poised to crash down on Rusty's head; and Roma screamed at the top of her lungs:

"Duck—Rusty—duck!"

Then she shut her eyes and leaned back against the wall.

*       *       *

The blank moment passed. She still carried her coat in her arms, and she realized of a sudden that some one had taken hold of it. When she saw the face of the creature that had done so she almost laughed with fright. All this was a nightmare, and this creature was beyond doubt an ogre. It was a squat, yellow, flat face, leeringly toothsome, an incredible false-face that spoke.

"Papa'll take charge o' this little fur-piece, sweetie. Turn it loose—and hold on to the holler." The yellow face developed arms which snatched the fur away from her; developed a body and legs which turned and made off toward the stairs. But in no time, unbelievingly, Roma saw the same body backing toward her, as though its departure had been a movie scene, which was now being run backwards. The uproar writhed about her like vapor, but out of the mist came one clear thing—Rusty grappling with the ogre, ogre's arms all clogged with fur, Rusty pressing the ogre back toward the place where he'd snatched the coat. The coat dropped—was kicked toward her.

Fire by Night                                                                    129

She stooped, caught it up. As she did so the ogre went sprawling into the nearest tangle of legs and feet, and Rusty himself was beside her, urging her out.

They almost fell down the stairs, Rusty explaining in staccato: "Stud Samson—rat—Club—thinks—I wanted—coat—" And Roma gathered between gasps that already the ogre and Rusty had been enemies; that they had fought at some time before, when Rusty had intensified the enmity by winning; that this last encounter must be Stud's cup, since, so far as he could see, Rusty's sole motive had been to deprive him of his spoil. Theft among thieves is unpardonable.

"Got to run—he'll be right on our heels—not a cop in sight—totes a gun, too—half-drunk and blood-mad—"

They struck sharp air, turned eastward toward the lights of Seventh avenue. Not till they broke into its brightness and crossed did Rusty realize his thoughtlessness.

"Good night!" he groaned. "Right in the light. He's seen us—he's seen us sure." Holding her arm he thrust her on, into the relative darkness of Harlem's middle strip. "Why the devil did I come this way? Why the devil—"

They were now just beyond Seventh Avenue, going toward Lenox along one of the numbered side streets. Rusty himself did not know what refuge he was seeking. His folly in crossing the avenue, his fear for Roma had paralyzed every mental resource. "I'm panicky," he thought. He looked ahead—the Club was that way, offering certainly no hopes. Stud Samson owned half the Club. He looked behind, into the dimness beyond the Avenue, whence they had come. At that moment he saw a flash and heard a report like a five-ton truck, back-firing. He stopped, caught Roma about the waist, turned, propelled her up the stairs of the nearest house, into its glass-doored vestibule.

They shrank back into the darkest corner.

"What—was—was he shooting?"

"Darned if I know. May've been cops. Why the devil I came this way—Maybe he saw your gray fur—he'd plug me, the fool. Look, you get out and haul it—No, he'd think I was with you and plug anyhow. What the devil made me come this way? I wouldn't care about myself if I could only get you to some safe place. What the devil—oh, Lord!"

"Rusty—I couldn't leave you now. He might—"

There was a long moment, a moment of heavy breathing, a moment in which they could imagine their pursuer coming nearer, red-minded, gin-reckless, running perhaps from one stoop to the next, ready to "plug" in the general direction of a gray fur coat, should he see one.

Then came from somewhere out in the dark a faint and far-away shriek. It drew closer, grew louder, till they recognized the penetrating scream, then the clangor and roar of headlong fire-engines.

"Firemen?" wondered Rusty. "Ought to be cops there by now. No. It's the other way. It's Lenox Avenue."

But it was not the noise of the engines alone that grew sharper now in consciousness. Something else was happening, something far more subtle and portentous, something felt, still uncomprehended, that held them expectant, like daybreak. Then from where they hid in the vestibule they saw that the sky, as much as they could see of it, was actually growing brighter; first a faint, flickering yellow, then successive waves of orange, pursuing each other like wind-flaws; and presently a steady, flame-red glow whose heat they could almost sense through the cold. And when they looked at each other they saw that their own faces faintly reflected the glow.

"Good Lord!" breathed Rusty. "'Tisn't half a mile away. If Stud comes past now, we're good-bygoners, that's all." And Roma heard him whisper over and over, "Lord, Lord," as if he were praying; nor did his eyes search the street, as they had searched, but were fixed on the vivid sky.

Suddenly something near caught Roma's eye. At first she shrank in alarm, then cried with relief: "Rusty—Rusty—it's all right now! He ran right past—that man—I saw him. He thinks it's his Club that's afire."

But Rusty seemed to have forgotten Stud Samson. He was still gazing into the sky; and now live wonder had recast his features and he was mumbling meaningless words:

"Pizen gin—doubled up 'n' died—you ain't been paid fo' it yit. . . ."

"Rusty—what are you saying?"

"Look, Romie!"

There was in his whisper discovery and awe, and he spoke without turning his head.

She pressed forward so that she, too, could see what held him so wholly absorbed. Together they stared. So might the children of Israel have stared upon the illumined tabernacle; so might Elijah have looked upon the approaching chariot of fire. High above the houses, black against the flame, a cross stood out in silhouette against the kindled sky; bold, untroubled, clear-cut, still—serenely terrible. . . .

The door of the house in whose entrance they had hidden grew bright and opened behind them. A kindly warmth touched their cold cheeks. Surprised, they turned, then gaped at each other in utmost, blankest amazement.

Rusty's father stood smiling upon them as if he had known they were coming.

# BLADES OF STEEL

I

Negro Harlem's three broad highways form the letter H, Lenox and Seventh Avenues running parallel northward, united a little above their midpoints by east-and-west 135th Street.

Lenox Avenue is for the most part the boulevard of the unperfumed; "rats" they are often termed. Here, during certain hours, there is nothing unusual in the flashing of knives, the quick succession of pistol shots, the scream of a police-whistle or a woman.

But Seventh Avenue is the promenade of high-toned dickties and strivers. It breathes a superior atmosphere, sings superior songs, laughs a superior laugh. Even were there no people, the difference would be clear: the middle of Lenox Avenue is adorned by street-car tracks, the middle of Seventh Avenue by parking [probably refers to the strip of turf with, possibly, trees in the middle of the street. Ed.].

These two highways, frontiers of the opposed extreme of dark-skinned social life, are separated by an intermediate any-man's land, across which they communicate chiefly by way of 135th Street. Accordingly 135th Street is the heart and soul of black Harlem; it is common ground, the natural scene of unusual contacts, a region that disregards class. It neutralizes, equilibrates, binds, rescues union out of diversity.

In a fraction of a mile of 135th Street there occurs every institution necessary to civilization from a Carnegie Library opposite a public school at one point to a police station beside an undertaker's parlor at another. But one institution outnumbers all others, an institution which, like the street itself, represents common ground: the barbershop overwhelmingly predominates.

Naturally on the day of the Barber's Annual Ball this institution clipped off among other things several working hours. The barbers had their own necks to trim, their own knots to conquer, their own jowls to shave and massage.

The inevitable last-minute rush of prospective dancers, eager for eleventh-hour primping, would have kept the hosts themselves from appearing at the dance-hall, in their best, on time. Hence the association had agreed that every member's door be closed and locked today at four.

Shortly before that hour in one of 135th Street's "tonsorial parlors," the head barber, for whom a half dozen men were waiting, dismissed a patron and called "Next!" Already Eight-Ball Eddy Boyd, whose turn it was, had removed coat and collar and started toward the vacated chair.

"Make it boyish, Pop," he grinned to the fat and genial proprietor. "And long as you trimmin' me, lemme have two tickets for the stom-down tonight."

Pop Overton smiled goldenly and assumed the grand manner. "You means to grace our function wid yo' attendance?"

The other's assent was typical Harlemese:

"I don't mean to attend yo' function with my grace."

As Eight-Ball put one foot on the foot-rest of the chair, someone pulled him back ungently.

"My turn, big shorty."

Eight-Ball turned, recognized Dirty Cozzens, an enemy of several days' standing.

"My turn," disagreed he evenly.

"Yo' mistake," Dirty corrected shortly, and moved to brush the smaller man aside.

The move was unsuccessful. The smaller man exhibited something of the stability of a fire-plug which one attempts to boot off the sidewalk. Dirty had bumped him without anticipating such firm footing, and now himself recoiled, careening off toward the mirrored wall with its implement-laden ledge. There was a little giggling jingle of instruments as his elbow struck this ledge. Then there was silence. Of the two barbers, one stopped pushing his clippers, but left them resting against the customer's neck while he gaped; the other halted, his razor poised, his thumb in one corner of his patron's mouth. Those who sat waiting dropped their papers, their conversation, and their lower jaws. Everybody stared. Everybody knew Dirty Cozzens.

Eight-Ball stood pat, as if awaiting an apology for the other's rudeness. Dirty also remained where he had landed, his elbow still amid the paraphernalia on the ledge, his eyes glaring, as if to let everyone see how he had been wronged.

The two made a striking contrast. Dirty Cozzens was a peculiar genetic jest. Heredity had managed to remove his rightful share of pigment even from his hair, which was pale buff. His eyes were gray, their lids rimmed red. His complexion had won him his nickname, "Dirty Yaller," of which "Dirty," was the familiar abbreviation. In every other particular his African ancestry had been preserved and accentuated. The buff hair was woolly, the nose flat with wide nostrils, the mouth big, bordered by so-called liver-lips, unbelievably thick. Within the shadow of a black skin, even, Dirty would have been a caricature; with the complexion that he actually had he was a cartoon, a malicious cartoon without humor.

So had heredity handed him over to environment, and environment had done its damnedest; had put sly cunning into the eyes, had distorted the lips into a constant sneer, had set the head at a truculent forward thrust on the large, lank body. With its present evil face, his was a head that might well have adorned the scepter of Satan.

His opponent was his antithesis. Eight-Ball had been nicknamed after that pool-ball which is black, and his skin was as dark as it is possible for skin to be, smooth and clean as an infant's. The close-cut hair hugged the scalp evenly, the bright black eyes were alive with quick understanding, the nose was broad but sharp-ridged, with sensitive nostrils, the lips thin and firm above a courageous chin. He was beautifully small, neither heavy nor slight, of proud erect bearing, perfect poise, and a silhouette-like clean-cutness.

In the silence, Dirty's fingers reaching along the marble ledge found and caressed a barber's tool; an instrument which is the subject of many a jest but whose actual use involves no element of humor; a weapon which is as obsolete as a blunderbuss, even among those whose special heritage it is commonly supposed to be—as obsolete and as damaging. Dirty, skilled in the wielding of steel, would not have considered this instrument in a set encounter, but the devil put the thing now in his hand. He decided it would be entertaining to run his enemy out of the shop.

Pop Overton saw the movement, and it lifted his out of his daze. He said: "Aimin' to shave yo'self, Dirty?"

"None yo' dam' business," snapped Dirty, still eyeing Eight-Ball.

"No," said Pop. "'Tain't none my business. But hit's my razor."

Dirty drew himself together, but not erect,—"You seen what he done?"—moved then with slow menace across the distance between himself and Eight-Ball. "You seen it, didn' y'?"

"Now, listen, big boy. Don't you go startin' nothin' in my shop, you hear?"

"I ain't startin' nothin'. I'm finishin' sump'm. Dis started a week ago. Hot nigger, dis black boy, but I'm goan turn his damper down."

Eight-Ball spoke: "Don't burn yo' fingers."

Dirty advanced another step, knees bent, one hand behind him. Had Eight-Ball retreated a single foot, Dirty would have tossed the razor aside with a contemptuous laugh; would have made a fly crack about fast-black, guaranteed not to run; would have swaggered out, proudly acknowledging that he had picked the quarrel. But Eight-Ball had not retreated. Eight-Ball had stood still and looked at him, had even taunted him: "Don't burn yo' fingers"; had watched him approach to arm's length without budging. Ought to take one swipe at him just to scare him good. Ought to make him jump anyhow—

Whatever might have happened didn't. Instead of the expected swift sweep of an arm Dirty's next movement was a quick furtive bending of his elbow to slip the armed hand into his coat pocket; such a movement as might have greeted the entrance of an officer of the law.

As a flame flares just before it goes out, so the tension heightened, then dropped, when eyes discovered that the figure which had darkened the door was only that of a girl. She was a striking girl, however, who at once took the center of the stage.

"Whew-ee!" she breathed. "Just made it. Hi, Pop. Hello, Eighty. One minute to four! And the head barber waitin' for me! Some service—I scream—some service." Wherewith she clambered into the vacant chair and effervesced directions.

The waiting customers first ogled, then guffawed. It struck them as uproarious that two men should appear to be on the point of bloodshed over a mere turn and neither of them get it. But the girl seemed quite oblivious.

Eight-Ball greeted her: "Hello, Effie,"—grinned, and returned to his seat. Dirty shuffled to the wall opposite the mirrors, got his hat and went toward the door. As he passed the head barber's chair he paused and spoke to the girl:

"It was my turn, Miss Effie—but you kin have it." He smiled so that his thick lips broadened against his teeth, and he touched his hat and went out.

His departure released comment:

"Nice felluh!"

"Doggone! Sposin' he really got mad over sump'n!"

"He wasn't mad. He was jes' playin'."

"He better not play wi' *me* like dat."

"Take 'at thing out'n his hand and he'd run."

"Leave it *in* his hand and *you'd* run."

Then, to everyone's astonishment, before Pop Overton had assembled the proper implements, the girl jumped down from the chair, scattering stealthy glances which had been creeping toward the crimson garters just below her crossed knees.

"Whose turn was it?" she asked Pop.

"Eighty's."

"Thought so. Come on, Eighty. I got mine this morning."

"What's the idea?" wondered Eight-Ball.

"Wasn't it a fight?"

"Pretty near. How'd you know?"

"Anything wrong with these?"

A purely rhetorical question. There was certainly nothing wrong with Effie Wright's eyes—nor with her hair, nor with that rare, almost luminous dark complexion called "sealskin brown." One might complain that she was altogether too capable of taking care of herself, or that she was much too absorbed in Eight-Ball. Beyond that no sane judgment criticized.

Effie ran a beauty-parlor directly across the street, and it was to this that she now referred.

"I was lookin' out the window over there. Saw you drive up in your boss's straight-eight. Your friend was standin' in front of the saloon—he saw you too, so he come in behind you. Pop's window's got too much advertisin' in it to see through, so I come on over. Seem like I spoiled the party."

"Ain't this sump'n?" Eight-Ball asked the world.

"Angels rush in when fools is almost dead," was Pop's proverb.

"Well, since you won't open a keg o' bay rum, I guess I'll breeze.—Say, Pop, got an extra safety razor blade?—Yes.—Huh?—Oh, a customer gimme a pair o' pumps to wear to the shin-dig tonight, and I got to whittle off here and there till I can get 'em on. Cheatin' the foot-doctor.—A single-edged blade, if you got it, Pop. Double-edged one cuts y' fingers before it cuts anything else.—Thanks. Shall I lock the door on my way out?—Stop by before you haul it, Eighty."

She was gone in a flurry of words.

"Can y' beat that, Pop?" Eight-Ball laughed.

"They ain't but two like her and she's both of 'em," admitted Pop. "But what's that Cozzens boy on you for?"

"We had a little argument in a dark-john game a while back."

"Yea? Well, watch 'im, boy. Bad boogy what knows he's bad. And don't think he won't cut. He will. Thass th' onliest kind o' fightin' he knows, and he sho knows it. They's nineteen niggers 'round Harlem now totin' cuts he gave 'em. They through pullin' knives too, what I mean."

"He's that good, huh?"

"He's that bad. Served time fo' it, but he don't give a damn. Trouble is, ain't nobody never carved *him*. Somebody ought to write shorthand on his face. That'd cure him.

"Yes? Whyn't you shave him sometime, Pop?"

"Mine's accidental. Somebody ought to carve him artistically."

"Well," Eight-Ball considered thoughtfully, "maybe somebody will."

II

The Barbers' Ball does not pretend to be a dicty affair. It is announced, not by engraved cards through the mails, but by large printed placards in barbershop windows. One is admitted, not by presenting a card of invitation, but by presenting a dollar bill in exchange for a ticket. It is a come-one, come-all occasion, where aspiring local politicians are likely to mount the platform between dances and make announcements and bow while influential bootleggers cheer. It was quite fitting, therefore, that this fête of, for, and in spite of the people should take place on 135th Street—this year in a second-floor dance-hall just east of Lenox Avenue.

"Well, hush my mouth!" exclaimed Eight-Ball as he and Effie entered somewhat before midnight.

"Do tell!" agreed she.

For there were decorations. Nothing subdued and elegant like the So-and-So's dance. Nothing "fly," like the Dirty Dozen's. Just color in dazzling quantity, presented through the inexpensive medium of crêpe paper—scarlet, orange, brilliant green, embracing the lights, entwining the pillars, concealing the windows, transforming the orchestral platform into a float.

The orchestra also made no pretenses. It was a so-called "low-down" orchestra and it specialized in what are known as shouts. Under the influence of this leisurely rhythm, steady, obsessing, untiring, you gradually forget all else. You can't make a misstep, you can't get uncomfortably warm, you can't grow weary—you simply fall more and more completely into the insistently joyous spirit of the thing until you are laughing and humming aloud like everyone else. You get happy in spite of yourself. This is the inevitable effect of shouts, to which the orchestra tonight largely confined its efforts.

The newcomers joined the gay, noisy dancers, finding their way not too swiftly around the crowded floor. Here someone advised them to "Get off that dime!" and there someone else suggested that they "Shake that thing!"

But the shout to which Eight-Ball and his girl inadvertently kept time had not yet saturated their emotions, and in spite of it they discussed less happy concerns.

"I been so mad I ain't had no dinner," said Eight-Ball.

"'Bout what?"

"Notice I didn't bring the car tonight?"

"Yes. Boss usin' it?"

"No.—Know when I left your place this afternoon, after you showed me that trick?"

"Yes."

"Notice anything wrong with the car when I drove off?"

"Nope. Too busy watchin' the driver."

"I went about half a block and felt somethin' wrong. Pulled up and got out to look. Two flat tires."

"No!"

"Uh-huh. Front and back on the side away from the sidewalk."

"They was O.K. when you parked?"

"Brand new."

"Blow-outs? Slow leaks?"

"No. Cuts."

"What are you ravin' about?"

"Both tires had a six-inch gash in 'em, made with a knife—"

"What!"

"Or a razor."

Effie stopped dancing. "The yellow son-of-a-baboon!"

"Everybody says they ain't nothin' he can't do with a knife. Looks like they ain't nothin' he *won't* do."

The shout, the rhythmically jostling crowd, impelled them back into step.

"Eighty, you ought to half kill 'im. Of all the low, mean, gutter-rat tricks— you ought to lay 'im up f' a year."

"How you know I can?" he grinned.

"Can't y'?"

"I can't prove nothin' on him. Who seen him do it?"

"Nobody didn't have to see him. You know he did it."

"Nope. I can wait. He's sore. He'll keep on messin' around. Thinks he can't be had."

"He can be had all right. All I'm 'fraid of is somebody else'll have 'im first. Everybody that knows that guy hates 'im and most of 'em's scared to boot. Whoever whittles 'im down will be a hero."

As the jazz relented, the object of her anger took form out of the crowd and approached.

"Evenin', Miss Effie," said he, ignoring Eight-Ball. "Been lookin' f' you. I give you my turn in d' barber-shop today. How 'bout givin' me mine now?"

Effie looked through him at the decorations surrounding a post. As if she and Eight-Ball had been discussing the colors, she commented:

"That's one color I'm glad they forgot—I can't stand anything yellow."

Dirty turned garnet; but before his chagrin became active resentment, the music returned with a crash. Eight-Ball and Effie moved on past him, their anger partially appeased by knowing that Effie's tongue had cut like steel.

And now the shout more easily took hold on them, hammering them inexorably into its own mould. The increasing jam of people pressed them more closely into each other's arms. The husky mellowness of soft-throated saxophones against the trumpet's urge, the caress of plaintive blues-melody against the thrill of strange disharmonies, the humor of capricious traps against the solidity of unfailing bass—to these contrasts the pair abandoned themselves. Harsh laughter, queer odors, the impact of the mob became nothing. They closed their eyes and danced.

They might have danced for an hour, only half aware of the jumble of faces about, of their own jests and laughter, of the occasional intervals of rest. Then something woke them, and they suddenly realized that it was at them that people nearby were laughing—that a little space cleared about them wherever they moved and people looked at them and laughed.

At first they were unconvinced and looked around them for something comic. Then Pop Overton appeared, smiling roundly.

"Thought monkey-backs was out o' style, son."

"What—?"

"Did you have yo' coat cut to order?"

Effie switched Eight-Ball around and gasped while onlookers frankly smiled. A triangle of white shirt-back, its apex between Eight-Ball's shoulder blades, shone through a vertical vent in his coat, a vent twice as long as any designed by a tailor. In the crush and abandonment of the dance a single downward stroke of a keen-edged instrument, light enough not to be noticed, had divided the back of the garment in two as cleanly as if it had been ripped down midseam. The white of the shirt gleamed through like a malicious grin.

As Eight-Ball examined himself unsmilingly, Pop Overton sobered. "I thought it was torn accidental," he said. "Judas Priest—I bet that—! Say, Eighty, fo' Gawd's sake don't start nothin' here. We ain't never had a row—"

Eight-Ball and Effie, faces set, stood looking at each other in silence.

*     *     *

Dirty Cozzens stood in the shadow of the doorway beside that leading to the Barbers' Ball and in return for a generous drink unburdened himself to a buddy.

"It was in d' back room at Nappy's place. Dis lil spade turns a black-jack and winds d' deal, see? Well, he's a-riffin' d' cards and talkin' all d' same time, and he says, 'You guys jes' git ready to loosen up, 'cause I'm gonna deal all d' dark-johns home. I promis' my boss I wouldn' gamble no mo', but dis is jes' like pickin' up money in d' street.' Fly line, see? Den he starts dealin'. Well, I figgers dis guy's been so lucky and jes' turned a black-jack for d' deal, it's time fo' his luck to change. So I ups and stops his bank fo' twenty bucks, see? And I be dam' if he don't deal himself another black-jack—makin' two in a row!

"Well, he picks up all d' money befo' we can git our breath, see? Everybody laffs but me. I figgers day's a trick in it. Wouldn' you?"

"Sho I would. Two black-jacks in a row. Huh!"

"So I calls 'im crooked. But he jes' laffs and tells me to talk wid mo' money and less mouf. Natchelly dat makes me mad. A guy pulls a crooked deal and says sump'n like dat. Wouldn' you 'a' got mad?"

"Sho I would. Sho, man."

"So I tells him to pass back my twenty, long as he said he wasn't gamblin'. Den he stops dealin' and asts me is I big enough to take it. Tryin' to start sump'n all d' time, see?"

"Sho he was. Tryin' to start somp'n."

"So I says I'll either take it out his pile or off his hips, see? But when I starts for him, d' guys won't let me put it on him, see? Fact dey puts me out d' game.—So natchelly I jes' got to get me some o' dis lil spade's meat, dass all. I got to. He can't git away wid nuthin' like dat."

"Tryin' to git away wi' sump'n. Huh!"

"Sho he is. But I'll git 'im."

"What you aim to do?"

"I been primin' 'im fo' a fight."

"Dey claim he's pretty good wif' 'is hands."

"Ain't gonna be no hands. See dis?"

He withdrew from his right-hand coat pocket what appeared to be a quite harmless pocket-knife. He pressed it under his thumb and a steel blade leaped forth, quick as the tongue of a snake, a blade five inches long with a sweeping curve like a tiny scimitar. It was hollow-ground and honed to exquisite sharpness. A little catch fell into place at the junction of blade and handle, preventing the protruding blade from telescoping shut. The steel gleamed like eyes in the dark.

"Whew-ee!" admired the observer.

"He won't be d' fuss one I ever put it on. And here's how I figger. His boss is tight, see. Fired two guys already fo' roughin'. Dis boogy's got two new tires to account fo' now. And when his boss sees he been out, he'll find out it's 'count o' some gamblin' scrape and fire him too. Dass where I laff. See?"

"'Deed, boy, it's a shame fo' all dem brains to go to seed in yo' head. You could sell 'em and buy Europe, no stuff."

Then abruptly both shrank into deeper shadow as Eight-Ball and Effie came out.

## III

Diagonally across the street from the dance-hall stands Teddy's place, an establishment which stays open all night and draws all manner of men and women by the common appeal of good food. Oddly, it was once a mere bar-room lunch, and the mahogany bar-counter still serves the majority of Teddy's patrons, those who are content to sit upon stools and rub elbows with anybody. But there is now a back room also, with a side entrance available from the street. Here there are round-top tables beside the walls, and here parties with ladies may be more elegantly served. It is really a "high-class" grill-room, and its relation to the bar-counter lunch-room, the whole situated on democratic 135th Street, marks Teddy a man of considerable business acumen.

In one corner of the grill-room there is an excellent phonograph which plays a record repeatedly without changing. A song ends; you wait a few moments while the instrument is automatically re-wound and adjusted; and the songs begins again.

Tonight the long-distance record was Tessie Smith's "Lord Have Mercy Blues," a curious mingling of the secular and the religious, in the tragic refrain of which the unfortunate victim of trouble after trouble resorts to prayer. The record was not playing loudly, but such was the quality of Tessie Smith's voice that you heard its persistent, half-humorous pain through louder, clearer sounds.

Just now there were no such sounds, for the room was almost empty. The theatre crowd had departed; the crowd from the dance-halls had not yet arrived. Three or four couples sat about tête-à-tête, and near the phonograph Eight-Ball and Effie. Eight-Ball's back was turned toward the wall to hide the gape in his coat.

The phonograph wailed:

My man was comin' to me—said he'd
    Let me know by mail,
My man was comin' to me—said he'd let me know by mail—
The letter come and tole me—
They'd put my lovin' man in jail.

Grief, affliction, woe, told in a tone of most heartbroken despair; desolation with the merest tincture of humor—yet those who listened heard only the humor, considered only the jest.

Mercy—Lawd, have mercy!
    How come I always get bad news?
Mercy—Lawd, have mercy!
How come I always got the blues?

"Them's the blues I ought to be singin'," said Eight-Ball.

"You'll feel better after you eat," soothed the girl.

"I'll feel better after I get one good crack at that half-bleached buzzard."

"You ought to pick your comp'ny, Eighty."

Her tone surprised him. He encountered her look, mingled tenderness and reproach, and his eyes fell, ashamed.

"All right, kid. I'm off gamblin' for life.—But if that dude keeps messin' around—"

"Don't forget—he cuts."

"He better cut fast, then."

As if willing to oblige, Dirty Cozzens appeared at the door. He stood looking about, head hunched characteristically forward, right hand deep in his right coat pocket; calmly observed the relative desertion of the dining-room; then slowly advanced across the open space in the center of the floor.

Quickly Effie reached into her bag, withdrew something, put it into Eight-Ball's hand. The movement could have been seen, but the object passed was too small for the closest observation to make out. She might merely have been indulging in a heartening handclasp. Eight-Ball looked at her, first with puzzlement, then with understanding and resolution.

This time Dirty ignored Effie. This afternoon he might have had a chance with her; now he knew he had not. Then he had hidden his weapon from her; now he wanted her to see. That, too, had been largely bullying; this was serious challenge. Then he had sought but a momentary satisfaction; the satisfaction pending now would last, arising as it would out of the infliction of physical injury which could cost the victim his job. Let Effie share all of this—by all means let her see.

"Gimme my twenty bucks."

Eight-Ball looked up, allowed his gaze to pause here and there over his enemy's frame; then patted his left trouser's pocket. "It's right here.—You big enough to take it?"

"Listen, lamp-black. You been tryin' to git fly wid me ev'r since las' week, ain't y'? Put d' locks on me wid a crooked deal. Tried to start sump'n in d' barber shop today. Tole yo' woman to freeze me at d' dance tonight. Aw right. I'm warnin' y', see? I done warned you twice. I put my mark on yo' two shoes today and I put it on yo' coat tonight. D' nex' time I'm gonna put it on yo' black hide. See?"

Eight-Ball sat quite still, looking up at the lowering face.

"I tole y' I'd either take it out yo' pile or off yo' hips. Now put up or git up, you—"

Eight-Ball went up as if he'd been on a coil-spring, suddenly released. Dirty staggered backward but did not lose his footing.

Naturally none of Teddy's three waiters was in sight—it is unlikely that they would have interfered if they had been. Indeed, had they seen the initial blow of Eight-Ball—a familiar patron—they would have been satisfied to let him take care of himself. As for the other guests, they were interested but not alarmed. One does not yell or run at such a time unless a pistol is drawn.

Recovering balance, Dirty Cozzens withdrew his right hand from his pocket. It is difficult to believe possible the expression of evil that now contorted his features. That expression, however, was not more evil than the glint of the miniature scimitar, whose handle his right hand grasped.

He held the weapon in what pocket-knife fighters consider best form— three fingers firmly encircling the handle, but the index finger extended along the posterior, dull edge of the blade, tending to direct, brace,and conceal it. A sufficient length of the curved point extended beyond the end of the index finger to permit the infliction of a dangerously deep wound.

Eight-Ball stood ready, leaning a little forward, arms lax, both palms open—and empty.

Dirty's scowl concentrated on Eight-Ball's hands, and that he did not move at once was probably due to his astonishment at seeing no weapon in them. Any such astonishment, however, promptly gave way to quick appreciation of an advantage, and he did what a knifer rarely does. He rushed bringing his blade swiftly across and back in a criss-cross sweep before him.

Eight-Ball neither side-stepped nor attempted to block the motion. Either might have been disastrous. Instead, he ducked by suddenly squatting, and, touching the floor with his left hand for balance, kicked suddenly out with his right foot. The sharp crack of his heel against his antagonist's shin must have almost broken it. Certainly he gained time to jump up and seize Dirty's wrist before it could execute a second descending arc.

One less skilled than Eight-Ball would have found this useless. From such a wrist-hold the knife-hand is effectively liberated by simply inverting the weapon, which the fingers are still free to manipulate. The blade is thus brought back against its own wrist, and any fingers surrounding that wrist usually let go at once. Eighty had forestalled this contingency by a deft slipping of his grip upward over the fingers that held the knife handle. The hold that he now fastened upon those fingers was the same that had yanked two slashed balloon-tires off their rims some hours before, and it held Dirty's fingers, crushed together around their knife, as securely as a pipe-wrench holds a joint.

And now those who had watched this little fellow empty-handed win the advantage over an armed and bigger adversary saw a curious thing occur. Regularly in the ensuing scuffle Eight-Ball's right hand landed open-palmed against Dirty's face—landed again and again with a surrounding smack;

and for every time that it landed, presently there appeared a short red line, slowly widening into a crimson wheal.

Before long Dirty, rendered helpless now, and losing heart, raised his free hand to his face and as his fingers passed across it, the crimson wheals that they touched all ran together. He looked at the tips of those fingers, saw they were wet and red; his mouth fell open; the hand which Eight-Ball held went limp, the knife fell to the floor; and Dirty Cozzens quailed, as craven now as he'd been evil a moment before.

He began to stammer things, to deprecate, to plead; but Eight-Ball was deaf. The muscles of the latter's left arm seemed about to burst through their sleeve, while the artificial vent in the back of the coat ripped upward to the collar, as with one tremendous twist he brought the other man to his knees.

In that mad moment of triumph no one may say what disproportionate stroke of vengeance might not have brought on real tragedy. But with that strange and terrible open palm raised, a voice halted Eight-Ball's final blow:

Have mercy—Lawd, have mercy—

Tessie Smith's voice, wailing out of an extremity of despair.

Letter come and told me—
They'd put my lovin' man in jail—

The entire engagement had occupied only the few moments during which the phonograph automatically prepared itself to repeat. Now the words came as warning and plea:

Have mercy—Lawd, have mercy—

Eight-Ball released Dirty Cozzens, stepped back, picked up a crumpled paper napkin from the table where Effie still sat.

"Wipe y' face with this. Go on 'round to the hospital." He urged Dirty, whimpering, out of the side door.

Then he turned back toward Effie, stood over the table a moment, returned her rather proud smile. Two of the men who'd looked on came up. Said one:

"Buddy, show me that trick, will you?"

Eight-Ball extended his right hand, palm downward, and spread the fingers wide open. Freed from its vise-like hiding place between firmly adjacent fingers, something fell upon the porcelain table-top. It fell with a bright flash and a little clinking sound not unlike a quick laugh of surprise— the safety-razor blade which Effie had borrowed that afternoon from Pop Overton.

# COMMON METER

The Arcadia, on Harlem's Lenox Avenue, is "The World's Largest and Finest Ballroom—Admission Eighty-Five Cents." Jazz is its holy spirit, which moves it continuously from nine till two every night. Observe above the brilliant entrance this legend in white fire:

TWO—ORCHESTRAS—TWO

Below this in red:

FESS BAXTER'S FIREMEN

Alongside in blue:

BUS WILLIAMS' BLUE DEVILS

Still lower in gold:

HEAR THEM OUTPLAY EACH OTHER

So much outside. Inside, a blazing lobby, flanked by marble stairways. Upstairs, an enormous dance hall the length of a city block. Low ceilings blushing pink with rows of inverted dome-lights. A broad dancing area, bounded on three sides by a wide soft-carpeted promenade, on the fourth by an ample platform accommodating the two orchestras.

People. Flesh. A fly-thick jam of dancers on the floor, grimly jostling each other; a milling herd of thirsty-eyed boys, moving slowly, searchingly over the carpeted promenade; a congregation of languid girls, lounging in rows of easy chairs here and there, bodies and faces unconcerned, dark eyes furtively alert. A restless multitude of empty, romance-hungry lives.

Bus Williams' jolly round brown face beamed down on the crowd as he directed his popular hit—*She's Still My Baby*:

You take her out to walk
And give her baby-talk.

But talk or walk, walk or talk—
   She's still my baby!


But the cheese-colored countenance of Fessenden Baxter, his professional rival, who with his orchestra occupied the adjacent half of the platform, was totally oblivious to *She's Still My Baby.*

Baxter had just caught sight of a girl, and catching sight of girls was one of his special accomplishments. Unbelief, wonder, amazement registered in turn on his blunt, bright features. He passed a hand over his straightened brown hair and bent to Perry Parker, his trumpetist.

"P.P., do you see what I see, or is it only the gin?"

"Both of us had the gin," said P.P., "so both of us sees the same thing."

"Judas Priest! Look at that figure, boy!"

"Never was no good at figures," said P.P.

"I've got to get me an armful of that baby."

"Lay off, papa," advised P.P.

"What do you mean, lay off?"

"Lay off. You and your boy got enough to fight over already, ain't you?"

"My boy?"

"Your boy, Bus."

"You mean that's Bus Williams' folks?"

"No lie. Miss Jean Ambrose, lord. The newest hostess. Bus got her the job."

Fess Baxter's eyes followed the girl. "Oh, he got her the job, did he?—Well, I'm going to fix it so she won't need any job. Woman like that's got no business working anywhere."

"Gin," murmured P.P.

"Gin hell," said Baxter. "Gunpowder wouldn't make a mama look as good as that."

"Gunpowder wouldn't make you look so damn good, either."

"You hold the cat's tail," suggested Baxter.

"I'm tryin' to save yours," said P.P.

"Save your breath for that horn."

"Maybe," P.P. insisted, "she ain't so possible as she looks."

"Huh. They can all be taught."

"I've seen some that couldn't."

"Oh you have?—Well, P.P., my boy, remember, that's you."

\*    \*    \*

Beyond the brass rail that limited the rectangular dance area at one lateral extreme there were many small round tables and clusters of chairs. Bus

Williams and the youngest hostess occupied one of these tables while Fess Baxter's Firemen strutted their stuff.

Bus ignored the tall glass before him, apparently endeavoring to drain the girl's beauty with his eyes; a useless effort, since it lessened neither her loveliness nor his thirst. Indeed the more he looked the less able was he to stop looking. Oblivious, the girl was engrossed in the crowd. Her amber skin grew clearer and the roses imprisoned in it brighter as her merry black eyes danced over the jostling company.

"Think you'll like it?" he asked.

"Like it?" She was a child of Harlem and she spoke its language. "Boy, I'm having the time of my life. Imagine getting paid for this!"

"You ought to get a bonus for beauty."

"Nice time to think of that—after I'm hired."

"You look like a full course dinner—and I'm starved."

"Hold the personalities, papa."

"No stuff. Wish I could raise a loan on you. Baby—what a roll I'd tote."

"Thanks. Try that big farmer over there hootin' it with Sister Full-bosom. Boy, what a side-show they'd make!"

"Yea. But what I'm lookin' for is a leadin' lady."

"Yea? I got a picture of any lady leadin' you anywhere."

"You could, Jean."

"Be yourself, brother."

"I ain't bein' nobody else."

"Well, be somebody else, then."

"Remember the orphanage?"

"Time, papa. Stay out of my past."

"Sure—if you let me into your future."

"Speaking of the orphanage—?"

"You wouldn't know it now. They got new buildings all over the place."

"Somehow that fails to thrill me."

"You always were a knock-out, even in those days. You had the prettiest hair of any of the girls out there—and the sassiest hip-switch."

"Look at Fred and Adele Astaire over there. How long they been doing blackface?"

"I used to watch you even then. Know what I used to say?"

"Yea. 'Toot-a-toot-toot' on a bugle."

"That ain't all. I used to say to myself, 'Boy, when that sister grows up, I'm going to—.'"

Her eyes grew suddenly onyx and stopped him like an abruptly reversed traffic signal.

"What's the matter?" he said.

Common Meter                                                        147

She smiled and began nibbling the straw in her glass.

"What's the matter, Jean?"

"Nothing, Innocence. Nothing. Your boy plays a devilish one-step, doesn't he?"

"Say. You think I'm jivin', don't you?"

"No, darling. I think you're selling insurance."

"Think I'm gettin' previous, just because I got you the job."

"Funny, I never have much luck with jobs."

"Well, I don't care what you think, I'm going to say it."

"Let's dance."

"I used to say to myself, 'When that kid grows up, I'm going to ask her to marry me.'"

She called his bluff, "Well, I'm grown up."

"Marry me, will you, Jean?"

Her eyes relented a little in admiration of his audacity. Rarely did a sober aspirant have the courage to mention marriage.

"You're good, Bus. I mean, you're good."

"Every guy ain't a wolf, you know, Jean."

"No. Some are just ordinary meat-hounds."

From the change in his face she saw the depth of the thrust, saw pain where she had anticipated chagrin.

"Let's dance," she suggested again, a little more gently.

*     *     *

They had hardly begun when the number ended, and Fess Baxter stood before them, an ingratiating grin on his Swiss-cheese-colored face.

"Your turn, young fellow," he said to Bus.

"Thoughtful of you, reminding me," said Bus. "This is Mr. Baxter, Miss Ambrose."

"It's always been one of my ambitions," said Baxter, "to dance with a sure-enough angel."

"Just what I'd like to see you doin'," grinned Bus.

"Start up your stuff and watch us," said Baxter. "Step on it, brother. You're holding up traffic."

"Hope you get pinched for speedin'," said Bus, departing.

The Blue Devils were in good form tonight, were really "bearin' down" on their blues. Bus, their leader, however, was only going through the motions, waving his baton idly. His eyes followed Jean and Baxter, and it was nothing to his credit that the jazz maintained its spirit. Occasionally he lost the pair: a brace of young wild birds double-timed through the forest, miraculously

Rudolph Fisher

avoiding the trees: an extremely ardent couple, welded together, did a decidedly localized mess-around; that gigantic black farmer whom Jean had pointed out sashayed into the line of vision, swung about, backed off, being fancy. . . .

Abruptly, as if someone had caught and held his right arm, Bus's baton halted above his head. His men kept on playing under the impulse of their own momentum, but Bus was a creature apart. Slowly his baton drooped, like the crest of a proud bird, beaten. His eyes died on their object and all his features sagged. On the floor forty feet away, amid the surrounding clot of dancers, Jean and Baxter had stopped moving and were standing perfectly still. The girl had clasped her partner close about the shoulders with both arms. Her face was buried in his chest.

Baxter, who was facing the platform, looked up and saw Bus staring. He drew the girl closer, grinned, and shut one eye.

They stood so a moment or an hour till Bus dragged his eyes away. Automatically he resumed beating time. Every moment or so his baton wavered, slowed, and hurried to catch up. The blues were very low-down, the nakedest of jazz, a series of periodic wails against a background of steady, slow rhythm, each pounding pulse descending inevitably, like leaden strokes of fate. Bus found himself singing the words of this grief-stricken lamentation:

Trouble—trouble has followed me all my days,
Trouble—trouble has followed me all my days—
Seems like trouble's gonna follow me always.

The mob demanded an encore, a mob that knew its blues and liked them blue. Bus complied. Each refrain became bluer as it was caught up by a different voice: the wailing clarinet, the weeping C sax, the moaning B-flat sax, the trombone, and Bus's own plaintive tenor:

Baby—baby—my baby's gone away.
Baby—baby—my baby's gone away—
Seems like baby—my baby's gone to stay.

Presently the thing beat itself out, and Bus turned to acknowledge applause. He broke a bow off in half. Directly before the platform stood Jean alone, looking up at him.

He jumped down. "Dance?"

"No. Listen. You know what I said at the table?"

"At the table?"

"About—wolves?"

"Oh—that—?"

"Yea. I didn't mean anything personal. Honest, I didn't." Her eyes besought his. "You didn't think I meant anything personal, did you?"

"Course not," he laughed. "I know now you didn't mean anything." He laughed again. "Neither one of us meant anything."

With a wry little smile, he watched her slip off through the crowd.

✻   ✻   ✻

From his side of the platform Bus overheard Fess Baxter talking to Perry Parker. Baxter had a custom of talking while he conducted, the jazz serving to blanket his words. The blanket was not quite heavy enough tonight.

"P.P., old pooter, she fell."

Parker was resting while the C sax took the lead. "She did?"

"No lie. She says, 'You don't leave me any time for cash customers.'"

"Yea?"

"Yea. And I says, 'I'm a cash customer, baby. Just name your price.'"

Instantly Bus was across the platform and at him, clutched him by the collar, bent him back over the edge of the platform; and it was clear from the look in Bus's eyes that he wasn't just being playful.

"Name her!"

"Hey—what the hell you doin'!"

"Name her or I'll drop you and jump in your face. I swear to—"

"Nellie!" gurgled Fessenden Baxter.

"Nellie who—damn it?"

"Nellie—Gray!"

"All right then!"

Baxter found himself again erect with dizzy suddenness.

The music had stopped, for the players had momentarily lost their breath. Baxter swore and impelled his men into action, surreptitiously adjusting his ruffled plumage.

The crowd had an idea what it was all about and many good-naturedly derided the victim as they passed:

"'Smatter, Fess? Goin' in for toe-dancin'?"

"Nice back-dive, papa, but this ain't no swimmin'-pool."

Curry, the large, bald, yellow manager, also had an idea what it was all about and lost no time accosting Bus.

"Tryin' to start somethin'?"

"No. Tryin' to stop somethin'."

"Well, if you gonna stop it with your hands, stop it outside. I ain't got no permit for prize fights in here—'Course, if you guys can't get on together I can maybe struggle along without one of y' till I find somebody."

Bus said nothing.

"Listen. You birds fight it out with them jazz sticks, y' hear? Them's your weapons. Nex' Monday night's the jazz contest. You'll find out who's the best man next Monday night. Might win more'n a lovin' cup. And y' might lose more. Get me?"

He stood looking sleekly sarcastic a moment, then went to give Baxter like counsel.

*　　*　　*

Rumor spread through the Arcadia's regulars as night succeeded night.

A pair of buddies retired to the men's room to share a half-pint of gin. One said to the other between gulps:

"Lord today! Ain't them two roosters bearin' down on the jazz!"

"No lie. They mussa had some this same licker."

"Licker hell. Ain't you heard 'bout it?"

"'Bout what?"

"They fightin', Oscar, fightin'."

"Gimme that bottle 'fo' you swaller it. Fightin'? What you mean, fightin'?"

"Fightin' over that new mama."

"The honey-dew?"

"Right. They can't use knives and they can't use knucks. And so they got to fight it out with jazz."

"Yea? Hell of a way to fight."

"That's the only way they'd be any fight. Bus Williams'd knock that yaller boy's can off in a scrap."

"I know it. Y'ought-a-seen him grab him las' night."

"I did. They tell me she promised it to the one 'at wins this cup nex' Monday night."

"Yea? Wisht I knowed some music."

"Sho-nuff sheba all right. I got a long shout with her last night, Papa, an' she's got ever'thing!"

"Too damn easy on the eyes. Women like that ain't no good 'cep'n to start trouble."

"She sho' could start it for me. I'd 'a' been dancin' with her yet, but my two-bitses give out. Spent two hardearned bucks dancin' with her, too."

"Shuh! Might as well th'ow yo' money in the street. What you git dancin' with them hostesses?"

"You right there, brother. All I got out o' that one was two dollars worth o' disappointment."

Two girl friends, lounging in adjacent easy chairs, discussed the situation.

"I can't see what she's got so much more'n anybody else."

"Me neither. I could look a lot better'n that if I didn't have to work all day."

"No lie. Scrubbin' floors never made no bathin' beauties."

"I heard Fess Baxter jivin' her while they was dancin'. He's got a line, no stuff."

"He'd never catch me with it."

"No, dearie. He's got two good eyes too, y'know."

"Maybe that's why he couldn't see you flaggin' 'im."

"Be yourself, sister. He says to her, 'Baby, when the boss hands me that cup—'."

"Hates hisself, don't he?"

"'When the boss hands me that cup,' he says, 'I'm gonna put it right in your arms.'"

"Yea. And I suppose he goes with the cup."

"So she laughs and says, 'Think you can beat him?' So he says, 'Beat him? Huh, that bozo couldn't play a hand organ.'"

"He don't mean her no good though, this Baxter."

"How do you know?"

"A kack like that never means a woman no good. The other one ast her to step off with him."

"What!"

"Etta Pipp heard him. They was drinkin' and she was at the next table."

"Well, ain't that somethin'! Ast her to step off with him! What'd she say?"

"Etta couldn't hear no more."

"Jus' goes to show ya. What chance has a honest workin' girl got?"

Bus confided in Tappen, his drummer.

"Tap," he said, "ain't it funny how a woman always seems to fall for a wolf?"

"No lie," Tap agreed, "When a guy gets too deep, he's long-gone."

"How do you account for it, Tap?"

"I don't. I jes' play 'em light. When I feel it gettin' heavy—boy, I run like hell."

"Tap, what would you do if you fell for a girl and saw her neckin' another guy?"

"I wouldn't fall," said Tappen, "so I wouldn't have to do nothin'."

"Well, but s'posin' you did?"

"Well, if she was my girl, I'd knock the can off both of 'em."

"S'posin' she wasn't your girl?"

"Well, if she wasn't my girl, it wouldn't be none of my business."

"Yea, but a guy kind o' hates to see an old friend gettin' jived."

"Stay out, papa. Only way to protect yourself."

"S'posin' you didn't want to protect yourself? S'posin' you wanted to protect the woman?"

"Hmph! Who ever heard of a woman needin' protection?"

*     *     *

"Ladies and gentlemen!" sang Curry to the tense crowd that gorged the Arcadia. "Tonight is the night of the only contest of its kind in recorded history! On my left, Mr. Bus Williams, chief of the Blue Devils. On my right, Mr. Fessenden Baxter, leader of the Firemen. On this stand, the solid gold loving-cup. The winner will claim the jazz championship of the world!"

"And the sweet mama too, how 'bout it?" called a wag.

"Each outfit will play three numbers: a one-step, a fox-trot, and a blues number. With this stop watch which you see in my hand, I will time your applause after each number. The leader receiving the longest total applause wins the loving-cup!"

"Yea—and some lovin'-up wid it!"

"I will now toss a coin to see who plays the first number!"

"Toss it out here!"

"Bus Williams's Blue Devils, ladies and gentlemen, will play the first number!"

Bus's philosophy of jazz held tone to be merely the vehicle of rhythm. He spent much time devising new rhythmic patterns with which to vary his presentations. Accordingly he depended largely on Tappen, his master percussionist, who knew every rhythmic monkey-shine with which to delight a gaping throng.

Bus had conceived the present piece as a chase, in which an agile clarinet eluded impetuous and turbulent traps. The other instruments were to be observers, chorusing their excitement while they urged the principals on.

From the moment the piece started something was obviously wrong. The clarinet was elusive enough, but its agility was without purpose. Nothing pursued it. People stopped dancing in the middle of the number and turned puzzled faces toward the platform. The tap-drummer was going through the motions faithfully but to no avail. His traps were voiceless, emitted mere shadows of sound. He was a deaf mute making a speech.

Brief, perfunctory, disappointed applause rose and fell at the number's end. Curry announced its duration:

"Fifteen seconds flat!"

Fess Baxter, with great gusto, leaped to his post.

"The Firemen will play their first number!"

Bus was consulting Tappen.

Common Meter         153

"For the love o' Pete, Tap—?"

"Love o' hell. Look a' here."

Bus looked—first at the trapdrum, then at the bass; snapped them with a finger, thumped them with his knuckles. There was almost no sound; each drum-sheet was dead, lax instead of taut, and the cause was immediately clear; each bore a short curved knife-cut following its edge a brief distance, a wound unnoticeable at a glance, but fatal to the instrument.

Bus looked at Tappen, Tappen looked at Bus.

"The cream-colored son of a buzzard!"

Fess Baxter, gleeful and oblivious, was directing a whirlwind number, sweeping the crowd about the floor at an exciting, exhausting pace, distorting, expanding, etherealizing their emotions with swift-changing dissonances. Contrary to Bus Williams's philosophy, Baxter considered rhythm a mere rack upon which to hand his tonal tricks. The present piece was dizzy with sudden disharmonies, unexpected twists of phrase, successive false resolutions. Incidentally, however, there was nothing wrong with Baxter's drums.

Boiling over, Bus would have started for him, but Tappen grabbed his coat.

"Hold it, papa. That's a sure way to lose. Maybe we can choke him yet."

"Yea—?"

"I'll play the wood. And I still got cymbals and sandpaper."

"Yea—and a triangle. Hell of a lot o' good they are."

"Can't quit," said Tappen.

"Well," said Bus.

Baxter's number ended in a furor.

"Three minutes and twenty seconds!" bellowed Curry as the applause eventually died out.

Bus began his second number, a fox-trot. In the midst of it he saw Jean dancing, beseeching him with bewildered dismay in her eyes, a look that at once crushed and crazed him. Tappen rapped on the rim of his trap drum, tapped his triangle, stamped the pedal that clapped the cymbals, but the result was a toneless and hollow clatter, a weightless noise that bounced back from the multitude instead of penetrating into it. The players also, distracted by the loss, were operating far below par, and not all their leader's frantic false enthusiasm could compensate for the gaping absence of bass. The very spine had been ripped out of their music, and Tappen's desperate efforts were but the hopeless flutterings of a stricken, limp, pulseless heart.

"Forty-five seconds!" Curry announced. "Making a total so far of one minute flat for the Blue Devils! The Firemen will now play their second number!"

The Firemen's fox-trot was Baxter's re-arrangement of Burleigh's "Jean,

Rudolph Fisher

My Jean," and Baxter, riding his present advantage hard, stressed all that he had put into it of tonal ingenuity. The thing was delirious with strange harmonies, iridescent with odd color-changes, and its very flamboyance, its musical fine-writing and conceits delighted the dancers.

But it failed to delight Jean Ambrose, whom by its title it was intended to flatter. She rushed to Bus.

"What is it?" She was a-quiver.

"Drums gone. Somebody cut the pigskin the last minute."

"What? Somebody? Who?"

"Cut 'em with a knife close to the rim."

"Cut? He cut—? Oh, Bus!"

She flashed Baxter a look that would have crumpled his assurance had he seen it. "Can't you—Listen." She was at once wild and calm. "It's the bass. You got to have—I know! Make 'em stamp their feet! Your boys, I mean. That'll do it. All of 'em. Turn the blues into a shout."

"Yea? Gee. Maybe—"

"Try it! You've got to win this thing."

An uproar that seemed endless greeted Baxter's version of "Jean." The girl, back out on the floor, managed to smile as Baxter acknowledged the acclaim by gesturing toward her.

"The present score, ladies and gentlemen, is—for the Blue Devils, one minute even; for the Firemen, six minutes and thirty seconds! The Devils will now play their last number!" Curry's intonation of "last" moved the mob to laughter.

Into that laughter Bus grimly led his men like a captain leading his command into fire. He had chosen the parent of blue songs, the old St. Louis Blues, and he adduced every device that had ever adorned that classic. Clarinets wailed, saxophones moaned, trumpets wept wretchedly, trombones laughed bitterly, even the great bass horn sobbed dismally from the depths. And so perfectly did the misery in the music express the actual despair of the situation that the crowd was caught from the start. Soon dancers closed their eyes, forgot their jostling neighbors, lost themselves bodily in the easy sway of that slow, fateful measure, vaguely aware that some quality hitherto lost had at last been found. They were too wholly absorbed to note just how that quality had been found: that every player softly dropped his heel where each bass-drum beat would have come, giving each major impulse a body and breadth that no drum could have achieved. Zoom-zoom-zoom-zoom. It was not a mere sound; it was a vibrant throb that took hold of the crowd and rocked it.

They had been rocked thus before, this multitude. Two hundred years ago they had swayed to that same slow fateful measure, lifting their lamentation to heaven, pounding the earth with their feet, seeking the mercy of a new God through the medium of an old rhythm, zoom-zoom. They had rocked so a thousand years ago in a city whose walls were jungle, forfending the wrath of a terrible black God who spoke in storm and pestilence, had swayed and wailed to the same slow period, beaten on a wild boar's skin stretched over the end of a hollow tree-trunk. Zoom-zoom-zoom-zoom. Not a sound but an emotion that laid hold on their bodies and swung them into the past. Blues—low-down blues indeed—blues that reached their souls' depths.

But slowly the color changed. Each player allowed his heel to drop less and less softly. Solo parts faded out, and the orchestra began to gather power as a whole. The rhythm persisted, the unfaltering common meter of blues, but the blueness itself, the sorrow, the despair, began to give way to hope. Ere long hope came to the verge of realization—mounted it—rose above it. The deep and regular impulses now vibrated like nearing thunder, a mighty, inescapable, all-embracing dominance, stressed by the contrast of wind-tone; an all-pervading atmosphere through which soared wild-winged birds. Rapturously, rhapsodically, the number rose to madness and at the height of its madness, burst into sudden silence.

Illusion broke. Dancers awoke, dropped to reality with a jolt. Suddenly the crowd appreciated that Bus Williams had returned to form, had put on a comeback, had struck off a masterpiece. And the crowd showed its appreciation. It applauded its palms sore.

Curry's suspense-ridden announcement ended:

"Total—for the Blue Devils, seven minutes and forty seconds! For the Firemen, six minutes and thirty seconds! Maybe that wasn't the Devils' last number after all! The Firemen will play their last number!"

It was needless for Baxter to attempt the depths and heights just attained by Bus Williams's Blue Devils. His speed, his subordination of rhythm to tone, his exotic coloring, all were useless in a low-down blues song. The crowd moreover, had nestled upon the broad, sustaining bosom of a shout. Nothing else warmed them. The end of Baxter's last piece left them chilled and unsatisfied.

But if Baxter realized that he was beaten, his attitude failed to reveal it. Even when the major volume of applause died out in a few seconds, he maintained his self-assured grin. The reason was soon apparent: although the audience as a whole had stopped applauding, two small groups of assiduous handclappers, one at either extreme of the dancing-area, kept up a diminutive, violent clatter.

Again Bus and Tappen exchanged sardonic stares.

"Damn' if he ain't paid somebody to clap!"

Only the threatening hisses and boos of the majority terminated this clatter, whereupon Curry summed up:

"For Bus Williams's Blue Devils—seven minutes and forty seconds! For Fess Baxter's Firemen—eight minutes flat!"

He presented Baxter the loving-cup amid a hubbub of murmurs, handclaps, shouts, and hisses that drowned whatever he said. Then the hubbub hushed. Baxter was assisting Jean Ambrose to the platform. With a bow and a flourish he handed the girl the cup.

She held it for a moment in both arms, uncertain, hesitant. But there was nothing uncertain or hesitant in the mob's reaction. Feeble applause was overwhelmed in a deluge of disapprobation. Cries of "Crooked!" "Don't take it!" "Crown the cheat!" "He stole it!" stood out. Tappen put his finger in the slit in his trap-drum, ripped it to a gash, held up the mutilated instrument, and cried, "Look what he done to my traps!" A few hardboiled ruffians close to the platform moved menacingly toward the victor. "Grab 'im! Knock his can off!"

Jean's uncertainty abruptly vanished. She wheeled with the trophy in close embrace and sailed across the platform toward the defeated Bus Williams. She smiled into his astonished face and thrust the cup into his arms.

"Hot damn, mama! That's the time!" cried a jubilant voice from the floor, and instantly the gathering storm of menace broke into a cloudburst of delight. That romance-hungry multitude saw Bus Williams throw his baton into the air and gather the girl and the loving-cup into his arms. And they went utterly wild—laughed, shouted, yelled and whistled till the walls of the Arcadia bulged.

Jazz emerged as the mad noise subsided: Bus Williams's Blue Devils playing "*She's Still My Baby.*"

# JOHN ARCHER'S NOSE

Whenever Detective Sergeant Perry Dart felt especially weary of the foibles and follies of his Harlem, he knew where to find stimulation; he could always count on his friend, Dr. John Archer. Spiritually the two bachelors were as opposite as the two halves of a circle—and as complementary. The detective had only to seek out the physician at the latter's office-apartment, flop into a chair, and make an observation. His tall, lean comrade in crime, sober of face but twinkling of eye, would produce a bottle, fill glasses, hold a match first to Dart's cigar then to his own, and murmur a word of disagreement. Promptly an argument would be on.

Tonight however the formula had failed to work. It was shortly after midnight, an excellent hour for profound argumentation, and the sounds from the avenue outside, still alive with the gay crowds that a warm spring night invariably calls forth, hardly penetrated into the consulting-room where they sat. But Dart's provocative remark had evoked no disagreement.

"Your folks," Dart had said, "are the most superstitious idiots on the face of the earth."

The characteristic response would have been:

"Perry, you'll have to cut out drinking. It's curdling your milk of human kindness." Or, "*My* folks?—Really!" Or, "Avoid unscientific generalizations, my dear Sherlock. They are ninety-one and six-thirteenths percent wrong by actual measurement."

But tonight the physician simply looked at him and said nothing. Dart prodded further:

"They can be as dark as me or as light as you, but their ignorance is the same damned color wherever you find it—black."

That should have brought some demurring comment on the leprechauns of the Irish, the totems of the Indians, or the prayer-wheels of the Tibetans. Still the doctor said nothing.

"So you won't talk, hey?"

Whereupon John Archer said quietly:

"I believe you're right."

Dart's leg came off its perch across his chair-arm. He set down his glass untasted on the doctor's desk, leaned forward, staring.

"Heresy!" he cried, incredulous. "Heresy, b'gosh!—I'll have you read out of church. What the hell? Don't you know you aren't supposed to agree with me?"

"Spare me, your grace." The twinkle which kindled for an instant in Dr. Archer's eyes flickered quickly out. "I've had a cogent example today of what you complain of."

"Superstition?"

"Of a very dark hue."

"State the case. Let's see if you can exonerate yourself."

"I lost a kid."

Dart reached for his glass. "Didn't know you had one."

"A patient, you jackass."

Dart grinned. "Didn't know you had a patient, either."

"That's not funny. Neither was this. Beautiful, plump little brown rascal— eighteen months old—perfectly developed, bright-eyed, alert—and it passes out in a convulsion, and I was standing there looking on—helpless."

"If it was so perfect, what killed it?"

"Superstition."

"Humph. Anything for an alibi, hey?"

"Superstition," repeated Archer in a tone which stilled his friend's banter. "That baby ought to be alive and well, now."

"What's the gag line?"

"Status lymphaticus."

"Hell. And I was just getting serious."

"That's as serious as anything could be. The kid had a retained thymus."

"I'll bite. What's a retained thymus?"

"A big gland here in the chest. Usually disappears after birth. Sometimes doesn't. Untreated, it produces this status lymphaticus—convulsions— death."

"Why didn't you treat it?"

"I did what I could. Been seeing it for some time. Could have cleared it up over night. What I couldn't treat was the superstition of the parents."

"Oh."

"Specially the father. The kid should have had X-ray treatments. Melt the thing away. These kids, literally choking to death in a fit, clear up and re-cover—zip—like that. Most spectacular thing in medicine. But the old man wouldn't hear of it. None of this new-fangled stuff for *his* only child."

"I see."

"You can't see. I haven't told you yet. I noticed today, for the first time, a small, evil-smelling packet on a string around the baby's neck. In spite of the shock immediately following death, my curiosity got the better of me. I suppose there was also a natural impulse to—well—change the subject, sort of. I asked what it was."

"You would."

"The father didn't answer. He'd gone cataleptic. He simply stood there, looking. It seemed to me he was looking rather at the packet than at the child, and if ever there was the light of madness in a man's eyes, it was in his. The mother, grief-stricken though she was, managed to pull herself together long enough to answer."

"What was it?"

"Fried hair."

"What?"

"Fried hair.—No—not just kinky hair, straightened with hot irons and grease, as the term usually implies. That packet—I examined it—contained a wad of human hair, fried, if you please, in snake oil."

Dart expelled a large volume of disgusted smoke. "The fools."

"A charm. The father had got it that morning from some conjure-woman. Guaranteed to cure the baby's fits."

"He'd try that in preference to X-rays."

"And his name," the doctor concluded with a reflective smile, "was Bright—Solomon Bright."

After a moment of silence, Dart said:

"Well—your sins are forgiven. No wonder you agreed with me."

"Did I?" Having unburdened his story, John Archer's habit of heckling, aided by a normal desire to dismiss an unpleasant memory, began now to assert itself. The twinkle returned to his eyes. "I am of course in error. A single graphic example, while impressive, does not warrant a general conclusion. Such reasoning, as pointed out by no less an authority than the great Bacon—"

"I prefer ham," cut in Dart as the phone rang. His friend, murmuring something to the effect that "like begets like," reached for the instrument.

"Hello . . . Yes . . . Yes. I can come at once. Where? 15 West 134th Street, Apartment 51 . . . Yes—right away."

Deliberately he replaced the receiver. "I'm going to post a reward," he said wearily, "for the first person who calls a doctor and says, 'Doctor, take your time.' Right away—right away—"

He rose, put away the bottle, reached for hat and bag.

"Want to come along?"

"You're not really going right away?"

"In spite of my better judgment. That girl was scared."

"O.K. All I've got to do before morning is sleep."

"Don't count on it. Got your gun?"

"Gun? Of course. But what for?"

"Just a hunch. Come on."

"Hunch?" Dart jumped up to follow. "Say—what is this? A shooting?"

"Not yet." They reached the street.

"So what?"

"Girl said her brother's been stabbed."

"Yea?—here—let's use my car!"

"Righto. But lay off that siren. It gives me the itch."

"Well, scratch," Dart said as his phaeton leaped forward. "You've got fingernails, haven't you?" And with deliberate perversity he made the siren howl.

\* \* \*

In three minutes they reached their destination and were panting up endless stairs.

"It's a cowardly trick, that siren," breathed the doctor.

"Why?"

"Just a stunt to scare all the bad men away from the scene of the crime."

"Well, it wouldn't work up here. This high up, they couldn't hear a thing in the street."

"You're getting old. It's only five flights."

Dart's retort was cut off by the appearance of a girl's form at the head of the stairway.

"Dr. Archer?" Her voice was trembling. "This way.—Please—hurry—"

They followed her into the hallway of an apartment. They caught a glimpse of a man and woman as they passed the front living-room. The girl stopped and directed them with wide, frightened eyes into a bed-chamber off the hall. They stepped past her into the chamber, Dart pausing automatically to look about before following the physician in.

An old lady sat motionless beside the bed, her distorted face a spasm of grief. She looked up at the doctor, a pitifully frantic appeal in her eyes, then looked back toward the bed without speaking.

Dr. Archer dropped his bag and bent over the patient, a lean-faced boy of perhaps twenty. He lay on his left side facing the wall, his knees slightly drawn up in a sleeping posture. But his eyes were open and fixed. The doctor grasped his thin shoulders and pulled him gently a little way, to reveal a wide stain of blood on the bedclothing below; pulled him a little farther over, bent in a moment's inspection, then summoned Dart with a movement of his head. Together they observed the black-pearl handle of a knife, protruding from the chest. The boy had been stabbed through his pajama coat, and the blade was unquestionably in his heart.

Dr. Archer released the shoulder. The body rolled softly back to its original posture. The physician stood erect.

"Are you his mother?" he asked the old lady.

Dumbly, she nodded.

"You saw the knife, of course?"

"I seen it," she said in almost a whisper, and with an effort added, "I—I didn't pull it out for fear of startin' him bleedin' ag'in."

"He won't bleed any more," Dr. Archer said gently. "He hasn't bled for an hour—maybe two."

The girl behind them gasped sharply. "You mean he's been—dead—that long?"

"At least. The blood stain beneath him is dry."

A sob escaped the old lady. "Sonny—"

"Oh Ma—!" The girl moved to the old lady's side, encircled her with compassionate arms.

"I knowed it," the old lady whispered. "I knowed it—the minute I seen him, I knowed—"

Dr. Archer terminated a long silence by addressing the girl. "It was you who called me?"

She nodded.

"When you said your brother had been stabbed, I knew the case would have to be reported to the police. Detective Sergeant Dart was with me at the time. I thought it might save embarrassment if he came along."

The girl looked at Dart and after a moment nodded again.

"I understand.—But we—we don't know who did it."

A quick glance passed between the two men.

"Then it's lucky I came," Dart said. "Perhaps I can help you."

"Yes.—Yes perhaps you can."

"Whose knife is that?"

"His own."

"His own?—Where did you last see it?"

"On the bureau by the head of the bed."

"When?"

"This afternoon, when I was cleaning up."

"Tell me how you found him."

"Just like that. I'd been out. I came in and along the hall on the way to my room, I noticed his door was closed. He hasn't been coming in till much later recently. I stopped to speak to him—he hadn't been well.—I opened the door and spoke. He didn't answer. I pushed on the light. He looked funny. I went over to him and saw the blood.—"

"Shall we go into another room?"

"Yes, please.—Come, Ma—"

Stiffly, with the girl's assistance, the mother got to her feet and permitted herself to be guided toward the door. There she paused, turned, and looked back at the still figure lying on the bed. Her eyes were dry, but the depth of her shocked grief was unmistakable. Then, almost inaudibly, she said a curious thing:

"God forgive me."

And slowly she turned again and stumbled forward.

Again Dart and Archer exchanged glances. The former's brows lifted. The latter shook his head thoughtfully as he picked up his bag. As the girl and her mother went out, he stood erect and sniffed. He went over to the room's one window, which was open, near the foot of the bed. Dart followed. Together they looked out into the darkness of an airshaft. Above, one more story and the edge of the roof. Below, an occasional lighted window and a blend of diverse sounds welling up: a baby wailing, someone coughing spasmodically, a radio rasping labored jazz, a woman's laugh, quickly stifled.

"God forgive her what?" said Dart.

The doctor sniffed again. "It didn't come from out there."

"What didn't?"

"What I smelt."

"All I smell is a rat."

"This is far more subtle."

"Smell up the answer to my question."

The physician sniffed again, said nothing, turned and started out. He and Dart overtook the others in the hallway. A moment later, they were all in the living-room.

*　　*　　*

The man and woman, whom they had seen in passing, waited there, looking toward them expectantly. The woman, clad in gold-figured black silk Chinese pajamas, was well under thirty, slender, with yellow skin which retained a decided make-up even at this hour. Her boyish bob was reddish with frequent "frying," and her eyes were cold and hard. The man, in shirt-sleeves and slippers, was approximately the same age, of medium build and that complexion known as "riny"—light, sallow skin and sand-colored kinky hair. His eyes were green.

The girl got the old lady into a chair before speaking. Then, in a dull, absent sort of way, she said:

"This is the doctor. He's already turned the case over to this gentleman that came with him."

"And who," the woman inquired, "is this gentleman that came with him?"

"A policeman—a detective."

"Hmph!" commented the woman.

"Fast work," added the man unpleasantly.

"Thank you," returned Dart, eyeing him coolly. "May I know to whom I owe the compliment?"

The man matched his stare before answering.

"I am Ben Dewey. This is my wife. Petal there is my sister. Sonny was my brother." There was unnecessary insolence in the enumeration.

"'Was' your brother?"

"Yes, was." Mr. Dewey was evidently not hard to incense. He bristled.

"Then you are already aware of his—misfortune?"

"Of course."

"In fact, you were aware of it before Dr. Archer arrived."

"What do you mean?"

"I mean that no one has stated your brother's condition since we came into this room. You were not in the bedroom when Dr. Archer did state it. Yet you know it."

Ben Dewey glared. "Certainly I know it."

"How?"

The elder brother's wife interrupted. "This is hardly the time, Mr. Detective, for a lot of questions."

Dart looked at her. "I see," he said quietly. "I have been in error. Miss Petal said, in the other room just now, 'We don't know who did it.' Naturally I assumed that her 'we' included all the members of the family. I see now that she meant only herself and her mother. So, Mrs. Dewey, if you or your husband will be kind enough to name the guilty party, we can easily avoid a 'lot of questions.'"

"That ain't what I meant!" flared the wife. "We don't know who did it either."

"Oh. And you are not anxious to find out—as quickly as possible?"

Dr. Archer mediated. "Sergeant Dart naturally felt that in performing his duty he would also be serving you all. He regrets, of course, the intrusion upon your—er—moment of sorrow."

"A sorrow which all of you do not seem to share alike," appended Dart, who believed in making people so angry that they would blurt out the truth. "May I use your phone?"

He went to the instrument, resting on a table near the hall door, called the precinct station, reported the case, asked for a medical examiner, and declined assistants.

"I'm sure the family would prefer to have me act alone for the time being."

Only Dr. Archer realized what these words meant: that within five minutes half a dozen men would be just outside the door of the apartment, ready to break in at the sergeant's first signal.

But Dart turned and smiled at the brother and his wife. "Am I right in assuming that?" he asked courteously.

"Yes—of course," Ben said, somewhat subdued.

Swiftly the courteous smile vanished. The detective's voice was incisive and hard. "Then perhaps you will tell me how you knew so well that your brother was dead."

"Why—I saw him. I saw the knife in—"

"When?"

"When Petal screamed. Letty and I had gone to bed. And when Petal screamed, naturally we jumped up and rushed into Sonny's room, where she was. She was standing there looking at him. I went over to him and looked. I guess I shook him. Anybody could see—"

"What time was that?"

"Just a few minutes ago. Just before the doctor was called. I told her to call him."

"About ten minutes ago, then?"

"Yes."

"How many times did your sister scream?"

"Only once."

"You're sure?"

"Yes."

"You had retired. You heard one scream. You jumped up and went straight to it."

"Why not?"

"Extraordinary sense of direction, that's all.—Whose knife is that?"

"Sonny's."

"How do you know?"

"I've seen him with it. Couldn't miss that black pearl handle."

"Who else was in the house at the time?"

"No one but Ma. She was already in the room when we got there. She's got an extraordinary sense of direction, too."

"Any one else here during the evening?"

"No—not that I know of. My wife and I have been in practically all evening."

"Practically?"

"I mean she was in all evening. I went out for a few minutes—down to the corner for a pack of cigarettes."

"What time?"

"About ten o'clock."

"And you've heard nothing—no suspicious sounds of any kind?"

"No. At least *I* didn't. Did you Letty?"

"All I heard was Sonny himself coming in."

"What time was that?"

"'Bout nine o'clock. He went in his room and stayed there."

"Just what was everyone doing at that time?"

"The rest of us were in the back of the flat—except for Petal. She'd gone out. Ben and I were in the kitchen. I was washing the dishes, he was sitting at the table, smoking. We'd just finished eating supper."

"Your usual supper hour?"

"Ben doesn't get home from the Post Office till late."

"Where was Mother Dewey?"

"In the dining-room, reading the paper."

"Anyone else here now?"

"Not that I know of."

"Do you mind if we look?"

"If I minded, would that stop you?"

Dart indulged in an appraising pause, then said:

"It might. I should hate to embarrass you."

"Embarrass me!—Go ahead—I've nothing to hide."

"That's good. Doc, if you can spare the time, will you take a look around with me?"

Dr. Archer nodded with his tongue in his cheek. Dart knew very well that a cash-in-advance major operation could not have dragged the physician away.

"Before we do, though," the detective said, "let me say this: Here are four of you, all closely related to the victim, all surely more or less familiar with his habits and associates. Yet not one of you offers so much as a suggestion as to who might have done this."

"You haven't given us time," remarked Letty Dewey.

Dart looked at his watch. "I've given you five minutes."

"Who's been doing all the talking?"

"All right. Take your turn now. Who do *you* think did it?"

Rudolph Fisher

"I haven't the remotest idea."

"M—m—so you said before—while I was doing all the talking."—He smiled. "Strange that none of you should have the remotest idea. The shock, no doubt. I should rather expect a flood of accusations. Unless, of course, there is some very good reason to the contrary."

"What do you mean?"

"I mean—" the detective was pleasantly casual—"unless you are protecting each other. In which case, if I may remind you, you become accessory.— Come on, Doc. No doubt the family would like a little private conference."

＊　　＊　　＊

During the next few minutes the two went through the apartment. Alert against surprise, they missed no potential hiding-place, satisfying themselves that nobody had modestly secreted himself in some out-of-the-way corner. The place possessed no apparent entrance or exit other than its one outside door, and there was nothing unusual about its arrangement of rooms—several bedchambers off a central hallway, with the living-room at the front end and a kitchen and dining-room at the back.

Characteristically, the doctor indulged in wordy and somewhat irrelevant reflection during the tour of inspection. Exchanges of comment punctuated their progress.

"Back here," Dr. Archer said. "I don't get it. But up there where they are, I do. And in the boy's room, *I* did."

"Get what—that smell?"

"M—m. Peculiar—very. Curious thing, odors. Discernible in higher dilution than any other material stimulus. Ridiculous that we don't make greater use of them."

"I never noticed any particular restriction of 'em in Harlem."

On the dining-room table a Harlem newspaper was spread out. Dart glanced at the page, which was bordered with advertisements.

"Here it is again," he said, pointing, "'Do you want success in love, business, a profession?' These 'ads' are all that keep this sheet going. Your folks' superstition—"

Dr. Archer's eyes traveled down the column but he seemed to ignore the interruption.

"Odors *should* be restricted," he pursued. "They should be captured, classified, and numbered like the lines of the spectrum. We let them run wild—"

"Check."

"And sacrifice a wealth of information. In a language of a quarter of a million words, we haven't a single specific direct denotation of a smell."

"Oh, no?"

"No. Whatever you're thinking of, it is an indirect and non-specific denotation, liking the odor in mind to something else. We are content with 'fragrant' and 'foul' or general terms of that character, or at best 'alcoholic' or 'moldy,' which are obviously indirect. We haven't even such general direct terms as apply to colors—red, green, and blue. We name what we see but don't name what we smell."

"Which is just as well."

"On the contrary. If we could designate each smell by number—"

"We'd know right off who killed Sonny."

"Perhaps. I daresay every crime has its peculiar odor."

"Old stuff. They used bloodhounds in *Uncle Tom's Cabin*."

"We could use one here."

"Do tell?"

"This crime has a specific smell—"

"It stinks all right."

"—which I think we should find significant if we could place it."

"Rave on, Aristotle."

"Two smells, in fact. First, alcohol."

"We brought that with us."

"No. Another vintage I'm sure. Didn't you get it in the boy's bedroom?"

"Not especially."

"It's meaning was clear enough. The boy was stabbed while sleeping under the effect of alcohol."

"How'd you sneak up that answer?"

"There was no sign of struggle. He'd simply drawn up his knees a little and died."

"Don't tell me you smelt alcohol on a dead man's breath."

"No. What I smelt was the alcoholic breath he'd expelled into that room before he died. Enough to leave a discernible—er—fragrance for over an hour afterward."

"Hm—Stabbed in his sleep."

"But that simply accounts for the lack of struggle and the tranquil posture of the corpse. It does indicate, of course, that for a boy of twenty Sonny was developing bad habits—a fact corroborated by his sister's remark about late hours. But that's all. This other odor which I get from time to time I consider far more important. It might even lead to the identity of the killer—if we could trace it."

"Then keep sniffing, Fido. Y'know, I had a dog like you once. Only he didn't do a lot of talking about what he smelt."

"Too bad he couldn't talk, Sergeant. *You* could have learned a great deal from him."

As they approached the front door the bell rang. Dart stepped to the door and opened it. A large pink-faced man carrying a doctor's bag stood puffing on the threshold. He blinked through his glasses and grinned.

"Dr. Finkelbaum!" exclaimed the detective. "Some service! Come in. You know Dr. Archer." He looked quickly out into the corridor, noted his men, grinned, signaled silence, stepped back.

"Sure. Hello, doctor," greeted the newcomer. "Whew!" Thank your stars you're not the medical examiner."

"You must have been uptown already," said Dr. Archer.

"Yea. Little love affair over on Lenox Avenue. I always phone in before leaving the neighborhood—they don't do things by halves up here. Where's the stiff?"

"In the second room," said Dart. "Come on, I'll show you."

"At least," murmured Dr. Archer, "it was in there a moment ago."

Despite his skepticism, which derived from sudden mysterious disappearances of corpses on two previous occasions in his experience, they found the contents of Sonny's bedchamber unchanged.

"Who did this?" inquired the medical examiner.

"At present," Dart said, "there are four denials—his mother, his sister, his brother, and his brother's wife."

"All in the family, eh?"

"I haven't finished talking to them yet. You and Dr. Archer carry on here. I'll go back and try some more browbeating."

"Righto."

Now Dart returned to the living-room. The four people seemed not to have moved. The brother stood in the middle of the floor, meditating. The wife sat in a chair, bristling. The girl was on the arm of another chair in which her elderly mother still slumped, staring forward with eyes that saw nothing—or perhaps everything.

The detective looked about. "Finished your conference?"

"Conference about what?" said Ben.

"The national debt. What's happened since I left here?"

"Nothing."

"No conversation at all?"

"No."

"Then who used this telephone?"

"Why—nobody."

"No? I suppose it moved itself? I left it like this, with the mouthpiece facing the door. Now the mouthpiece faces the center of the room. One of the miracles of modern science or what?"

Nobody spoke.

"Now listen." There was a menacing placidity in the detective's voice. "This conspiracy of silence stuff may make it hard for me, but it's going to make it a lot harder for you. You people are going to talk. Personally, I don't care whether you talk here or around at the precinct. But whatever you're holding out for, it's no use. The circumstances warrant arresting all of you, right now."

"We've answered your questions," said Letty angrily. "Do you want us to lie and say one of *us* did it—just to make your job easier?"

"Lawd—Lawd!" whispered the old lady and Petal's arm went about her again, vainly comforting.

"Who else lives here?" Dart asked suddenly.

As if sparing them the necessity of answering, the outside door clicked and opened. Dart turned to see a young man enter the hallway. The young man looked toward them, his pale face a picture of bewilderment, closed the door behind him, mechanically put his key back into his pocket, and came into the living-room.

"What's up," he asked. "What do those guys want outside?"

"Guys outside?" Ben looked at Dart. "So the joint's pinched?"

"Not yet," returned Dart. "It's up to you people." He addressed the newcomer. "Who are you?"

"Me?—I'm Red Brown. I live here."

"Really? Odd nobody's mentioned you."

"He hasn't been here all day," said Letty.

"What's happened?" insisted Red Brown. "Who is this guy?"

"He's a policeman," Petal answered. "Somebody stabbed—Sonny."

"Stabbed Sonny—!" Dart saw the boy's wide eyes turn swiftly from Petal and fix themselves on Ben.

"A flesh wound," the detective said quickly.

"Oh," said Red, still staring with a touch of horror at Ben. His look could not have been clearer had he accused the elder brother in words.

"You and Sonny are good friends?" pursued Dart.

"Yea—buddies. We room together."

"It might make it easier for Ben if you told me why he stabbed his brother."

Red's look, still fixed, darkened.

"Why should I make it easier for him?"

There was silence, sudden and tense. Ben drew a deep, sharp breath, amazement changing to rage.

"Why—you stinking little pup!"

He charged forward. Letty yelled, "Ben!" Red, obvious child of the city, ducked low and sidewise, thrusting out one leg, over which his assailant tripped and crashed to the floor. Dart stepped forward and grabbed Ben as he struggled up. There was no breaking the detective's hold.

"Easy. What do you want to do—prove he's right?"

"Let me go and I'll prove plenty! I'll make him—"

"It's a lie!" breathed Letty. "Ben didn't kill him."

Unexpectedly Dart released Ben.

"All right," said he. "Get to proving. But don't let me have to bean you."

The impulse to assault was spent. Ben pulled himself together.

"What's the idea?" he glowered at Red. "I even call up the poolroom where you work, trying to keep you out of this. And you walk in and try to make me out a murderer."

"Murderer?" Red looked about, engaged Dart. "You—you said—flesh wound."

"Yes," the detective returned drily. "The flesh of his heart."

"Gee! Gee, Ben. I didn't know you'd killed him."

"I didn't kill him! Why do you keep saying so?"

Red looked from Ben to Letty, encountering a glare of the most intense hatred Dart had ever seen. The woman would obviously have tried to claw his eyes out had not circumstances restrained her.

"Go on," she said through her teeth. "Tell your tale."

Her menace held the boy silent for an uncertain moment. It was outweighed by the cooler threat of Dart's next words:

"Not scared to talk, are you, Red?"

"Scared? No, I ain't scared. But murder—gee!"

"You and Sonny were buddies, weren't you?"

"Yea—that's right."

"Slept in the same bed."

"Yea."

"Supposing it had been you in that bed instead of Sonny?"

"Yea—it might 'a been."

"Sonny wouldn't have let you down, would he?"

"He never did."

"All right. Speak up. What do you know?"

"I know—I mean—maybe—maybe Ben figured there was somethin' goin' on between Sonny and—." He did not look at Letty now.

"Was there?"

"Wouldn't matter whether there was or not—if Ben thought so."

"True enough. Well, Mr. Dewey, what about that?"

Ben Dewey did not have an answer—seemed not to have heard the detective's last word. His mouth hung open as he stared dumbfounded at his wife.

His wife, however, still transfixed Red with gleaming eyes.

"It should have been you instead of Sonny," she said evenly. "You rat."

Abruptly Dart remembered the presence of the old lady and the girl. He turned toward them, somewhat contrite for not having spared them the shock of this last disclosure, but got a shock of his own which silenced his intended apology: The girl's face held precisely the expression of stunned unbelief that he had expected to find. But the old lady sat huddled in the same posture that she had held throughout the questioning. Her steadfast gaze was still far away, and apparently she had not heard or seen a single item of what had just transpired in the room.

Dart stepped into the hall to meet Dr. Archer and the medical examiner as they returned from the death room.

"I'm through," said Dr. Finkelbaum. "Immediate autopsy on this. Here's the knife." He handed Dart the instrument, wrapped in a dressing. "I don't believe—"

Dart interrupted him with a quick gesture, then said loudly enough to be heard by those in the living-room:

"You don't believe it could have been suicide, do you, doctor?"

"Suicide? I should say not." The medical examiner caught Dart's cue and matched his tone. "He wasn't left-handed, was he?"

Dart turned back, asking through the living-room doorway, "Was your brother left-handed, Mr. Dewey?"

Ben had not taken his eyes off Letty.

"Seems like he was," he said in a low voice, which included his wife in his indictment.

"Is that true, Miss Petal?"

"No, sir. He was right-handed."

"Then it wasn't suicide," said the medical examiner. "The site of the wound and the angle of the thrust rule out a right hand. The depth of it makes even a left hand unlikely."

"Thanks, doctor. We can forget the fact that it was his own knife."

"Absolutely."

"And," Dart winked as he added, "we can expect to find the killer's fingerprints on this black pearl handle, don't you think?"

"Oh, unquestionably," replied Dr. Finkelbaum. "That handle will name the guilty party even if he wore a glove. The new method, you know."

"So I thought," said Dart. "Well, on your way?"

"Yep. I'll get him downtown and let you have a report first thing in the morning. See you later, gentlemen."

172                    Rudolph Fisher

"I'm afraid you will," murmured Dr. Archer.

Dr. Finkelbaum departed. Dr. Archer and the detective conferred a brief moment in inaudible tones, then entered the living-room.

"Mr. Dewey," said Dart. "do you deny having committed this crime in the face of the circumstances?"

"What circumstances?"

"The existence of ample motive, as testified by Red Brown, here, and of ample opportunity, as testified by your wife.

"What do you mean, opportunity?"

"She corroborated your statement that at about ten o'clock you went out for a few minutes on the pretext of getting a pack of cigarettes."

"I did go out and I got the cigarettes."

"The time when you say you went out happens to correspond with the time when the doctors say the crime was committed."

"And if I was out, how could I have done it?"

"You couldn't. But suppose you weren't out? Suppose you went down the hall, opened and shut the front door, crept back silently into Sonny's room—only a few steps—did what you had to do, and, after the proper lapse of time, crept back to the front door, opened and shut it again, and walked back up the hall as if you had been out the whole time? Your wife says that you went out. But she can not swear that you actually left the apartment."

"Of course I can!" said Letty sharply.

"Yes? Then, Mrs. Dewey, you must have been in the hallway the whole time Mr. Dewey was out. You can not see the length of that hallway from any room in this house. The only way you can swear there was nobody in it throughout that time is to swear that you were in it throughout that time. Could you swear that?"

Letty hesitated only a moment before answering hotly, "Yes!"

"Careful, Mrs. Dewey. Why should you stand idle for ten minutes alone in an empty hallway?"

"I—I was measuring it for wallpaper."

"Strange. I noted that it had recently been re-papered."

"I didn't like the new paper. I was planning to have it changed."

"I see. Then you insist that you were in that hallway all that time?"

"Yes."

"And that Mr. Dewey was not?"

"Yes."

"And that no one else was?"

"No one."

"Madam, you have accused yourself."

"Wh—what?"

"You have just accused yourself of killing your brother-in-law."

"What are you talking about?"

"I'll make it plainer. The only doorway to Sonny's room is on the hall. Assuming that the doctors are right about the time of death, and assuming that the killer used the only door, which is on the hallway you so carefully kept under observation, no one but yourself was within striking distance at the time Sonny was stabbed. You follow my reasoning?"

"Why—"

"Therefore by your own statement—which you are willing to swear to—you must have killed him yourself."

"I never said any such thing!"

"You wish to retract your statement?"

"I—I—"

"And admit that your husband may have been in the hallway?"

Completely confused and dismayed, the woman burst into tears.

But disloyal or not, this was Ben Dewey's wife; he came to her rescue:

"Wait a minute, officer. At least you had a reason for accusing me. What would she want to do that for?"

"I'd rather not guess, Mr. Dewey. But it shouldn't be hard."

Only Letty's sobs broke the next moment's silence. Finally Ben said in a dull, low voice:

"She didn't do it."

"Did you?" asked Dart quickly.

"No. I didn't either. It's—it's all cockeyed."

The man's change of attitude from arrogance to humility was more touching than the woman's tears.

"Are we under arrest?"

Dart's answer was surprising. "No."

"No?"

"No. You are free to go about as usual. You will all hold yourselves ready for questioning at any time, of course. But I shall not make an arrest until this knife is examined."

Letty stopped sobbing to follow the general trend of eyes toward the gauze-wrapped knife in Dart's hand.

"Here's the answer," said the detective, looking about and raising the object. "Of course—a confession would save us a bit of time and trouble."

Nobody uttered a word.

"Well—in the morning we'll know. Dr. Archer put this in your bag, please. And do you mind keeping it for me until morning? I've got a bit of checking up to do meanwhile."

"Not at all." The doctor took the knife, placed it carefully in a side pocket of his bag. "It'll be safe there till you come for it."

"Of course. Thanks a lot. We'll be going now."

The two started out. Dart halted as his companion went on toward the outside door.

"I might say before going, Mr. Dewey," he remarked, "that anything that happens to Red Brown here will make things look even worse for you and your wife. Both of you threatened him, if I remember."

"I can take care of myself," said Red Brown coolly.

"I'm glad to know that," returned Dart. "And—oh yes. I'd like to see you all here in the morning at nine. That's all. Good night."

"From your instructions to your men," observed Dr. Archer, as he and the detective rode back toward his office, "I gather the purpose of not making an arrest."

"It's the only way," Dart said. "Let 'em go and keep an eye on 'em. Their actions will always tell more than their words. I hadn't got anywhere until Red Brown looked at brother Ben. Yet he didn't say a word."

"And," Dr. Archer continued, "I gather also that Exhibit A, which rests enshrouded in my bag, is to be a decoy."

"Sure. That was all stuff—about prints and the new method. Probably not a thing on that knife but they don't know that. Somebody's going to try and get that lethal weapon back."

"But—" the doctor's words disregarded the detective's interruptions— "what I fail to gather is the reason for dragging in me and my bag."

"You dragged me in, didn't you?"

"I see. One good murder deserves another."

"No. Look. The thing had to be planted where the guilty person figured it could be recovered. They wouldn't attempt to get it away from me. But you're different."

"Different from you?"

"Exactly."

"It's a relief to know that."

"You're no happier over it than I am."

"You'll be nearby, I trust?"

"Under your bed, if you like."

"No. The girl might come for it."

"That's just why I'll be nearby. Leave you alone and she'll get it."

"Shouldn't be at all surprised. Lovely little thing."

"But not too little."

"Nor too lovely."

"Aren't you ashamed of yourself?"

John Archer's Nose            175

"Not at all. You see—"

"Yea, I see. Never mind the long explanation. Adam saw, too."

"Ah, but what did Adam see? An apple. Only an apple."

"Well, if it's the girl—which it won't be—she'd better bring an apple along—to keep the doctor away."

"Sergeant, how you admire me. What makes you think it won't be the girl?"

"You don't think she killed her brother, do you?"

"I hope not. But I wouldn't—er—express an opinion in cash."

"Couldn't you just say you wouldn't bet on it?"

"Never use a word of one syllable, sergeant, when you can find one of six."

"Why wouldn't you bet on it? She's just a kid. A rather nice kid."

"How did you find out?"

Dart ignored him. "She screamed. She telephoned for you."

"Nice girls of nineteen have been known to do such things."

"Kill their sweethearts, maybe—their ex-sweethearts. Not their brothers."

"True. Usually it is the brother who kills his sister's sweetheart, isn't it? Whereupon the sweetheart is known as a betrayer."

"Yea. Family honor. Course I've never seen it, but—"

"Cynic. Here we are."

But Dart drove on past the doctor's apartment.

"Whither, pray?"

"Get smart. They may recognize the detective's license-plates. Around the corner'll be better."

"And me with no roller-skates."

Shortly they returned to the apartment on foot, and soon were engaged in smooth hypotheses, well oiled.

"One of these things is going to fool us yet," meditated the physician between sips.

"They all fool us."

"Modesty ill becomes you, Perry. I mean the party who obviously did the thing from the outset sometimes does it."

"The party is always obvious from the outset—when it's all over. What I'd like to see is a case in which the party who is obvious from the outset is obvious *at* the outset."

"The trouble is with the obviousness—the kind of obviousness. One person is obviously guilty because everything points to him. Another is obviously guilty because nothing points to him. In the present case, Ben is the one example, Red the other."

"You're drinking. How can a man be guilty because nothing points to him?"

"Because, of course, too perfect an alibi is no alibi, just as too perfect a case is no case. Perfection doesn't exist. Hence the perfect thing is false."

"This is false whiskey."

"May it continue to deceive us. Consider this: Can you imagine a lad like Red Brown living in a house with a girl like Petal and not being—er—affected?"

"So what?"

"I was thinking of the brother-sweetheart complex you suggested."

"With the brother getting the worst of it? But Letty said Red had been out all day. How could Red—?"

"Just as you said Ben could. Only he didn't slam the front door."

"Of course Letty was lying about being in the hall all that time. Maybe Red could have sneaked in and out, at that. But that's taking it pretty far. Nothing that we know indicates Red."

"Nothing except that he's altogether too un-indicated."

"Well, if you really want to get fancy, listen to this."

"Go ahead."

"Red knows that Letty is two-timing."

"Yes."

"Ben doesn't."

"No."

"If Ben finds out, it's her hips."

"Yes."

"She's rather partial to her hips."

"Naturally."

"A blab from either Sonny or Red—and bye-bye."

"Hips."

"So, tired of Sonny and afraid of Red, she decides on what is known as murder for elimination."

"Murder of Sonny?"

"No. Of Red. With Sonny implicated by his knife."

"Go on. How'd she get Sonny and Red mixed?"

"She heard Sonny come in—'way down the hall where she couldn't see. But Sonny, having developed bad habits, never comes in so early. She believes this is Red. When Ben steps out, she slips into the dark room and hurriedly acts in self-defense."

"Hip-defense."

"M—m. Only it happens to be Sonny. Well, what about it?"

"Utterly fantastic. Yet not utterly impossible."

"O.K. Your turn."

"You leave me the most fantastic possibility of all."

"The old lady?"

"No. The mother." The doctor paused a moment, then said, "There's quite a difference. Can you imagine anything that would make a mother kill her son?"

"That smell you mentioned, maybe."

"No. Seriously."

"I don't know. It's pretty hard to believe. But it could happen, I suppose. By mistake, for instance. Suppose the old lady thought it was Red—just as Letty might have. Red—leading her child down the road to hell. . . . That would explain why she said, 'God forgive me!'"

"Let's forget your 'mistake' for a while."

"Well then, look. When I was walking a beat, a woman came to me once and begged me to put her son in jail. He was a dope. She said when she saw him like that, she wanted to kill him."

"But did she?"

"No. But why can't mother-love turn to hate like any other love?"

"I guess the fact that it doesn't is what makes it mother-love."

"What about those hospital cases where unmarried girls try to smother their kids—and sometimes succeed?"

"Quite different, I should say. Those girls aren't yet mothers, emotionally. They're just parents, biologically. With a wholly unwanted and recently very painful obstruction between themselves and happiness. Mother-love must develop, like anything else. It grows as the child grows, becomes a personal bond only as the child becomes a person."

"All right. But mothers can go crazy."

"Yes. There are cases of that kind."

"That old lady acted kind o' crazy, I thought."

"Probably just grief. Or concern over the whereabouts of Sonny's soul."

"Maybe. I wouldn't press the point. But as long as we're guessing, I don't want to slight anybody."

"I did have a case once where, I believe, a fairly sane mother would have killed her son if she'd been able. He was a lad about Sonny's age, with a sarcoma of the jaw. It involved half his head—he suffered terrifically. Death was just a matter of time. She repeatedly begged me to give him an overdose of morphine."

"What prevented her from killing him?"

"I sent him to a hospital."

"Well—"

"Yes, I know. Sonny could have had a sort of moral sarcoma—eating up his soul, if you like. The sight of him going down and down might have been more than his mother could bear. But unless she was actually insane at the moment, she'd keep hoping and praying for a change—a turn for the better. That hope would prevent any drastic action. After all, sarcoma of the soul is not incurable."

"The only way it could be his mother, then, is if she went temporarily off her nut?"

"Exquisitely phrased, my friend. Have another drink."

Dr. Archer's apartment, which combined office and residence, was on the ground floor of a five-story house. Its front door was immediately within and to one side of the house entrance, off a large rectangular foyer at the rear of which a marble staircase wound upward and around an elevator-shaft. At this hour the elevator was not running.

Inside, the front rooms of the apartment constituted the physician's office—waiting-room, consultation-room, laboratory. Beyond these were a living-room, bedroom and kitchen.

It was agreed that Dart should occupy the bedroom for the rest of the night, while Dr. Archer made the best of the living-room couch. Dart could thus remain behind the scene for any forthcoming action, observe unseen, and step forward when occasion demanded.

Neither undressed, each lying down in shirt-sleeves and trousers. In the event of a caller, Dart agreed that, barring physical danger, he would not interfere unless the doctor summoned him.

"Still hoping it'll be the girl, hey?" grinned the detective.

"Nothing would amaze me more," returned Archer. "Go on—lie down. This is my party." He stretched his considerable length on the couch. Dart went into the adjacent bedroom, leaving the intervening door ajar.

As if some unseen director had awaited this moment, the apartment bell promptly rang, first briefly, timidly, then longer, with resolute determination. "I didn't want to sleep anyway," murmured the doctor. "Keep your ears open. Here goes."

He went through the office rooms to the front door, cracked the little trap-window designed against rent-collectors and other robbers, snapped it to with a gasp of astonishment, unlocked and opened the door.

His preliminary glance was corroborated. Before him stood Petal, bare-headed, with a handbag under her arm.

"I know it's late," she was saying, a little breathlessly, "but—"

"Not at all. Come in."

"Thank you." She looked behind her.

He closed the door quickly. "Someone following you?"

"I—I thought so. Just—nervousness I hope."

"Come back this way."

She followed him through the waiting-room into the consulting office. He slipped on an office coat from a rack.

"Who would be following you at this hour?" he asked, giving her a chair and seating himself at his desk.

"Detectives, maybe."

"Hardly. You're the last person suspected in this affair."

She was silent a moment. Her eyes rested on the doctor's bag, which sat conspicuously on top of his desk. Then she began still breathlessly to talk. She leaned forward in her chair, dark eyes wide and bright, gentle breasts rising and falling, small fingers moving restlessly over the flat handbag on her lap.

"Are—are we alone?"

He smiled. "Would you care to look about?"

She accepted this with a feeble reflection of his smile.

"I came here to—to warn you. About Ben."

"Ben?"

"He's—wild. He blames you. He says if you hadn't brought in that detective, he wouldn't be in a jam."

"But that's ridiculous. The thing couldn't have been covered up. The same facts would have been brought out sooner or later."

"I know. But he—he's a little crazy, I guess. Finding out about Letty and everything. He thinks he could have managed."

"Managed—what?"

"Keeping the thing quiet."

"Why should he want to keep it quiet?"

"I don't know. His job—his wife—it's all such a mess. I guess he wants to take it out on somebody and he can't—on Sonny."

"I see. What does he intend to do?"

"He's coming here and hold you up for that knife. If you refuse to give it to him—he'll take it."

"How?"

"He has a pistol. He has to have it when he's loading mail, you know. The way he is now, he'd use it."

"In which case he might be actually guilty of a crime of which he is now only suspected."

"Yes. He might kill you."

"And naturally you want to save him from that."

"Him—and you."

"Hm . . . What do you suggest?"

"Give me the knife."

He smiled. "But I've promised Sergeant Dart to turn it over to him in the morning."

"I know. But I'll give it back to you, I swear I will."

"My dear child, I couldn't do that. Don't you see—it would make my position very awkward? Obstructing the due course of justice and all that?"

"Oh—I was afraid you wouldn't—Please! Don't you see? It may mean your life—and Ben's. I tell you he's crazy."

"How is it that he didn't get here first?"

"He had to stay with Ma. She passed out. I'm supposed to be out looking for medicine. As soon as I get back, he's coming."

"As soon as you get back. Well, that makes it simple."

"What do you mean?"

"Don't go back. Stay here. Sergeant Dart will come for the knife at eight o'clock in the morning. It's three now. When it has been examined, he will come back for us. It will be too late for Ben to do anything to me then."

"Stay here the rest of the night?"

"You'll be quite safe. I should hardly be—ungrateful for your effort to protect me."

"But—but—what about Ma's medicine?"

"If she simply fainted, she's in no danger."

"I couldn't stay away. If anything happened to Ma—"

The physician meditated.

"Well," he said after a moment, "strange how the simplest solution is often the last to occur to one. I can easily take care of both the danger to myself and the further implication of your brother."

"How?" Petal asked eagerly.

"By just spending the rest of the night elsewhere. Parts unknown."

"Oh."

"Come. That will settle everything. You run along now. Get your mother's medicine. When brother Ben arrives I'll be far, far away."

Reluctantly the girl arose. Suddenly she swayed, threw a hand up to her face, and slumped back down into the chair. Dr. Archer sprang forward. She was quite limp. He felt her pulse and grinned. She stirred, opened her eyes, smiled wanly.

"A little water—?" she murmured.

He filled a paper cup from the washstand faucet in the corner and brought it to her.

"It's so warm," she protested.

"I'll get a bit of ice."

He went through the next room into the kitchen, put ice in a glass, filled it and returned. She had not apparently moved, but the flap of his bag on the desk was unsecured at one end. She drank the water.

"Thank you. That's so much better. I'm sorry. I feel all right now."

Again she arose and now preceded him through the waiting-room. At the front door she turned and smiled. She was really very pretty.

"You've been swell," she said. "I guess everything will turn out all right now."

"I hope so. You've done bravely."

She looked at him, turned quickly away as if eluding some hidden meaning in his words, and stepped across the threshold. As she did so, the bang of a pistol shot shook the foyer. Archer reached out, seized the girl's arm, yanked her back, slammed the door. He secured its lock, then hustled her back into the consulting-room.

There, both drew breath.

"Somebody means business. Sit down."

She obeyed, wordless, while he went back to reassure Dart. When he returned a moment later, he found a thoroughly frightened girl.

"I—I heard it hit the side of the doorway," she breathed. "Who—who'd shoot at me?"

"I can't imagine who'd shoot at either of us. Even your brother would try to get what he came for before shooting."

"It was at me," she insisted. "You were still inside the room. It was from the stairs at the back."

"Well. Looks as if we both have to stay here a while now."

"There's no other way out?"

"Yes. The kitchen. But that door opens on the same foyer."

She gave a sign of despair. Slowly her eyes filled.

"Spoils your whole scheme, doesn't it?"

She said nothing.

"Don't feel too bad about it. It was spoiled already."

Her wet eyes lifted, questioning.

"Look in your bag," he said.

She opened the handbag, took out a gauze-wrapped object.

"Unwrap it."

She obeyed. The knife was not Sonny's pearl-handled weapon, but a shining surgeon's scalpel.

"I anticipated some such attempt as you made, of course. The real thing is already under inspection."

He felt almost ashamed at her look.

After a brief silence, she shrugged hopelessly. "Well—I tried."

Rudolph Fisher

He stood before her. "I wish you'd tell me the whole story."

"I can't. It's too awful."

"I'd really like to help you if I could."

"You could give me the knife."

"What could you do with it now? You don't dare leave, with somebody shooting at you."

"If Ben comes—"

"Ben has surely had time to come—come to his senses, anyway. If Ben would go so far as to kill—as you claim—to get that knife, it can only mean one thing: He knows whom it would implicate." He paused, continued: "That might be himself."

Inspiration kindled her eyes for a brief instant. Before he was sure he saw it, the lids drooped.

"Or," he leaned a little closer, "would it be Letty? Letty, who killed Sonny for betraying her, then begged her husband to forgive her and recover the one thing that would identify her?"

She looked up at him, dropped her eyes again, and said:

"Neither."

"Who then?"

"Me."

"You!"

"Me." She drew deep breath. "Don't you think I know what it means for me to come here and try to get that thing? Why make it hard? It means I killed Sonny, that's all. It means I told them tonight after you left. Ben would have come here and done anything to get the knife, to save me. But Ma passed out when I told. And I ran out while Ben was holding her, saying I'd get something for her. And then I came here . . . Why would I let Ben risk his neck for something I did?"

Dr. Archer sat down. "Petal, you're lying."

"No. It's true. I did it. I didn't know it was Sonny. I didn't go out as Letty said. I hid in the room closet. I thought it was Red that came in. When he went to sleep I came out of the closet. It was dark . . . I meant to—to hang on to the knife, but I couldn't pull it out." She halted, went on: "Then I went out, quietly. It was Ma who really discovered him as I came back in later. That's why I screamed so when—" She halted again.

"But Petal—why?"

"Can't you guess?" she said, low.

"Good Lord!" He sat back in his chair. "If that's a lie, it's a good one."

"It's not a lie. You said you'd help me if you could. Will you give me the knife now? Just long enough to let me clean the handle?"

He was silent.

"It's my life I'm asking for."

"No, Petal," he said gently. "The beauty of your story is that if it stands up you might get off very lightly. Juries are funny about a woman's honor. It's certainly not a question of your life."

"Lightly! What good is a jailbird's life?"

"I can't believe this."

She stood up, her bag dropping to the floor.

"Look at me," she said. He looked. "I'll do anything you want me to, any time, from now till I die, if you'll give me the knife for five minutes. Anything on earth."

And, whatever her falsehood up to that moment, he had no doubt of her sincerity now.

"Sit down, Petal."

She sat down and began to cry softly.

"It's a lie. But it's a grand lie."

"Why do you keep saying that?"

"Because it's so. Don't you see how inconsistent you are?"

She stopped crying.

"Look," he went on. "You've come to me, whom you know nothing about except that I'm a doctor. Nothing personal at all. You say you've killed for the sake of your—let us say—honor. Yet the same honor, which you prize highly enough to commit murder for, you offer to sacrifice to me if I will save you from the consequences of what you've done for it. Does that make sense?"

She did not answer.

"How can you hold so cheap now a thing which you held so dear a few hours ago?"

"I'm not. It's worth all it ever was. Something else is worth more, that's all."

"How you must love your brother."

"Myself."

"No. You wouldn't do this for yourself. If you were the only one involved, you'd still be defending your honor—not trading it in."

"Please—you said you'd help me."

"I'm going to help you—though not in the way you suggest—nor at the price."

"Then—how?"

"You'll have to leave that to me, Petal."

There was complete defeat in her voice. "It certainly looks that way."

"Now call your home and say that you've been detained by the police, but will be there in the morning. Tell Ben you were detained for trying to see me. That will keep him safe at home."

She obeyed, replaced the receiver, turned to him. "Now what?"

"Now lie down on that sofa and rest till morning. I'll be in the next room, there."

With utmost dejection in every movement, she went toward the sofa. John Archer turned and went out, back through the living-room into the bedroom where Dart waited, and went into whispered close communion with the detective.

An hour later he came softly back to the consulting-room, cracked the door, looked through. Petal lay face-down on the sofa, her shoulders shaking with silent sobs.

*     *     *

During that hour of whispered conference, the physician and the detective had engaged in one of their characteristic disagreements.

"You yourself said," Dart reminded the doctor, "that the party who is obviously guilty *is* guilty. That party is Ben. He is the only one with sufficient motive. This Letty and Petal stuff is hooey. Women don't kill guys that trick 'em any more. They sue 'em. But men still kill guys that trick their wives."

"You're barking up the wrong sycamore, Perry. Ben didn't know anything about Letty's two-timing—delightful phrase, 'two-timing'—till Red spilt it over two hours *after* the stabbing. The way you say he acted proves that. Why, he was still staring dumbfounded at Letty when the medical examiner and I came back on the scene. Men may kill guys that trick their wives—if I may borrow your elegant diction—but surely not till after they know the worst. It is still customary, is it not, for a cause to precede its effect?"

"You needn't get nasty. Maybe there was some other motive."

"You wouldn't abandon your motive, would you Sergeant? 'Love is all,' 'Seek the woman' and all that?"

"It's been known to play a part," said the other drily.

"I wish I could place that smell."

"I wish you could place it, too—as far away as possible."

"Let's see now. I got it in the dead boy's room when we first went in. But I didn't get it when the medical examiner and I went in."

"So?"

"So it must have been upon someone who was present the first time and absent the second."

"Yea."

"Don't growl—you're not the hound you think you are. That would mean it was on one of four people—Sonny, Petal, Ma, or you."

"Wake me when this is over."

"Then I got it in the front flat during the first period of questioning. So it couldn't have been Sonny. And I did not get it anywhere else in the flat when you and I were looking around. Hence it couldn't have been you."

"Nope. I use Life-Buoy."

"That leaves Petal and Ma. But I didn't get it when Petal greeted us at the head of the stairs, nor while I was talking to her just now. I actually leaned close to her to be sure."

"You leaned close to her—why?"

"To be sure."

"Oh. To be sure."

"That leaves Ma."

"Hmph. So Ma killed Sonny. I begin to smell something myself."

"I didn't say the bearer of the odor killed Sonny."

"No. You only said the odor would lead to the killer. You had a hunch."

"I've still got it—bigger than ever. Ma may not have killed Sonny, but I'll bet you champagne to Rochelle salts that if it hadn't been for Ma, Sonny wouldn't have been killed."

"It's a bet. And the one that wins has to drink his winnings on the spot."

"In other words, Ma is inextricably bound up in the answer to this little riddle."

"Anything besides an odor leading you on?"

"Yes. There are two things I can believe out of Petal's story: First, Petal is awfully anxious to protect somebody. Second, Ben—who was coming here also if Petal had returned home—is also very anxious to protect somebody. There was time for plenty of talk after we left, so it's unlikely that Ben and Petal are concerned over two different people. Ben and Petal, brother and sister, are trying to protect the *same* person. It wouldn't be Red, whom Ben tried to beat. It wouldn't be Letty, whom Petal has shown no special affection for. But it would be Ma, their mother, the one person in the picture whom both love."

"Are you trying to say that Ma killed her own son, and that Ben and Petal know she did?"

"Not exactly. I'm saying that Ben and Petal believe that that knife will incriminate Ma."

Dart became serious for a moment. "I get it. Ben's ignorance of Letty's two-timing eliminates him. Petal's inconsistency eliminates her. Yet each of them wants the knife, because it may incriminate Ma."

"Beautifully summarized, professor. With the aid of a smell."

"Where do you want to smell next?"

"At their apartment in the morning. Have everybody there—and a few trusty fallen arches. I'm going to locate that odor if it asphyxiates me."

"Y'know, maybe I ought to put you on a leash."

"Have the leash ready. I'll get you somebody to put on it."

*　　*　　*

In the morning about eight-thirty the two men and the girl had coffee together, Dart pretending to have just arrived. Petal exhibited a forced cheerfulness that in no wise concealed the despair in her eyes.

Even the hard habits of long police experience had not wholly stifled the detective's chivalry, and in an effort to match the girl's courageous masquerade, he said lightly:

"You know, this case is no cinch. I'm beginning to believe some of your folks must walk in their sleep."

As if struck, the girl jumped up. It was as if the tide of her terror, which had receded during the early morning hours, suddenly swung back with his remark, lifting her against her will to her feet. Controlling herself with the greatest effort, she turned from the table and disappeared into the next room.

"Gee!" said Dart. "Bull's eye—in the dark."

"M—m," murmured Archer. "Ma. But I hope I'm wrong."

"I hope so, too."

Petal reappeared.

"I'm sorry. I'm so upset."

"Better finish your coffee," said the doctor.

"My fault," Dart apologized. "I might have let you out a few more minutes."

"It's all right—about me. But there's someone I wish you would let out— as far as you can."

"Who?"

"Ma."

"I don't understand. Surely you don't mean that your mother—"

"No. Of course not. But—perhaps I should have mentioned it sooner— but it's not something we talk much about. You ought to know it though."

"I'll certainly try to protect your confidence."

"My mother is—well—not entirely—right."

"You mean she's—insane?"

"She goes off—has spells in which she doesn't know what she's saying. You saw how she was last night—she just sat there."

John Archer's Nose　　　　　187

"But," the physician put in, "anybody—any mother, certainly—might act that way under the circumstances. The shock must have been terrific."

"Yes, but it is more than that. Ma has—I don't know—she sees things. As long as she's quiet it doesn't matter. But when she starts talking, she says the most impossible things. When you see her again, she's likely to have a complete story of all this. She's likely to say anybody did it—anybody." Her voice dropped. "Even herself."

The two men looked at her, Dart quizzically, Archer gravely.

"That's why I'm asking you to—let her out. If ever she had reason to be unresponsible for what she says, it's now."

"Quite so," the doctor said. "I'm sure Sergeant Dart will give your mother every consideration."

Dart nodded. "Don't worry, young lady. Policemen are people, too, you know."

"I just thought I'd better tell you beforehand."

"Glad you did. Now let's get around to your place and see if we can't clear up the whole thing. Some of the boys are to meet me there at nine. Perhaps something has developed that will put your mind at rest."

"Perhaps," said the girl with no trace of conviction or hope.

When, a few minutes later, they reached the Dewey apartment, they found a bluecoat in the corridor outside the door and two of Dart's subordinates already awaiting him, with the other members of the family, in the living-room.

"Isn't Red Brown here?" was the detective's first question.

"No," Ben told him. "He left right after you did last night and hasn't come back."

"The first law of nature," murmured Dr. Archer.

"Yea," Dart agreed, "but who is he protecting himself from—Mr. and Mrs. Dewey here or the law?"

"It could be both," remarked the tight-lipped Letty.

"Or neither," the doctor added. "He's probably stayed out all night before. And I doubt that I should care to occupy Sonny's bed under the circumstances."

"I told him to be here," Dart said. "This doesn't look good for him."

One of the headquarters men called Dart aside.

"Autopsy report," he said, low. "Tuberculosis both lungs. Due to go anyway, sooner or later."

"M−m."

"Here's the knife."

"Anything on it?"

"Nothing."

And the detective, knowing that every Dewey's eyes had followed where their ears could not reach, pretended a satisfaction which only valuable information could have given.

"Thanks," said he aloud. "This is all I've been waiting for."

He surveyed the four members of the household—Ma, seated in the same chair she had occupied last night, much as if she had not left it since; Petal, again protectively by her side; Letty, still disagreeably defiant, standing beside Ben, her scowling husband. But the far-away expression was no longer in Ma's eyes; she was staring now at the detective with the same fearful expectancy as the others.

After a moment of complete silence, Dart, looking meditatively at the knife which he balanced in his hand, said almost casually:

"If I were the guilty party, I think I'd speak now."

Ma Dewey drew a quick breath so sharply that all eyes turned upon her.

"Yes," she said in a dull but resolute voice. "Yes. That's right. It's time to speak."

"Ma!" cried Petal and Ben together.

"Hush, chillun. You all don' know. I got to tell it. It's got to come out."

"Yes, Mrs. Dewey?"

"Oh Ma!" the girl sobbed, while Ben shoulders dropped suddenly and Letty gave a sardonic shrug.

"I don't know," Ma said, "what you all's found on that knife. It don't matter. One thing I do know—my hand—this hand—" she extended a clenched, withered fist—"had hold o' that knife when it went into Sonny's heart."

Petal turned desperate, appealing eyes to Dart. No one else moved or spoke.

"I told the chillun las' night after you all had lef'."

Dr. Archer gave Petal a glance that at last comprehended all she had tried to accomplish in his office last night.

"You all don' know," the old lady resumed with a deliberate calmness of voice that held no hint of insanity. "You don' know what it means to a mother to see a child goin' down and down. Sonny was my youngest child, my baby. He was sick, body and soul."

She stopped a moment, went doggedly on.

"He got to runnin' around with the wrong crowd here in Harlem. Took to drinkin' and comin' in all hours o' the night—or not at all. Nothin' I say or do seem to have no effect on him. Then I see he's beginnin' to fall off—gettin' thinner by the minute. Well, I made him go 'round to the hospital and let them doctors examine him. They say he got the T.B. in his lungs and if he don' go 'way to a cemetarium he'll die in a year. And I knowed it was so, 'cause his father died o' the same thing."

She was looking back over the years now, and into her eyes came last night's distant stare.

"But he wouldn' go. Jes' like his father. Say if he go'n' die he go'n die at home and have a good time befo' he go. I tried ev'ything—prayer, charms—God and the devil. But I'd done seen his father go and I reckon I didn' have no faith in neither one. And I begun to think how his father suffered befo' he went, and look like when I thought 'bout Sonny goin' through the same thing I couldn' stand it. Seem like sump'm kep' tellin' me, 'Don' let him suffer like that—Don' let him suffer like that.'

"It weighed on my mind. When I went to sleep nights I kep' dreamin' 'bout it. 'Bout how I could save him from goin' through all that sufferin' befo' he actually come down to it. And las' night I had sech a dream. I seen myself kneelin' by my bed, prayin' for strength to save him from what was in store for him—strength to make his death quick and easy, 'stead o' slow and mis'able. Then I seen myself get up and slip into the hall and make into Sonny's room like sump'm was leadin' me. Same sump'm say, 'If he die in his sleep he won' feel it.' Same sump'm took my hand and moved it 'long the bureau-top till it hit Sonny's knife. I felt myself pick it up and move over to the bed . . . and strike. . . ."

Her voice dwindled to a strained whisper.

"That's all. When I opened my eyes, I was in my own bed. I thought it was jes' another dream . . . Now I know better. It happened. I killed him."

She had straightened up in her chair as she spoke. Now she slumped back as if her strength was spent.

Dr. Archer went quickly to her. Dart saw him lean over her, grow abruptly rigid, then fumble at the bosom of her dress, loosening her clothing. After a moment, the doctor stood erect and turned around, and upon his face was the light of discovery.

"She's all right," he said. "Wait a minute. Don't do anything till I get back."

He went into the hallway, calling back, "Petal, just fan your mother a bit. She'll be all right"—and disappeared toward the dining-room at the rear of the apartment.

In a few moments, during which attention centered on reviving Ma Dewey, he returned with a newspaper in his hand.

"This was on the dining-room table, open at this page, last night," he said proffering the paper to Dart. "Read it. I'll be right back."

He turned and went out again, this time leaving the apartment altogether, by way of its front door.

Dart looked after his vanished figure a moment, wondering perhaps if his friend might not also be acting in a trance. Then his eyes fell on the page which advertised columns of guaranteed charms.

Before he could find just what it was Dr. Archer had wanted him to read, a curious sound made him look up. From the hallway, in the direction of the rear, came a succession of sharp raps.

"What's that?" whispered Letty, awe-struck.

Dart stepped into the hallway, Ben, Letty, and the two officers crowding into the living-room doorway behind him. Again came the sharp succession of taps, and this time there was no mistaking their source. They came from within the closed door of Sonny's room.

Letty stifled a cry as Dart turned and asked, "Who's in that room?"

"Nobody," Ben answered, bewildered. "They took Sonny away last night—the door's locked."

Again came the taps.

"Where's the key?"

Ben produced a key, Dart seized it, quickly unlocked the door and flung it wide.

Dr. Archer stood smiling in the doorway.

"What the hell?" said Dart.

"Unquestionably," returned his friend. "May I give an order to your two men?"

He wrote something on his prescription pad and handed it to one of the two men behind Dart. The latter read it.

"O.K., Doc. Come on, Bud."

They departed.

"As I remarked before," Dart growled, "what the hell?"

The physician backed into the room. "The missing link," he said blandly.

"Red Brown?"

"You heard Ma Dewey's story?"

"Of course I heard it."

"She was quite right. She did kill Sonny. But not in the way she believes. I'm just working out the details. See you in the living-room. Lock this door again, will you?" And he shut the door between himself and the detective.

With consummate self-control Dart suppressed comment and question and obeyed.

Then he went back into the living-room with the others. The local newspaper was still in his hand, somewhat crumpled. He smoothed the pages.

"Take it easy, everybody," he advised the members of the family, with whom he was now alone. "We'll wait for Dr. Archer and Red Brown." And he began to peruse in earnest the columns of ads:

BLACK CAT LODESTONE

Draw anything you want to you.

Free—Hot foot and attracting

Powders with your order.

Pay the postman only $1.95 on delivery and it is all yours to keep and enjoy forever.

Burn Lucky Stars and surround yourself with good fortune.

Win Your Loved One.

Let us send you our Sacred Controlling Love Powder.

Do you suffer from lack of Friends, Money, Health?

Oriental Wishing Ring

He had to read to the bottom of the right-hand column before something caught his eye, an address which seemed somehow familiar.
"15 West 134th Street, Apt. 51—Why, that's here!"
He re-read the advertisement:

Faith Charm
Faith can move mountains.
Develop your faith by using our special charm.
Secret formula. Bound to bring health and happiness to the wearer.

"Say!"
The front door rattled. Dart stepped out and admitted Dr. Archer. "What kind of hide-and-seek is this?"
"It isn't," smiled the physician. "It's a practical demonstration in entrances and exits. It shows that even if Sonny's door had been locked, his assailant could have entered and left his room, undetected."
"How."
"The next apartment is empty. Its entrance is not locked—you know how vacant apartments are hereabouts: the tenants bring their own locks and take them when they move. One room has a window on the same airshaft with Sonny's, at right angles to it, close enough to step across—if you don't look down."
"You jackass! You'd risk your hindquarters like that?"

"Sergeant—please."

"But what's the use? We've got the old lady's confession, haven't we?"

"Yes."

"And you admitted she did it—you were working out details. Good grief—would she go around to the next apartment and climb across an air-shaft—at her age? What do you want me to believe?"

"Believe in the value of an odor, old snoop. Come on."

They re-entered the living-room. Dr. Archer went to Ma Dewey.

"Tell me, Mother Dewey, where do you keep the oil?"

She looked up at him. "I don't keep it. I gets it jes' as I needs it."

"When did you last need it?"

"Yestiddy mornin'."

"After it had failed so long to help Sonny?"

"I didn' have faith. I'd done seen his father die. But somebody else might 'a' had faith."

"Curious," reflected the doctor, "but common."

Dart's patience gave out.

"Would you cut the clowning and state in plain English what this is all about?"

"I mean the mixture of Christian faith and primitive mysticism. But I suppose every religion is a confusion of superstitions."

The doorbell saved Dart from exploding. He went to the door and flung it open with unnecessary violence.

His two subordinates stood before him, holding between them a stranger—a sullen little black man whose eyes smoldered malevolence.

As they brought him into the living-room, those eyes first encountered Ben. Their malevolence kindled to a blaze. The captive writhed from the hands that held him and leaped upon the brother, and there was no mistaking his intention.

His captors got hold of him again almost before Ben realized what had happened.

"Who the devil's this?" Dart asked the physician.

"Someone for your leash. The man that killed Sonny."

"Yea—" panted the captive. "I got him. And—" indicating Petal—"I come near gettin' her las' night. And if you turn me loose, I'll get *him*." Vainly he struggled toward Ben.

"Three for one," said the doctor. "Rather unfair, isn't it, Mr. Bright?"

"She took all *we* had, didn' she? Give my wife that thing what killed *our* kid. We got to pay her back—all for all."

"Solomon Bright," breathed Dart. "The guy that lost his kid yesterday."

Dr. Archer said to the man, "What good will it do to pay Mother Dewey back?"

The little man turned red eyes on the quiet-voiced physician. "They ain' no other way to get our chile back, is they?"

Dr. Archer gave gesture of despair, then said to Dart:

"Mother Dewey made the charm yesterday."

"'Twasn' no charm," Solomon Bright glowered. "'Twas a curse. Cast a spell on our chile, tha's what it done."

"Its odor," John Archer went on, "was characteristic. But I couldn't place it till Mother Dewey fainted just now and I saw the cord around her neck. On the end of it hangs the same sort of packet that I saw on Mr. Bright's baby."

Dart nodded. "I get it . . . When she made that charm, she was unwittingly killing her own son. This bird's poison."

"Grief-crazed—doesn't realize what he's doing. Look at him."

"Realize or no realize, he killed Sonny."

"No," said the doctor. "Superstition killed Sonny." He sighed. "But I doubt that we'll ever capture that."

# WORKS OF RUDOLPH FISHER

## NOVELS

*The Walls of Jericho.* New York: Knopf, 1928.
*The Conjure Man Dies.* New York: Covici-Friede, 1932.

## SHORT STORIES

"The City of Refuge." *Atlantic Monthly* 135 (1925):178–87.
"The South Lingers On." *Survey Graphic* 14 (1925):644–47. Reprinted, with one
    sketch deleted, as "Vestiges" in *The New Negro*, edited by Alain Locke, 75–84.
    New York: Boni, 1925.
"Ringtail." *Atlantic Monthly* 135 (1925):652–60.
"High Yaller." *The Crisis* 30–31 (1925):281–86; 33–38.
"The Promised Land." *Atlantic Monthly* 139 (1927):37–45.
"Blades of Steel." *Atlantic Monthly* 140 (1927):183–92.
"The Backslider." *McClure's Magazine* 59 (1927):16–104.
"Fire by Night." *McClure's Magazine* 59 (1927):64–102.
"Common Meter." *Negro News Syndicate*, February 1930. Reprinted in *Black
    Voices*, edited by Abraham Chapman, 74–86. New York: New American Library,
    1968.
"Dust." *Opportunity* 15 (1931):46–47.
"Ezekiel." *American Junior Red Cross News* 14 (1932):151–53.
"Ezekiel Learns." *American Junior Red Cross News* 15 (1933):123–25.
"Guardian of the Law." *Opportunity* 19 (1933):82–90.
"Miss Cynthie." *Story Magazine* 4 (1933). Reprinted in *Dark Symphony*, edited by
    James Emanuel and Theodore Gross, 112–23. New York: Free Press, 1968.
"John Archer's Nose." *Metropolitan Magazine* 1 (1935):10–82.

## ESSAYS

"The Caucasian Storms Harlem." *American Mercury* 11 (1927):393–98.

## SCIENTIFIC ARTICLES

"Action of Ultraviolet Light upon Bacteriophage and Filterable Viruses." Co-authored with Earl B. McKinley and Margaret Holden. *Proceedings of the Society of Experimental Biology and Medicine* 23 (1926):408–12.

"The Resistance of Different Concentrations of a Bacteriophage of Ultraviolet Rays." Co-authored with Earl McKinley. *Journal of Infectious Diseases* 40 (1927):399–403.

## BOOK REVIEWS

"A Black Machiavelli." Review of *Mamba's Daughters* by DuBoise Heywood. *Book League Monthly*, May 1929, p. 201.

"A Novel That Makes Faces." Review of *Black No More* by George Schuyler. *Books* (*New York Herald-Tribune*), 1 February 1931, p. 5.

"Where Negroes Are People." Review of *The Chinaberry Tree* by Jessie Fauset. *Books* (*New York Herald-Tribune*), 17 January 1932, p. 6.

"Harlem Manor." Review of *Infants of the Spring* by Wallace Thurman. *Books* (*New York Herald-Tribune*), 21 February 1932, p. 16.

"Revealing a Beauty That Is Black." Review of *One Way to Heaven* by Countee Cullen. *Books* (*New York Herald-Tribune*), 28 February 1932, p. 3.

"White, High Yellow, Black." Review of *Gingertown* by Claude McKay. *Books* (*New York Herald-Tribune*), 27 March 1932, p. 3.

## UNPUBLISHED STORIES

A. Held at John Hay Library at Brown University

"Across the Airshaft"
"The Lindy Hop"
"The Lost Love Blues" (three versions)
"The Man Who Passed"

B. Held by Mrs. Jane Ryder Fisher

"One Month's Wages"
"A Perfect Understanding"
"Skeeter"